Overcoming Drugs

Overcoming Drugs: A Program for Action

The Drug Scene

Nightmare Drugs (*by Donald B. Louria and Mel Sokolow*)

Overcoming Drugs

A Program for Action

Donald B. Louria, M.D.

McGraw-Hill Book Company
New York St. Louis San Francisco Düsseldorf
London Mexico Sydney Toronto

To the three of you from the two of us, with love and thanks.

Library of Congress Catalog Card Number: 74-151499

FIRST EDITION

07-038779-6

Contents

Introduction

This is the third work I have written in the last five years on the subject of illicit drug use. The first was a brief pamphlet covering the drugs in vogue in 1967. The second was a comprehensive analysis of the drug scene as it stood in mid-1968. Because of the publicity that inevitably accompanied these two works, and because of my position as president of the New York State Council on Drug Addiction, I have been besieged with requests for speeches by a variety of high school, college, and community groups. On my speaking tours I met with many parents and students, and I have come to realize that—despite a welter of publications over the last three years, my own included—there is immense confusion about virtually every aspect of the drug scene. Part of this is due to the fact that the drug scene changes with astounding rapidity. A drug that is popular today may be discarded tomorrow; new fads are constantly cropping up to replace the old.

This appears to be a particularly propitious moment for a new work on drugs for four reasons. First, the concern among responsible persons over the increase in drug abuse by young people has never been greater. Second, a concerted attempt is being made to revise our entire legal structure as it relates to illicit drugs. Third, now that books and monographs have delineated the nature of the drug abuse problem, it is time to focus on potential approaches and remedies.

Fourth, we have the recent phenomenon of Bethel, New York. In that small hamlet in August, 1969, some 450,000 young people gathered in rain and mud to hear a rock music festival. Besides the mud and rain, there were colossal traffic jams, dearth of food, inadequate sanitation, and frequent inability to hear the music. The youngsters tolerated all this with astounding equanimity. There was no violence and, considering the circumstances, there was a minimum of property damage. For the majority of participants, the road to tranquility was made substantially smoother by the extensive use of marihuana and hashish and lesser use of more potent agents, including lysergic acid diethylamide (LSD), Methedrine (methamphetamine, or speed), mescaline, and heroin. The police, hoping to avoid possibly inflammatory confrontations, allowed open use of drugs and even their sale.

The seraphic facade of the youngsters has been applauded with rhetorical abandon by some of the Bethel residents, the majority of communications media representatives, politicians, the police, and most of the general public. To me, Bethel was a tragedy. There was one death directly attributed to drugs, and possibly another. There were an assortment of drug-induced accidents and an untold number of bad drug trips, far above the official number of 797. Yet the public willingly accepted severe mental disturbances —even death—because violence and property destruction did not occur, and it rationalized flagrant disregard of laws as desirable because this allegedly reduced the generation gap. Thus we encourage young people to use any drug, regardless of the potential harm, as long as our status quo is not disturbed. I think this is appalling. Since when are one or two deaths during a brief gathering acceptable? What makes us so enthusiastic about mass use of drugs, some of which can have terrible effects on the users?

I don't think Bethel was a gigantic success. We owe our young people a lot more than approval of illicit drug use in the name of nonviolence; we owe them more than monumental indifference to the ephemeral or permanent harmful consequences of promiscuous drug use. And the summer of 1970 showed us that acceptance of the drug aspects of a Bethel festival leads ineluctably to the far more serious drug experimentation seen at festivals such as Powder Ridge, Connecticut.

The major objective of this book is to enable each individual reader—be he user, potential user, parent, educator, legislator, or just an interested citizen—to deal more sensibly and effectively with our society's drug problem.

As the table of contents indicates, I have directly addressed the specific concerns of various social groups. In addition, I have included feedback—chapter 3 is based on the question-and-answer sessions that have followed my talks to high school, college, and community groups. I hope this framework will permit a realistic approach both to mild drugs such as marihuana, which produce pleasure for many and problems for a few, and to more dangerous agents such as heroin, LSD, and speed, which carry a very high risk-to-pleasure ratio.

1.

Where It's At—and Why

One thing is clear: drug abuse in the United States is increasing at an extraordinary rate. In recent years shibboleth-minded politicians have labeled our society The Affluent Society, The Great Society, and The New Frontier. As we move into the 1970s, it appears that a more appropriate title would be The Intoxicated Society.

For purposes of background, the major categories of illicitly used drugs can be considered sequentially.

First, there are the potent hallucinogens. Lysergic acid diethylamide (LSD) is the prototype and best known, but others are mescaline, psilocybin, dimethyltryptamine, and STP—an amphetamine derivative. As the enormous dangers of LSD became known to the medical community and then, through the media, to the general public, it became widely believed that the use of LSD was on the wane.

This was probably a premature judgment. In 1967 a variety of college and high school surveys indicated that the percentage of students using LSD ranged from zero to 15. Two of the better studies of 1968 appear to epitomize the situation in that year. At Ithaca College in New York State the amount of potent hallucinogen use in the different classes ranged from 3.8 to 5.4 per cent in males and from 0.6 to 2.2 per cent in females. In California, a very careful study by Richard Blum and his associates indicated that 17 per cent of the college sample and 20 per cent of the high school sample had tried potent hallucinogens. Data from 1968 thus suggest that, although there was no profound increase in LSD use during that year, neither was there a substantial decrease—and the same applies to 1971. A recent national survey places LSD use among college students at 14 per cent, and in a survey taken in a New Jersey suburban school during the 1969–1970 academic year, we found that 10 per cent of the junior and senior classes claimed experience with LSD.

Perhaps the most intriguing study recently published was that by Drs. George L. Mizner, James T. Barter, and Paul H. Werms of the University of Colorado Medical School, who presented their data at the American Psychiatric Association meetings in May, 1969. They noted that 5 per cent of a very large collegiate sample had used LSD at least once. Of this sample, 60 per cent had discontinued use, while 40 per cent planned to use LSD again. This seems to be a general pattern. Most of those who have tried LSD no longer use it, and others who thought of trying the drug have been frightened off by the publicity accorded its startling adverse effects. But a small percentage of non-LSD-using college students still indicate on questionnaires that they would like to try the drug. In addition, an increasing number of individuals who are afraid of LSD are turning on with other hallucinogens, particularly mescaline. Interviews with students from many college campuses convince me that the battle against the use of LSD is far from won. In large part this is because many students are told by their LSD-using colleagues that the alleged dangers of the drug have been much exaggerated and that, if taken under suitable circumstances, LSD is still quite a safe drug.

The marihuana situation is quite different. There has been a profound and obvious increase in the use of this drug in high schools and colleges. Nonetheless, statistics about use must be interpreted cautiously, particularly those quoted offhand by the student users themselves. Students frequently insist that 75 to 90 per cent of their colleagues use marihuana at least occasionally, but whenever their vague generalizations have been put to the test by careful analysis, they have turned out to be marked exaggerations; actual use was often two- to fivefold less. Unfortunately, these offhand, notoriously inaccurate, student statistics are often accepted as gospel by journalists and the public.

It is also important to point out that in almost every survey conducted, a significant percentage of respondents either failed to fill out the forms or in some other way made their answers unusable; in some of the best surveys no answers were obtained from one-third to almost one-half of those questioned. This obviously introduces a major bias in the results. Additionally, the marihuana scene changes so quickly that results obtained one month may differ substantially from data obtained from the same student population three months later.

Even if one acknowledges these shortcomings in survey figures, it is still clear that the use of marihuana in high schools and colleges has grown precipitously. In 1967 most experts agreed that about 15 per cent of college students used the drug on one or more occasions during a four-year college career. According to Blum's intensive studies in California (a leader in the marihuana sweepstakes, incidentally), the average use in one college was 21 per cent in 1967, and in a small sample in 1968 this had increased to 57 per cent. Blum's projection for 1969–1970 was approximately 70 per cent. The recent University of Colorado study placed the figure at 26 per cent, this being very close to a nationwide Gallup poll released on October 25, 1969, that gave a figure of 22 per cent. In a survey of ten high schools in Michigan, use ranged from zero to 33.7 per cent, and a college study revealed that 44 per cent had tried marihuana. Our own New Jersey study puts the figure at 25 per cent. An educated guess as of early 1971 would be that at least 35 per cent of college students will use marihuana on one or more occasions during a four-year college career, and that in some areas the figures will be strikingly higher, probably approaching the 75 to 90 per cent estimates of the students themselves. Thus, depending on whose figures you choose to accept, marihuana use among students has increased 100 to 200 per cent in just three years. In 1967 a prominent New York City psychiatrist suggested that use was so prevalent that anyone who did not smoke marihuana during his four years in college might well be atypical and could perhaps be considered inordinately rigid. Many drug educators decried his statement at the time, but now more and more people are beginning to believe that marihuana use rapidly is becoming the norm, so much so that the nonuser either is now or soon will be in the clear minority and therefore, in conventional sociological terms, indeed atypical.

As marihuana use increased, so did the use of hashish, a drug that contains the same active principle as marihuana but is five to eight times as potent. Hashish use is now epidemic; whenever marihuana becomes scarce, hashish is the drug usually turned to.

There are no accurate data on the abuse of stimulant drugs of the amphetamine variety. This is in part due to the fact that studies conducted in 1967 and early 1968 co-mingled heavy use of oral amphetamines for kicks, use in small dosage solely at examination time, and the intravenous use of methamphetamine (Methedrine, or speed). However, it was found that 2 per cent of Blum's 1968 undergraduate sample had injected Methedrine. Our New Jersey high school survey of 1969–1970 put the figure at 1 per cent. In high schools and colleges all across the country, especially on the east and west coasts, a small minority are using speed intravenously, the number increasing slowly but surely each month. Since use of Methedrine is characteristically continued once it has been started, the number of people so involved will continue to grow.

Equally alarming is the striking change in the pattern of heroin abuse in this country. There is no evidence that the total number of heroin addicts increased substantially in the United States between 1953 and 1965. Although the data are imprecise, a reasonable estimate is that there were in the range of 120,000 chronic heavy heroin users in the country each year during that period. However, in the last five years the number has risen considerably. The New York City narcotics registry recorded 62,938 heroin users in New York City alone during the five-year period 1964–1968 and has reported that, in late 1969, there was an additional sudden spurt in reported cases. Since it is estimated that for every known case there is one unreported, the 1970 figure for New York City is probably in the 100,000-to-120,000 range, and for the nation as a whole 200,000-to-250,000. Thus it would appear that the number of chronic users has doubled in the last five years. More alarming, the number of experimenters has grown precipitously, and no longer is heroin use confined to ghetto areas of large urban centers.

Heroin, of course, produces a high, and in our drug-inundated, kicks-oriented society it is hardly surprising that the notoriety surrounding this particular agent would assure its spread into middle- and upper-class neighborhoods and into colleges and high schools. More and more, those who seek pleasure or relief in drugs have turned to multiple drug use, and heroin and other opiates have become part of this pattern. This is borne out in a study conducted by Erich Goode in New York State, in which he analyzed the drug use pattern among 200 marihuana smokers, most of them students or affluent professionals. Of those tested, 49 per cent had tried LSD at least once, and 13 per cent had experimented with heroin. Among Blum's undergraduate college sample, of which 57 per cent had tried marihuana or some other cannabis preparation and 17 per cent had experimented with potent hallucinogens, it was found that 10 per cent had tried at least one of the opiate preparations. During the first years of LSD's extraordinary popularity, those who entered Bellevue Hospital in New York City with LSD-induced mental derangement had characteristically used marihuana and LSD and perhaps other hallucinogens, but they had not taken heroin. One year later, 50 per cent of those admitted to the hospital with LSD-induced psychiatric disorders had experimented with heroin. These studies have been confirmed by investigators at the Texas Research Institute of Mental Sciences in Houston, where it was found that among seventy-two patients studied primarily for their hallucinogen use, 29 per cent also had been involved with heroin. In our suburban New Jersey schools 1 per cent of the students admitted heroin use—a phenomenal figure when you realize that a few years ago the figure would have been zero in such a population.

It is, of course, the experimenter—who injects various amounts of heroin before his body is acclimated to the drug—who is most likely to die of acute heroin overdose. This may help explain the fact that in 1967 and 1968, in New York City, deaths from acute heroin intoxication rose so spectacularly that it became the leading cause of death in the fifteen- to thirty-five-year-old age group. In 1968 alone over 700 young people died from heroin overdose. In June, 1969, the situation dramatically worsened: One hundred and three persons died of heroin overdose, fifty of them on two successive weekends; one-third of them were under twenty years of age. For all of 1969 there were about 900 deaths due to heroin and in 1970 the number of heroin-related deaths increased to more than 1000. In small but increasing numbers, students will leave a school assembly or classroom, walk into a lavatory, inject heroin directly into the vein, and either be found in the bathroom stuporous or comatose or return to the classroom to sit nodding in drug-induced torpor. There have even been some reported cases of young people returning to their classrooms after taking heroin, suddenly experiencing overdose, and promptly dying as their classmates watched in horror. Perhaps no statement summarizes the discouraging situation better than that of a New Jersey school teacher who told me: "You know, in the last two years in our community more young people have died from drugs than from auto accidents and the Vietnam war combined."

Another grim fact: The age at which experimentation begins and the age groups in which use is maximal are becoming lower every year. The majority of the surveys conducted in 1966 and

1967 showed that the greatest percentage of marihuana, hallucinogen, and stimulant use occurred in the twenty-one- to twenty-two-year-old age group—that is, among college juniors and seniors. By 1968 the situation had changed. A survey by M. E. Rand, J. D. Hammond, and P. J. Moscou at Ithaca College in New York State showed that there was as much use of these drugs among freshmen and sophomores as among juniors and seniors. This study also pointed out that among marihuana users 29 per cent had their initial experience before entering college, and an additional 30 per cent had theirs during freshman year. The situation in regard to potent psychedelics such as LSD and mescaline was even more striking: 42 per cent had their initial experience before college, and an additional 24 per cent during their freshman year. Blum's studies in California also convincingly demonstrate the rapid increase of drug use within high schools. Blum surveyed three schools in 1967 to determine the prevalence of use and found that 7 to 31 per cent of the students had tried marihuana and, at the time of the survey, between 3 and 24 per cent were still smoking. The Blum group surveyed a single school in 1968 and found that 55 per cent had tried marihuana, and 39 per cent were continuing to use it. Maximum use was found in the twelfth grade. But that was all in 1968. In 1970, high school juniors, sophomores, and freshmen and even junior high and grade school students are rapidly catching up to the seniors. In our own high school survey we found that in some schools there was as much illicit drug use among freshmen and sophomores as there was among juniors and seniors. Thus we see how the marihuana fad, initiated by college juniors and seniors, has rapidly spread so that, at present, the majority of students are entering college with their drug habits already established. In regard to drugs a generation gap now exists between college seniors and incoming freshmen.

Other indications confirm this pattern of younger and younger drug users. In 1966 the average age of those in the New York City narcotics registry was 27.9 years. A year later it was 26.4 years, a decrease of 1½ years in that short period of time. In

New York City in 1967, 16,779 persons who were arrested admitted drug use. The figure for 1968 was 17,039—an increase of 15 per cent. But a breakdown of these figures is far more informative. Between 1967 and 1968 the total increase of those admitting drug use was 15 per cent, but among those in the sixteen- to twenty-year age group there was a 40 per cent increase, while in the twenty-one-year-and-older group there was actually an 8 per cent decrease.

Everywhere younger and younger individuals are experimenting and committing themselves to the drug scene. In New York City the entire eighth grade of a well-known private school was threatened with expulsion because of illicit use of stimulants and sedatives. Seven-, eight-, and nine-year-olds are swallowing stimulants or sedatives, smoking marihuana, and even injecting heroin. An indication of the severity of this problem may be found in a report from San Mateo County, California; in 1969 about 20 per cent of its eighth-graders had smoked marihuana, and approximately 10 per cent of its ninth-graders had tried LSD. Perhaps the most horrifying thing about use among the very young is that they have no capacity for discriminating among the various agents available. Although marihuana and pills are the most popular agents, many will take anything, including heroin, as long as there is the promise of intoxication. This accounts for the fact that of the approximately 900 heroin-induced deaths in New York City in 1969, 55 occurred in individuals sixteen years of age or younger. In 1968 no heroin deaths were reported in that age category.

The inhaling of volatile material is epidemic among this age group. They sniff glue, gasoline, decongestants, hair sprays, deodorants, spray-on foot medicaments, spot removers—even the ink in ball-point pens. Most, but not all, get away with it. There is a substantial number of cases of accidents or violent behavior under the influence of these materials. In 1969 the United States government released a report covering forty-four deaths of young persons who inhaled various sprays. Many died of suffocation, because they placed the volatile materials in a plastic bag, breathed deeply, and then lost consciousness with the plastic bag still around the head. A small number who inhaled glue, gasoline, or decongestants died from sudden swelling of the brain. One young boy sniffed a deodorant, became giddy and sick to his stomach, vomited, aspirated the vomitus into his lungs, and died therefrom. Another group of young people who sniffed glue developed serious depression of their bone marrow, leading in one case to bleeding, infection, and death.

In another report, in the June 22, 1970, issue of the *Journal of the American Medical Association,* Dr. Millard Bass summarized 110 additional sniffing deaths not due to suffocation and hypothesized that severe irregularities in heart rhythm were the cause of death. Here are two typical cases from that report:

> A 17-year-old white boy was offered the use of a plastic bag and spray can of hair shampoo at a beach party. The hair shampoo was sprayed into a plastic bag and then this teenager put his mouth to the open end of the bag and inhaled the spray. Upon inhaling the contents he exclaimed, "God, this stuff hits ya fast!" He got up and ran about 100 to 150 yards down the beach and collapsed. He was dead on arrival at the hospital. Complete autopsy: No anatomical cause of death.

> A 15-year-old white girl sprayed frying-pan aerosol into a plastic bag. She placed the opening of the bag over her nose and mouth and took several deep breaths. She said she felt funny, then sprayed more of the aerosol mist into the bag, and took another deep breath. Suddenly she became hysterical and began running about the house, picked up the phone and, without dialing, requested a doctor and hung up. She ran out of the house into the yard, then back into the house, and collapsed. She was dead on arrival at the hospital.

Some inhaled materials damage other organs. In the spring of 1969, ten persons aged twelve to sixteen were admitted to Montefiore Hospital in New York City with severe liver and /or kidney damage due to spot-remover inhalation.

As the average age of those involved in drug abuse gets

younger, some of the new fads become progressively more bizarre. Young persons are smoking toothpaste and injecting peanut butter, milk, meat tenderizer, perfume, or mayonnaise by vein. Some people have even injected marihuana directly into the vein. As one might anticipate, the frequency of severe complications, death included, is very high indeed.

In all age groups the taking of pills of unknown content is rampant. At Bethel, New York, some of the medical records of those who had bad trips read: "Took 2 blues, 2 reds, 3 greens." And that was the extent of the information. The users, their friends, and the treating physicians were all equally ignorant of what had been taken and what the potential toxicity might be. This willingness to take any pill that offers the promise of intoxication, regardless of possible dangers and without any knowledge of the content, is illustrated most dramatically by certain parties currently being held in many cities around the United States. Each partygoer brings a variety of unlabeled pills or capsules. These are all placed on a central table, and everyone at the party then chooses, by color or configuration, his intoxicants for the evening; no one gets a chance to know exactly what he or she is taking.

Although the United States leads in drug abuse this has become a world-wide problem. Sweden's stimulant problem is worse than America's. Drug abuse in England is rampant; in London a recent and disturbing fad is heavy intravenous use of barbiturates. France and Italy, long unaffected by drug abuse, both indicate increasing concern about drug use by their young. Even the Soviet Union acknowledges growing marihuana use. It now appears that no developed area of the world is immune from the ravages of drug abuse.

As the drug problem has increased, explanations as to why young people turn to drugs have proliferated. In a 1967 survey at Princeton University students placed relief of boredom at the top of the list. In other studies they emphasized curiosity, kicks, relaxation, a pleasant high, diminution of inhibitions, an urge to have a drug experience, and peer-group pressure. The search for insight was also frequently listed in 1967, especially by those using LSD and to a lesser extent by those experimenting with marihuana. Today there is much less emphasis on acquisition of insight. In a recent Colorado study of those who continued using marihuana, 68 per cent said they did so because it was fun and only 7 per cent because they felt the drug helped them achieve insight. In striking contrast, only 31 per cent who continued using LSD felt that the drug was pleasurable, while 38 per cent said they were continuing use primarily because it gave them increased insight. There are obviously many other factors. Blum, for example, found that drug users were more likely to be irreligious and opposed to their parents, felt they had experienced more interpersonal disruptions, and tended to be more curious, more adventuresome, and more responsive to social pressures than their non-drug-using peers. Blum also found that the committed drug user, as contrasted with the experimenter, tends to be more pessimistic and more dissatisfied; he will have experienced greater rebellion against his parents, and he feels emotionally alone.

In 1969, a whole new set of explanations became popular. More and more sociologists and psychologists, as well as educators, began to tie together drug abuse and the mood of rebellion sweeping this country. They suggested that to some extent drug use could be ascribed to the generation gap, to the war in Vietnam, to racial injustice, to urban decay, to environmental pollution, and to the threat of nuclear holocaust. I have followed the drug scene closely over the last few years, and my personal conviction is as follows: In 1967 the study of drug abuse among young people became extraordinarily popular. At that time, as I have indicated, the major reasons given by students for use included boredom, curiosity, and peer group influence. But those who began to investigate the drug scene in depth, and many more who were seeking material for speeches, began to look for less obvious causes than those listed by the students themselves. Thus the generation gap, the Vietnam war, and the inability to control one's future, none of which was listed in 1967, began to creep into talks and articles about the drug scene. Of course, as soon as such explanations were publicized, they were duly acknowledged by the most avid readers of drug scene literature—namely, the students themselves. Therefore, when students were asked in 1969 why they used drugs, they talked about the terrible war in Vietnam and the arms race—most likely because they had been told that these were tenable reasons for their drug use. This does not mean that dissatisfaction with the quality of life on our planet can be disregarded; unquestionably, this contributes to drug use. However, discussions with large numbers of students suggest that the reasons for using drugs have not changed substantially in the last few years. Indeed, more than ever before, curiosity, pleasure-seeking, and peer group influence appear to be the three major causes of drug experimentation, but it seems to me that at present we are underemphasizing another important cause—boredom. Kenneth Keniston has pointed out that our system of higher education, together with our affluence, now demands that youth spend a long time at an interface between the end of adolescence and mandatory commitment to the responsibilities of adulthood, such as earning a living and raising a family. During this period of prolonged adolescence our educational system provides far more knowledge than ever before, but it also allows so much flexibility and elective time in its curricula that many of today's students find themselves with an inordinate amount of free time. This is augmented by the all too common conviction of high school and college students that merely getting by is satisfactory. The combination of diminished responsibility, increased free time, and insouciance leads to boredom, and to the search for new and exciting experiences; in our society that search often leads to drugs.

Another factor I believe to be relevant is the lack of relief through commercial entertainment. People occasionally need to use fantasy to escape from the dreary or unpleasant aspects of their lives or to enhance their self-image. In the past this escape was often provided by motion pictures or the theater. No longer. Today movies and plays caricature life or depict its most unpleasant aspects, dwell on self-destructive sexual behavior, wallow in violence, or emphasize angry confrontation. Such "entertainment" provides little relief from the burdens of everyday life. Many desperately need their dreams and fantasies but, unable to use conventional entertainment as a mechanism for fantasy projection, and finding that they cannot create the illusions without external help, they enter their world of illusion through drugs of the marihuana and LSD types.

There are other aspects to escapism, namely, the use of drugs in reaction to academic pressures or the frustrations of everyday life. As competition for colleges and graduate schools increases, academic pressure grows. Some use drugs out of frustration because they cannot handle the academic demands; others compete successfully but use drugs such as marihuana for transient relief from the pressures.

There are, of course, all sorts of frustrations young persons must face, some real, others imagined. Use of drugs in an attempt to cope with these frustrations is a cop-out in that it contributes in no way to solving the problems that initiated the frustrations.

In addition to boredom and escapism, there is another factor of enormous importance that all too often has been almost totally neglected. This factor I shall call "ambivalent loneliness"—a concept emphasized by Dr. John Massey, an Oklahoma psychiatrist. The phenomenon is as follows: Many of us are afraid to give of ourselves; we hesitate to express our emotions openly, and we fear that if we get too close to others we may be threatened by that very intimacy. Living within a shell behind a facade of self-control creates loneliness that we both desire and dislike. When that loneliness becomes too great, we search desperately for an intimacy with others, for an opportunity to reach out and feel close to others. But it's not easy; one can't turn on intimacy at will. Because of this, we search for ways to sunder the barriers we have put between ourselves and others. Yet we do not want these barriers completely eradicated, because the sharing we seek, once

REASONS FOR DRUG USE

General	*Familial*	*Societal*	*Personality*
Curiosity	Broken family	Lack of escapism	Drug-prone
Peer group pressure	Unresolved problems	External boredom	Need to cope with sexual confrontation anxieties
Affluence (can afford drugs)	Bad parental example in regard to drug use	Lack of leadership	Depression
Free availability	Boredom	Hedonism (pleasure-seeking society)	Anxiety
Faddism		Disciplinary breakdown	Psychosis-neurosis
Desire to reduce social inhibitions		Communications media	Alienation
Adolescent rebellion		Milieu of ghetto	Internal boredom
Escape from academic pressures or frustrations with which he cannot cope			Normal adolescent turmoil
			Loneliness
			Inability to tolerate mental pain

achieved, soon becomes as threatening as the loneliness from which we fled. What is needed then, is a mechanism that disrupts our protective shell for a brief period and then permits its re-establishment. Certain drugs, especially marihuana, hashish, and the hallucinogens, fulfill this need. For a brief period they reduce inhibitions, penetrate loneliness and permit the individual to feel intimate with others. And there is no threat that the closeness, the sharing, and the free expression of ordinarily restrained emotions will be overwhelming, for the drug user knows he can return to his comfortable shell as soon as the drug's effects wear off. Many individuals live in a cycle of accepted loneliness, rejected loneliness, drug-induced rapport with others and, finally, a return to accepted loneliness. Depending on the individual's tolerance of his loneliness, drug use may occur once a year, once a month, once a week, or even once every few hours. Of course, there are many in our society who learn to live with their ambivalent loneliness without ever turning to illicit drugs. Some persons use alcohol, others sublimate by throwing themselves into work or athletics, and others adjust in a variety of different ways.

Curiosity, peer group pressure, and the desire for kicks are easy to reject as excuses for illicit drug use, but this is not true of loneliness. Those who cannot find relief from loneliness in alcohol or in other agents deemed acceptable by society, and so turn to illegal drugs, should be regarded with compassion and understanding, not cold condemnation. What percentage of those who use drugs do so in large part from loneliness? I have no idea; neither does anyone else. But among those who experiment with drugs the number is certainly substantial, and it is even greater among those who use drugs to excess. Clearly, there is an enormous difference between the use of an illicit drug for kicks and its use to escape loneliness. This fact should deter us from seeking either simplistic explanations or simplistic remedies for our growing drug problem.

The last year has brought a new facet of drug use into focus: Among the rebellious, drugs such as marihuana are frequently used merely to document anti-establishment attitudes and utter disdain for society's conventions or laws. For these persons drug use becomes a badge of rebellion and the very fact of illegality a specific reason for use.

Finally, it must be admitted that the media are inadvertently promoting the problem. Writers and reporters often cannot undertake detailed valid surveys of the actual extent of drug use. As a result, they often depend on superficial observations and on the statements of users. The resulting figures almost uniformly overestimate the amount of drug use. When they are presented on television, on radio, in newspapers and national magazines, no matter how cautiously, the impression is given that certain drugs, particularly marihuana, are being used by everybody. And it is natural for the young to then say to themselves: "If everybody else is doing it and almost everybody is getting away with it, why not take a chance?"

To sum up, it would seem that the reasons for illicit drug use by young people have not changed substantially over the last few years. It also seems that, as the prevalence of drug abuse grows, the internal and external pressures upon the nonuser to at least experiment with drugs have increased enormously. Furthermore, in our troubled nation pervasive unhappiness has become characteristic of a significant percentage of our young people and, because of our effective communications media, this unhappiness has literally become a contagious disease among the young, and more than any other group the unhappy are propelled to drug abuse.

2.

Approaching Young People

Obviously, ukases from on high, pedantic monologues, and unwarranted scare tactics are going to be ineffective in discussing drug use with young people. Anyone in an avuncular relationship to young people will have to develop his own particular methods, and surely there is no one right approach. Inevitably, a high school or college audience will view a representative of the so-called establishment with skepticism and even some hostility. If the speaker is to be effective, he must realize that he will have to be impeccably honest in his approach to drugs. Further, he will have to convince his audience that he knows a great deal more about drugs than they do. Most important, he must make his audience believe in his sincerity.

Long speeches are usually self-defeating. Rather, the speaker should present his own views in precise and unemotional fashion, concentrating on facts, and then the session should be opened to questions so that a dialogue ensues between speaker and audience. My own experience is that the question-and-answer period is always better received than the formal presentation. The speaker's objectives should be to make it clear where he stands and why, set the record straight as to the facts about drug use, and allow as few questions as possible to remain unanswered. Many speakers dislike extensive audience participation because they are afraid of questions they cannot answer. If, however, a speaker has done his homework and knows more than his audience, he need not be afraid of saying he doesn't know the answer to a question. That will not destroy his credibility with his audience; giving a dishonest or evasive answer will.

Here are some of the data I included in formal presentations given during the 1969–1970 academic year, starting with LSD:

Taken under strict and careful medical control, LSD may be helpful in the treatment of chronic alcoholism, and it may have some value in the treatment of certain psychoses in that it may permit more effective transference between patient and psychiatrist and may cause deeply repressed materials to surface. Furthermore, in a small number of cases LSD has been given to patients with terminal diseases associated with pain. In approximately half of these cases, the administration of LSD has been followed by a striking reduction in narcotic requirement and, in about half, it has permitted the patients to meet their imminent death with a great deal of equanimity. In none of these situations have the therapeutic effects of LSD been proven, but the results have been promising enough to warrant continued research.

There is no evidence that LSD taken under nonmedical aegis has beneficial effects. At first, its proponents said it augmented creativity, but there is no evidence that this is so. Indeed, a very careful study by Drs. W. H. McGlothlin, S. Cohen, and M. S. McGlothlin in the *Archives of General Psychiatry* shows that LSD has no effect on creativity. The LSD proselytizers said it was a potent aphrodisiac, but certainly it is not. People may have sexy thoughts under the influence of LSD and experience erotic illusions, but they rarely do anything about it, and that's not my definition of an aphrodisiac. Finally, it was insisted that LSD gave people important insights or permitted them to have extraordinary religious experiences. It appears that the insights are superficial and the religious experiences are ephemeral delusions.

A typical insight was described by a patient who entered Bellevue Hospital after taking an enormous amount of LSD. He was grossly psychotic for several days. After he became lucid, we asked him why he had taken such a fantastic dose. He said he had deliberately taken a very large amount of LSD in an attempt to gain insight, and he insisted that despite his hospitalization and psychotic break, the whole LSD experience had been worthwhile because he had indeed acquired insight. Our curiosity aroused, we asked him what he had learned. He said: "I have learned that I am egotistical." That is the type of insight that one gets; he could have found that out merely by sitting down in a quiet room and doing a little reflecting for a short period of time. LSD taken promiscuously under non-medical aegis has no demonstrable benefits; most of those who are still taking the drug are taking it not for benefits but simply for kicks.

What about the dangers of LSD? The evidence is overwhelming that LSD can cause almost indescribable panic. In Los Angeles alone, over 2,000 bad LSD trips were reported in a 1½-year period. A small number of homicides have taken place under the influence of the drug, and a substantial number of suicides. An interesting point about the suicides is that some of them clearly have not been intentional. For example, a friend of mine—a physician who took LSD before the dangers were fully documented—had to be forcibly restrained from jumping out of a fourth-floor window. When he came down from his LSD high, he told us that he remembered trying to jump out of the window and that he had been aware of what he was doing at the time. He said, however, that when he had looked out of the window, there was such beauty that he had an overwhelming desire to immerse himself in it immediately. Wherever LSD has become popular, suicides and accidents have followed. I saw two young men in New York City who got high on LSD and then walked into fires, remaining there—oblivious to pain—until they were horribly burned. Others have taken LSD during winter months and then, ignoring the cold and snow, have remained outside in freezing weather until they suffered serious frostbite, which in some cases resulted in gangrene of the fingers and toes.

Three additional dangers are psychosis, recurrence, and chromosomal abnormalities. It is now abundantly clear that a single ingestion of LSD may result in a mental breakdown requiring hospitalization for days, weeks, months, or even years. The individual does not have to have any severe underlying personality disturbance for a breakdown to occur. As far as his parents, his schoolmates, and his school's administration are concerned, a student may be perfectly normal and functioning adequately in his environment. Yet if he takes LSD just once, in conventional dosage, he may have a mental breakdown lasting for months or years. It is true that such extended psychotic reactions occur infrequently in a previously normal individual; nonetheless, they do occur.

The recurrence phenomenon is quite intriguing. If you take LSD today and have a typical trip, consisting of some pleasure but with some unpleasant aspects, the latter may come back days, months, or even years later—even if you take no more LSD or any other hallucinogens in the interim. A friend of mine—again a physician and, again, before the dangers of LSD were fully established—took LSD on a single occasion and for twelve hours had an absolutely beautiful trip; for the next twelve hours he experienced relentless panic. He called me some two and a half years later because during that entire two-and-a-half-year period, at unpredictable intervals, his panic had returned. It is also true that if you take LSD or mescaline, then, at some later time smoke marihuana, you may get an LSD-like reaction instead of the conventional, relatively mild, marihuana-like reaction.

The final point about LSD is its potential for genetic harm. First, it is necessary to explain how chromosomes are damaged. In essence, there are two major categories of drug-induced chromosomal abnormality. In the first type, the center of the chromosome or one of its arms may be broken. These chromosomal breaks are unstable abnormalities. They tend to be repaired rapidly, and they are not passed on from generation to generation. The second type of deformity is the so-called rearrangement, or translocation: Part of the chromosome is broken off, then attaches itself to another chromosome. This tends to be a stable abnormality often persisting in the individual for a long time, and it can be passed from generation to generation. Of course our physical and mental attributes are in large part directly related to our chromosomal makeup. Ordinarily, chromosomes are analyzed by taking blood from the arm, preparing some of the white blood cells by using easy chemical techniques, and then directly examining the chromosomes of these cells under the microscope.

There is still enormous controversy over the effects of LSD on chromosomes. The following is a summary of the information as of early 1971: There have been seventeen studies performed on groups of persons who took LSD. (I have excluded reports covering only one or two individuals.) In six of the seventeen studies, chromosomal breaks accompanied by rearrangements were found in up to 80 per cent of the users. Nine other studies either were negative or revealed breaks, but no significant number of rearrangements. In the final two investigations, the experts themselves could not decide whether they were negative or positive. The changes reported in the positive studies tend to persist. Some of the users with rearrangements have been followed for two and one-half years and continue to show the chromosomal defects. One geneticist studied forty children whose mothers took LSD early in pregnancy. In twenty of the forty, chromosomal defects were found, and these too appear to persist, in some cases having been followed for a minimum of two years. It is important to note that chromosomal abnormalities can be found after a single ingestion of conventional amounts of LSD. So it isn't necessary to take many or large doses to get into trouble.

These studies have been buttressed by experiments on animals. In three of five such studies LSD was given early in pregnancy, and its administration was followed by a very high incidence of stillbirths or fetal malformations. In the other two studies no such defects were found. For a considerable period of time the detractors of these studies said: "All right, there may be defects in blood cells, but what about reproductive tissues? If defects are found there, it is much more significant." Three such studies have now been published. In two of these studies LSD was given to mice and the same chromosomal defects found in the blood cells were detected in reproductive tissues. The third study was negative.

Finally, there are two studies analyzing the effects of LSD on the outcome of pregnancies. Drs. Chester Berlin and Cecil Jacobson of George Washington University observed 127 pregnancies in 112 women who took LSD during or before pregnancy. They found about double the expected incidence of spontaneous abortion and reported a sixteenfold increase in fetal abnormalities; especially prevalent were defects of the nervous system. On the other hand, William McGlothlin and his colleagues, reporting in the June 1, 1970, issue of the *Journal of the American Medical Association,* found no increase in birth defects in 121 pregnancies, although they did report an increased likelihood of spontaneous abortion if the mother used the drug before or during pregnancy.

Some people have criticized the LSD studies because the individuals evaluated often were taking drugs other than LSD. This is a valid point; however, in at least three cases the LSD was known to be the chemically pure laboratory investigation material. Thus we clearly have a drug that produces genetic harm in the test tube, in experimental animals, and apparently in some of the young people who use it.

What does all this mean? What do we look for in the user or in the user's children? The major disease sought in the user himself is leukemia, that is, cancer of the white blood cells, a disease almost invariably fatal. This can occur months or years after the ingestion of LSD, as long as the chromosomal abnormalities persist. As far as the user's children are concerned, it could be any physical or mental defect occurring at birth, early in life, or later in life. The first generation could carry the defect without any overt expression, but there could be major physical or mental abnormalities in the second generation. Unfortunately, it will take us two generations to make a valid judgment as to the kind and degree of harm the LSD already used has done to the user or his progeny. If we accept the potential of LSD for genetic harm, how many cases have there actually been of disease due to LSD? At present there are at least ten LSD users with either leukemia or a closely related disease, lymphoma. In addition, there are six cases reported of defects in the infants of women who took LSD during pregnancy; in four cases the child was born with a markedly deformed limb, and in another the bones of the chest and back were defective. In the final case there were multiple abnormalities that led to death at birth. There are also two cases of infants of LSD users being born with leukemia, a very uncommon disease in that age group. Does this mean there is a definite association between LSD use and leukemia, limb deformities, or any other abnormality? No. But it does seem clear that LSD has the potential for causing genetic mischief and that the increasing number of reported cases of either leukemia or other defects is a matter for considerable concern.

There are many people, including a substantial number of physicians, who disparage these findings; they say that measles vaccine, tranquilizers, aspirin, or caffeine can do exactly the same thing. I personally think these are irresponsible statements. It is indeed true that measles vaccine or naturally occurring measles can cause chromosomal breaks, but as soon as the acute effects of the vaccine or the measles are over, the breaks are repaired, and there is no evidence of the far more dangerous relocations. As far as tranquilizers are concerned, a definitive recent article from Mount Sinai Hospital in New York City, published in the *Journal of the American Medical Association,* indicates that no significant chromosomal abnormalities are found after use of tranquilizers. What about aspirin? It is true that aspirin in the test tube will produce chromosomal breaks, but not chromosomal rearrangements. If aspirin in considerable doses is given to mice during pregnancy, the newborns may show cleft palates, but no chromosomal defects. People taking very large amounts of aspirin for a substantial period of time have been carefully studied and no chromosomal abnormalities detected. Finally, there is caffeine. Caffeine is a mutagenic potentiator and will augment the potential of other chromosome-damaging drugs but, by itself, it can cause little damage of a severe nature in mammals. It can produce chromosome breaks in the test tube but appears to almost protect against rearrangement of the broken chromosomes. Caffeine has produced abnormalities in fruit flies and in rats. Although it is a bit unfair to compare experimental and human dosages, the fact is that the dosage used in the fruit fly would be equivalent to thirty gallons of coffee per day for a man. Recently, a seventeen-year-old high school boy in Detroit repeated the studies in the fruit fly and failed to detect any abnormalities. Up to this time, there has been not a single instance of caffeine-induced chromosomal abnormality in man.

It is one thing to say the studies are contradictory and that LSD has not been proved to be genetically harmful to man. That is a fair and honest statement. It is quite another thing to say that because the studies in man are not conclusive, there is no genetic harm associated with LSD. Such a statement is unfair and does a disservice to young persons who might then be encouraged to take the drug thinking it is safe. The fact of the matter is that we cannot dismiss the potential genetic harm of LSD. At the very least, it is our obligation to point out to young people that although a final judgment cannot now be made, if they opt for LSD, they also must accept the possibility of genetic damage. I would note that cyclamates were removed from the market because they produced cancer in the bladder of rats after prolonged treatment with large doses. And monosodium glutamate was removed because, in one set of experiments, it produced brain lesions in mice. Everyone applauded the government for these acts even though there was no evidence of harm to humans and little reason to believe those particular experiments are applicable to man. We know a hundred times as much about the dangers of LSD, yet many in the drug subculture continue to urge young people to try it. The evidence that some LSD users may show genetic damage, the impressive experimental studies, and the small number of cases of disease or defects following LSD ingestion should make any potential user think twice. Indeed, I personally carry this a step further. Anyone who uses LSD today under nonmedical aegis, given its extraordinary dangers, has to be either foolhardy, sick, or ignorant; I'm afraid there isn't any other rational way to look at it.

After data appeared on the dangers of LSD, its most vocal proponents issued what amounted to a blanket denial. One of them said: "The greatest hoax perpetrated on the American people in the twentieth century is that LSD is a dangerous drug." Then, as the evidence mounted against LSD, they began to change their tune, and what they said in essence was: "It may be true that LSD is a dangerous drug, but it really doesn't matter because we are now beyond LSD and we're taking new drugs that produce longer trips and are both safe and legal." I must say I don't think it's all that simple. The drug proselytizers seem to think they can advocate a drug and then abandon it if and when they find it is in reality dangerous. But what about the young people whose minds are perhaps permanently impaired by LSD? What about the young people who have seriously injured themselves under its influence? What about the young woman who might develop chromosomal damage and then would have to go through life with the threat of leukemia or damage to her children? Those who urge LSD on young people cannot simply walk away from all the problems caused by the drug they so enthusiastically promoted.

Two of the newer drugs they were talking about were STP and Asthmador. When I first heard about STP in the spring of 1967, I thought they were telling us that they were now taking a gasoline additive. If they had been, it might have been safer. In the early summer of 1967, somewhere between 5,000 and 20,000 doses of STP were given out free at a San Francisco "love-in," and within two weeks the young people were flocking to the Haight-Ashbury free medical clinic, some sick but others merely coming to the clinic to give back their supply. What is this allegedly safe drug? STP is an amphetamine derivative with atropine-like toxicity. What does this mean? Those who take the street variety frequently experience wild auditory and visual hallucinations. Additionally, they often have unpleasant reactions which include blurred vision, dry mouth, difficulty in swallowing, difficulty in breathing, agitated psychoses, marked increase in heart rate, stupor, coma, and occasionally even death from respiratory paralysis. Furthermore, if a physician thought a patient had taken LSD instead of STP and inadvertently gave him a drug called Thorazine (to some extent an LSD antidote), it would make the STP reaction worse and could even precipitate fatal cardiovascular collapse. Yet STP was ebulliently advertised as a new kick that was much safer than LSD!

The story with Asthmador is very similar. Asthmador is a proprietary preparation for asthmatics. Inhaled, it may be beneficial and is ordinarily quite safe. Members of the drug subculture learned that they could hallucinate if they swallowed a teaspoon to several tablespoons of the drug. Asthmador contains belladonna alkaloids, and the toxicity is very similar to that of STP.

I think the point to emphasize is that young people are not being told the truth. The Freon story is a good example. Freon is a substance used in refrigerators and to frost glasses. When used as intended, it causes no harm whatsoever. The drug proponents learned that if they sprayed Freon, not into a glass, but directly into their mouths, they would subsequently hallucinate. College newspapers were enthusiastically telling their readers that here was a new kick that was fun, safe, inexpensive, and legal. There are just two caveats they should have added to their pronouncements. First, there is evidence that when users hallucinate, they do so because they have displaced oxygen from the lungs and there is too little oxygen reaching the brain. Second, Freon sprayed directly into the respiratory tract can literally freeze it. This safe new kick was a drug whose mechanism of action was probably reduction of the oxygen supply to the brain and whose major acute toxic effect was death by asphyxiation. There were perhaps twenty to thirty deaths due to this fad. It temporarily ended when a nineteen-year-old college student who had taken Freon and had had no unpleasant effects sprayed it into the respiratory tract of his thirteen-year-old sister. She was promptly asphyxiated and died. But the drug subculture is inventive, imaginative, and undaunted by contretemps such as asphyxiation. In early 1969 in upper New York State, the proselytizers were once again urging young people to try Freon. This time they admitted that you could indeed die if you sprayed Freon directly into the mouth, but they insisted all you had to do was heat the Freon or let it come to room temperature and you could have your kicks without danger. Of course, if you heat Freon it may explode, but even to just let it warm up and then spray it into the respiratory tract doesn't obviate all the dangers. The medical division of the company which produces Freon says its studies suggest that about half the deaths were indeed due to freezing of the respiratory tract and subsequent asphyxiation, whereas the other half appear to be due to the brain being deprived of oxygen. Still, the irresponsible drug subculture was able to start another Freon fad, ignoring the possibility of more Freon-induced deaths.

What it amounts to is that young people are being urged to try any drug or any combination of drugs that may offer the potential for intoxication—regardless of the potential for harm. In Canada, for example, they are using a pill called the peace pill that on chemical analysis proves to be a combination of LSD, cocaine, and mescaline—a combination hardly calculated to give you a peaceful trip. In the United States, the "peace pill" contains entirely different ingredients from those found in the Canadian pill of the same name. In 1968 there was a pill, whose initials undoubtedly will be changed, called "LBJ stay away." It proved to be a combination of LSD and strychnine. Studies on the West Coast have suggested that capsules of LSD frequently contain about 10 per cent LSD and about 90 per cent adulterants that include atropine, strychnine, and amphetamines. Another Canadian pill, with the scatological initials FUK consisted mainly of phosgene. There have been several deaths from strychnine poisoning in persons who thought they were taking LSD.

Nowadays you can't even trust what is being sold as marihuana. "Pure grass" may be filled with inactive twigs and stems, oregano, alfalfa, or beet roots; in one case in New York State what was being smoked as marihuana was actually dehydrated horse manure. There is increasing evidence that some marihuana is laced with opium; in other cases either it is soaked in scopolamine or dimethyltryptamine is added to it before it is smoked. Both of these are potent drugs and give the user either a very agitated trip or an LSD reaction, not an ordinary marihuana high. And the increasingly popular marihuana cookies frequently contain mixtures of marihuana-like compounds and either stimulants of the amphetamine variety or hallucinogens of the belladonna-atropine group. Again the point to emphasize is that young people are not being told the facts about the contents of the drugs urged upon them. I think we have every right and indeed every obligation to urge young people who feel they must try illicit drugs to at least try to make sure that what they obtain is really that drug and nothing else. And they had better be very certain that they know the potential dangers thereof. Lack of knowledge and the failure of the proselytizers to tell them the truth may cost them dearly. Indeed, the price of a few hours of ephemeral pleasure may be terror, coma, acute mental breakdown, or even death. To quote an old saying: "Pleasure may be more trouble than trouble."

Perhaps I can sum up the whole area of deception in the illicit market by describing a case recently called to my attention. A young man who had no previous psychiatric difficulties and had never smoked marihuana was given three marihuana cigarettes by a friend. He smoked one and said it had no effect on him; so he smoked half of the second cigarette, after which he became agitated and confused. He refused his wife's request to go to a hospital and ran out of the apartment. The next she heard he had gone to an overpass they knew well and either jumped or fell to his death.

The question his young widow asked was, "Could this be due to marihuana?" The friend who provided the cigarettes was quite sophisticated about drugs and swore he had good marihuana that was absolutely pure. Before telling the widow this was due to marihuana we asked her to go through her husband's effects and let us have the third cigarette. This she did. On analysis, the tobacco was indeed pure, good-grade marihuana. But what the unfortunate dead young man, and even his friendly supplier, did not know was that the cigarette paper used to wrap the marihuana was loaded with LSD. LSD is destroyed by heat but the dead man still could have absorbed the drug while holding the cigarette in his mouth prior to lighting it or during the early smoking phases. I suspect this death was not due to marihuana but rather to LSD. Here was a young person whose life was snuffed out probably because LSD was added to his marihuana without his knowledge.

As the popularity of LSD leveled off, that of another group of drugs, the stimulants, increased. The history of stimulant abuse is intriguing. It started in Japan after World War II. During the war the Japanese had freely administered stimulants by mouth to their troops preparatory to combat. When the war was over, they had very large supplies of amphetamines—so-called wake-amines—which were then dumped on the open market where one could readily obtain the pills without prescription. By 1954, depending on whose account you accept, there were between 500,000 and 1½-million Japanese who were chronic heavy users of stimulants, about half taking them by mouth and the other half by needle. In 1954 the Japanese decided they had had enough, and thereafter they rigidly controlled supplies, conducted an educational campaign, and imposed penalties both for illicit possession and for illegal sale or manufacture. Within a year the problem had diminished profoundly.

As the problem lessened in Japan, it increased in Sweden, where a group of bohemians began to use substantial amounts of oral amphetamines. Shortly thereafter, an enterprising and apparently overage medical student discovered that a far greater kick could be obtained by injecting the drug intravenously. By the early 1960s, far and away the most popular stimulant used in Sweden was phenmetrazine, which goes by the trade name Preludin and is ordinarily taken in pill form in attempts to lose weight. The Swedes also used a stimulant drug called Ritalin, and either amphetamines by mouth or, more commonly, methamphetamine by vein. The latter, of course, is the same as the Methedrine used in the United States and colloquially called speed.

The most important thing to recognize about the illicit use of stimulants is the enormous amount used by those who are chronically and heavily habituated. For example, if a doctor prescribes Preludin or Dexedrine, he will give one tablet three times a day, which is the equivalent of 75 milligrams of Preludin or 15 milligrams of amphetamine. The abusers, both in Sweden and the United States, tend to take not three, but 20 to 200 pills daily. In Sweden users inject 1,800 to 3,000 milligrams of Preludin into their veins daily and, in the United States, 150 to 15,000 milligrams of Methedrine. In other words, they are using between ten and one thousand times the usual dosage. Stimulants taken in such gigantic doses are fantastic energizers and inhibition releasers. In Stockholm there are now estimated to be between 5,000 and 10,000 heavy users of these drugs, most of them taking them intravenously, and the number of people involved doubles every two years. Characteristically, the user takes four to six injections a day, eats little, and sleeps almost not at all. He may go for days or even as long as two weeks with hardly any sleep. After this period he injects himself with a sedative, sleeps for forty-eight hours, and then starts the cycle over again. In both experimental animals and in man the use of very large amounts of these stimulants produces stereotyped behavior. An animal, for example, may open and close a paw for hours on end, and people who have taken Preludin or Methedrine have been known to dismantle and then reassemble a lamp or a motor and repeat this cycle endlessly for nine to twelve hours. I well remember one young lady who abhorred housework and used to get her kicks from injecting intravenous Methedrine while she was sitting in a bathtub. As soon as the needle was out of her vein and the drug began to take effect, she could hardly wait to get out of the tub, grab a broom, and vigorously clean her one-room apartment—continuing to do so for as long as five, six, or ten hours at a stretch.

The most important adverse effect of any of these stimulants taken in large dosage is paranoia, that is, delusions of persecution. This is so well known in Sweden that it is simply called "noia" there. When noia hits the Swedes, a temperamentally nonaggressive people, they tend to behave ludicrously but harmlessly. For example, one man took all the furniture out of his apartment, dragged it to the roof of his building, and then threw it off—because, he said, there were gnomes below who were out to get him. Another man bought a gigantic dog and walked him around the block over and over again in a futile search for imaginary enemies. One man who got his noia during the middle of the day jumped out of his chair screaming that the police were after him, jumped into his Volvo and rushed through the middle of Stockholm as fast as the car would take him. Stockholm at midday is a driver's nightmare, and by the time the gentleman with his noia had proceeded about a mile he was exactly right—the entire local constabulary was indeed after him. Eventually he smashed up his car, but nobody was seriously hurt. The Swedes' reactions may be ludicrous or humorous, but violence occurs infrequently.

The situation is not the same in America. After all, we are an aggressive society, and if you introduce into such a society a drug that simultaneously energizes, reduces inhibitions, increases all sorts of activity including sexual activity, and induces delusions of persecution, you are openly inviting rape, mayhem, or murder—and this kind of crime is precisely what has happened. A perfect example is the Haight-Ashbury district in San Francisco. When the young people first formed their community there it was, at least by many standards, a kookie area; but it was peaceful, with marihuana and LSD as the drugs of choice. The San Francisco police, who abhorred the "hippie" community, were the first to admit that there was virtually no violence in it. Pretty soon, however, the area attracted certain groups with sociopathic tendencies who went there solely because it was well known that the Haight-Ashbury was where the action was and that the girls were readily available. Those who came included members of motorcycle gangs who brought with them their amphetamines—a virtual staple of their diets. Thus, within a year and a half of the time the Haight-Ashbury district achieved notoriety, it was inundated with amphetamines. Large numbers of young people began to use them both by mouth and by vein in very large dosages. Today that community is repulsive. The original flower children have gone, and now the most popular drugs, aside from marihuana, are Methedrine and heroin. As one might anticipate, the peace has been replaced by violence. Precisely the same sequence of events is now taking place in a similar community in Atlanta, Georgia.

In the first six months of 1969 there were over thirty murders in the Haight-Ashbury district directly related to the heavy use of amphetamines. Similarly, on the Lower East Side of New York, in an enclave where Methedrine became equally popular, a celebrated homicide took place in which a young girl was raped and then she and her boyfriend were bludgeoned to death. According to the newspapers, the murders followed an extended LSD party, but all the evidence suggests that those involved were actually Methedrine users. And in Queens, New York, in June, 1969, a twenty-two-year-old man went berserk on Methedrine and shot three friends and himself. If you give Methedrine to an angry, basically aggressive individual and he becomes paranoid, violent behavior almost inevitably follows. I would hasten to say that the heavy amphetamine use by pill or needle in our colleges and high schools, which is increasing very substantially, has been associated with marked behavioral abnormalities, but thus far with no significant amount of violence, presumably because those using the central nervous system stimulants excessively in student communities are not people with an extraordinary amount of latent aggression.

Nonetheless, I think we can predict with considerable assurance that if this pattern of abuse continues to evolve, there will be violent behavior even in colleges and high schools.

The other major toxic effect to be concerned about when considering stimulants is permanent brain damage. Studies in Japan and more recent ones in Sweden suggest that habitual users of these stimulants by the intravenous route develop a so-called organic brain syndrome, as evidenced by long-standing personality changes and persisting abnormalities on brain-wave testing. Physicians in these two countries believe strongly that stimulant drugs taken heavily and habitually can permanently injure the brain, and there are experimental data to back them up.

Let us turn to what appears to be the young generation's favorite drug, marihuana. It is not a hallucinogen; rather, it should properly be classified as a euphoriant. Those who favor the drug and enjoy its effects say it makes them feel good. Marihuana users tend to become talkative, have a carefree and happy feeling, laugh easily, may enjoy music more than ordinarily, and often note a feeling of togetherness with their companions who are sharing in the marihuana experience. This is not a drug with the capacity to alter the mind in the manner that LSD does. During the early phases of the LSD fad, those who used and advocated it insisted that it had fantastic effects on the mind. Although we could warn them about the potential dangers of LSD, we had to admit that the effects on the mind were so overwhelming and dramatic that for some individuals the lure of the drug was virtually irresistible. This is not the case with marihuana. It is for most people a mild drug if taken in moderate dosage. In point of fact, exactly the same effects can be produced if someone merely thinks he is smoking marihuana. The following story, which has been told to me in similar versions by many different groups of young people, will illustrate this:

One weekend five college students decided to obtain some marihuana. Four of them had never smoked the drug; the fifth had had considerable experience, and he knew where to buy it. He purchased some, and then they sat around in an apartment smoking and enjoying themselves. After they had lit their cigarettes and taken deep puffs, one of them noticed that he was very talkative, and a second felt unusually happy; a third listened to music and said it had never sounded so beautiful, and a fourth sat quietly suffused with feelings of good will toward his companions. The fifth smoked carefully and intently, but he was getting no effect at all. He was the purchaser of the marihuana, the only one who had had any experience with the drug. He knew perfectly well they all had been burned—that what they had bought was ersatz marihuana and not the real thing. The next night they purchased some real marihuana, and this time the purchaser made certain good stuff was obtained, and all five experienced the desired high. The four neophytes had had a marihuana-like experience without ever touching marihuana because they thought they were smoking it. In other words, the drug is so impotent that suggestion alone can virtually reproduce its effects.

This anecdote was confirmed through a controlled study by Drs. Reese Jones and George Stone, presented at the American Psychiatric Association meetings in Florida in May, 1969. They found that even experienced marihuana smokers could not distinguish between a cigarette containing a very substantial amount of tetrahydrocannabinol, the active ingredient in marihuana, and a non-marihuana-containing placebo. To quote them: "This evidence of the unreliability of human assay utilizing heavy smokers should cause investigators to exercise some caution and should cause marijuana peddlers some joy." To put it another way, just think how embarrassing it would be to find you had been having a great high and that in reality the cigarette contained, not marihuana, but alfalfa, oregano, or horse dung. This, of course, could never happen with LSD, for that drug is so powerful that you cannot mimic or simulate its effects through mere suggestion. Those advocating marihuana have tried to glorify it and invest it with grandeur. Unwittingly, our society has helped them by overreacting so strenuously to marihuana that young people have become convinced there must be something important about it. This is bad, for the first step in understanding this drug fad and in handling it sensibly is to deglamorize marihuana and restore it to its rightful place as a minor-league modifier of human consciousness. That's all it is. It often intoxicates and gives pleasure, but it's no big deal.

The second point to discuss is whether or not marihuana is a dangerous drug. Those who urge it on us say it is innocuous, totally harmless. Yet all the data available to our society since 1850 contradict them. What are the facts about the potential dangers of marihuana? These must be divided into two categories: first, the acute dangers, and second, the chronic dangers.

There are five acute dangers: panic, depression, paranoia, psychosis, and accident proneness. In 1956 the noted author William Burroughs, certainly no opponent of drug use, summarized in typically concise and articulate fashion the panic and depression. He said: "Marijuana is a sensitizer and the results are not always pleasant. It makes a bad situation worse, depression becomes despair, anxiety panic." This is precisely correct. If an individual smokes marihuana, even one cigarette, when he feels somewhat anxious, his anxiety may be transformed into overwhelming panic; and if at the time he smokes he is a bit unhappy, his unhappiness may grow into overwhelming despair. Under these conditions, a few young people have even attempted suicide. Panic and despair are of course highly unpleasant and undesirable reactions. The obvious question is how frequently they occur. The answer is: infrequently. If a hundred young people smoke marihuana, many will have no effects at all, many others will have what they would describe as a pleasant trip, and perhaps only one or two will experience severe fear or depression. And so it is clear that these adverse effects occur infrequently after one or two marihuana cigarettes. Nonetheless, they do occur. It is distortion of the facts to suggest that they do not.

Sometimes those who smoke marihuana have feelings of persecution, or paranoia; this is usually short-lived but may persist for hours or in rare instances for days. Some people say the paranoia results from legitimate fear of detection, and this may well be so, but there are those who have experienced feelings of persecution in situations where there was no possibility of detection. Therefore one must conclude that the paranoia is not solely related to our society's reaction to marihuana use. Acute psychosis occurs very infrequently after smoking small amounts of our type of marihuana, but as the use of marihuana grows, so does the number of reports documenting this complication. If a person has no significant underlying personality disturbance, mental breakdown is unlikely and the reaction, should it occur, is usually transient. But, if one has substantial personality disturbances or psychiatric problems, marihuana can precipitate an acute mental derangement that may require hospitalization and last for a considerable period of time. Dr. Doris Milman of New York City, writing in the *Journal of Pediatrics* in February, 1969, has described her experience with eleven such breakdown cases. And Drs. Martin Keeler, Clifford Reifler, and Myron Liptzin, writing in the *American Journal of Psychiatry* in September, 1968, have pointed out that if an individual has an unpleasant reaction from marihuana, it may recur spontaneously for up to three weeks after he has stopped smoking the drug. Marihuana also distorts time and space perception, and those driving under its influence are accident-prone and therefore potentially dangerous to themselves and to others. The majority of studies that have adequately tested motor performance show that even if simple motor acts are performed adequately under the influence of marihuana, complex ones are impaired. This would apply to driving an automobile.

It is clear, then, that marihuana, smoked in moderation, is not necessarily innocuous; it is a potentially harmful drug. But to state the case with impeccable honesty, one must emphasize that, excluding driving under its influence, the adverse reactions I have described will occur in only a small percentage of marihuana users. Acute dangers thus are limited, but they unequivocally are present.

Of far more concern are the dangers of chronic use. These include loss of goals, becoming a pothead, the dosage phenomenon, and closely related to this, escalation. I shall take these up in turn.

If an individual smokes marihuana every day or several times a week and on each day his total consumption is only two to four cigarettes, he may nevertheless experience a complete change in his outlook on life and lose his goals. A student who is doing well academically may begin to fail. One who plans to go on to graduate school may find that every time he faces the stress of an examination he smokes a marihuana cigarette and under its influence decides the exam is not so important, that his goals are illusory after all. So he does not study, smokes his marihuana, and fails his examination. Others may become forgetful and may find that they do not think nearly as clearly as they did before they used marihuana regularly. There are those in the drug cult who say: "So what?" They insist the original goals were ridiculous and the users are much better off having lost them. But that glib statement is not really fair, because many young people are coming to health services, physicians, or clergymen and asking to be given guidance to restore them to a goal-oriented life. For the most part, this can be done with counseling and discontinuation of marihuana use. Yet not all are aware enough to seek help. A complaint heard most often from friends of chronic marihuana users is that "he just isn't thinking right and he doesn't even seem to know it." I would emphasize that you do not have to be a sick personality to lose your goals or thinking powers under the influence of chronic marihuana smoking even if you are only smoking two, three, or four cigarettes daily or several times each week. Indeed, there is increasing evidence that this may happen to people under seventeen years of age even if they never smoke more than one or two cigarettes three or four times weekly.

Then there is the problem of the pothead. It is exactly the same as the problem of the alcoholic. The pothead no longer controls the drug, the drug controls him. For him, marihuana is the center of the universe. He smokes as much as he can, is high most of the time, and his whole life revolves around the marihuana experience. And he almost invariably undergoes psychological deterioration. It is currently estimated that 1 to 3 per cent of those who smoke on more than ten occasions will become potheads. A psychiatrist, after careful evaluation, might be able to predict who among the chronic marihuana smokers would be likely to develop into a pothead, but the young people who use the drug cannot make this judgment. What this means at a practical level is that any person using marihuana habitually must accept the risk that he might lose control and become a pothead.

Another potential danger of repeated use is related to the dosage phenomenon, by which I mean the following: An individual who smokes marihuana is using a drug that generically is termed cannabis. There are many forms of cannabis. Our marihuana is one of the weakest. Hashish, a form popular in England, contains far more tetrahydrocannabinol, the pure active ingredient in all forms of cannabis. Hashish is far more powerful than marihuana and also somewhat more dangerous. All the adverse effects I have described for marihuana occur more frequently and more predictably with hashish. Perhaps the dosage phenomenon can be best illustrated by describing experiments that have been performed with tetrahydrocannabinol. If you give someone a small amount of this substance, called THC, either by mouth or in cigarette form, he will have a marihuana reaction—that is, talkativeness, giddiness, euphoria, etc. If you take the same person under exactly the same circumstances on the following day and give him three to four times the amount of tetrahydrocannabinol, he will experience illusions, delusions, hallucinations and feelings of depersonalization—a reaction that could legitimately be described as an acute psychotic break. Thus if an individual smokes two, three, four, five, or ten marihuana cigarettes at one sitting or uses substantial amounts of hashish or THC, the chances for a bad reaction are greatly increased. There are those who say that cannabis users will always automatically limit their intake at any one session, but this is ridiculous. If given the opportunity, quite a few young people will smoke any number of marihuana cigarettes in a short period of time or will use large amounts of hashish or take THC. In 1968 and 1969 tetrahydrocannabinol tablets were sold for as much as $5 each, and each tablet was supposed to contain the equivalent of five marihuana cigarettes. Four tablets at one ingestion—the equivalent of twenty marihuana cigarettes—would make the adverse reaction rate enormous. Initially, such reactions were not noticed, for a very simple reason: Synthetic tetrahydrocannabinol is still unstable and deteriorates if removed from refrigeration for even a very short time. Consequently, those who thought they were getting a tablet containing the equivalent of five marihuana cigarettes were really getting no drug at all. But the problem of the instability of the THC will surely be solved in the near future, and then we will all have to face the realities of the dosage phenomenon. When that happens, it will be clear that it is silly to suggest that marihuana and marihuana-like drugs are entirely harmless.

The last of the important chronic consequences of marihuana use is escalation. What percentage of those who start with marihuana are likely to progress to more dangerous drugs such as LSD, tetrahydrocannabinol, Methedrine, or heroin? Virtually every expert now agrees that there is nothing about marihuana itself that compels an individual to go on to any other more dangerous drug. The relevant question for students in high schools and colleges is what percentage of them will elect voluntarily to do so. The answer, according to studies at numerous schools and colleges across the country during the period when LSD was at the zenith of its popularity, was 10 to 45 per cent. It is clear then, that the majority of students who smoke marihuana will not move on to LSD or similarly dangerous drugs, but the minority who will do so is still very sizable; indeed, in some schools it is almost half the total population of marihuana users. This is a very important and significant figure. It indicates that those who claim that if you use marihuana you will inevitably go to LSD or something else are absolutely wrong. But those who say that marihuana does not lead to more dangerous drugs are equally wrong.

There are increasing numbers of studies indicating that the likelihood of moving on to more potent drugs is directly related to the number of times one smokes marihuana. Most young people who experiment with it do so only transiently. Studies from numerous colleges indicate that at least 60 per cent of marihuana users do not use the drug more than ten times in their college careers. Among those who do, there is a direct correlation between the amount used and later experimentation with more dangerous agents. This is documented in a recent study by Erich Goode of the Stony Brook campus of the State University of New York. He found that if an individual in the population he studied used marihuana less than monthly, he had a 22 per cent chance of trying LSD when it was popular and readily available. If he used marihuana one or two times a week, the likelihood of trying LSD rose to 49 per cent. If marihuana was smoked every day, then the chances of using LSD were 82 per cent. What this amounts to, very simply, is that the more marihuana one smokes, the more one is likely to be involved in the drug subculture and the more one is likely to have a coterie of friends who use more than one drug. Under these circumstances it is more likely that a person will escalate to other drugs. Again, I am not saying that marihuana forces anyone to go on to more dangerous drugs; rather, the more you smoke it, the more likely it is that if you enjoy the experience you will opt for experimentation with LSD or THC or the central nervous system stimulants. Furthermore, there is now increasing evidence that some individuals, even in schools and colleges, who smoke marihuana on more than ten occasions will choose to experiment not only with potent hallucinogens and stimulants but also with heroin. Except under unusual circumstances, they will not become addicted to it, but they will try to see what the kick is like. For example, in Goode's series of 200 marihuana users, a very high percentage of whom were students, professional people, or affluent individuals, an astounding 13 per cent had used heroin. Very clear dangers then, are associated with the use of marihuana, and the more one smokes, the more one is likely to run into trouble of one sort or another.

A great many people insist on comparing the effects of marihuana to those of alcohol. They say that marihuana is no more dangerous and therefore should be legalized. It is certainly true that marihuana is no worse than alcohol, but if one wishes to compare the two, the comparison must be made between, for example, two shots of alcohol and one or two marihuana cigarettes. Or, at the other end of the spectrum, the alcoholic should be compared with the pothead. Those who wish to state the case strongly for marihuana very often glibly try to compare the smoking of one or two cigarettes with chronic severe alcoholism. This simply isn't fair. If one honestly compares two shots of alcohol and one or two marihuana cigarettes, then the evidence suggests that marihuana is a little bit more dangerous. It is more likely that the marihuana smoker may experience panic or depression or even an acute mental break, and driving under the influence of marihuana is more dangerous than driving under the influence of an equivalent amount of alcohol. This is true because even though both are intoxicants, the marihuana smoker may feel omnipotent and not recognize his perceptual defects, whereas the alcohol drinker is much more likely to realize that he is drunk and drive accordingly. On the other hand, alcohol is more likely to release aggressive tendencies. If we speak of chronic use, alcohol clearly is worse. A pothead will show psychological deterioration, but the severe chronic alcoholic will show psychological deterioration plus physical manifestations such as brain, liver, and nerve damage.

If the question before our society were simply whether to choose alcohol or marihuana, I personally would choose marihuana. But the question before us as a society is whether we should add marihuana to alcohol. We now have 6 to 9 million alcoholics. If marihuana were legalized and use grew markedly, the percentage of potheads might increase to 5 or even 10 per cent of the users. Are we prepared to add perhaps 1 to 3 million potheads to our 6 or more million alcoholics? And if so, where do we stop? There are many people in Sweden and some in this country who tell us: "I don't like alcohol and I don't want marihuana, I want my amphetamines. I will take only a few and they won't hurt me." And in a sense they make a valid point, for one to three amphetamine tablets a day taken by mouth are no more dangerous than a moderate amount of alcohol or one or two marihuana cigarettes. Therefore, if we are to add to alcohol any other drug that in moderation is no worse than alcohol, our society will have to legalize a veritable farrago of drugs, each with limited dangers if taken in moderation and each with far greater dangers if used to excess. And I would submit that no society can survive with unlimited intoxicants.

It appears to me, then, that marihuana does have certain potential dangers and that there are sensible reasons for opposing its legalization. But it is also true that the laws in our society governing marihuana are absolutely atrocious. We continue to treat a minor-league drug as if it were a heinous offense, and this makes no sense at all. It only glamorizes the drug and lures young people into using it merely because the laws are so abominable. (I shall discuss in some detail the current laws and their viciousness in Chapter 8.)

Finally, it seems to me important to point out to young persons that becoming involved in and then committed to the drug scene is a waste of time. Over the past few years a great many students have begun to question whether or not our society can change the world for the better by dint of its own efforts. This is a disturbing phenomenon. Given our incredible drug cornucopia, if young people become convinced that they cannot resolve the major problems facing our times, there is an excellent chance they will eventually turn to drugs. After all, if there is no tomorrow, one might as well enjoy as much as possible the pleasures of today, including the pleasures derived from mind-altering drugs. Today, with greater and greater frequency, young people are saying that they do not believe they have any chance at all of solving the world's greatest problems during their lifetime. The population boom, poverty, pollution, urban decay, and potential nuclear holocaust appear too overwhelming. Once they convince themselves that these problems are insoluble, they say, "Let us enjoy ourselves now any way we can and not worry about the risks." If these problems were indeed insoluble, then I and many other educators would not expend our efforts in stating the case against drugs. But this is not the case. We have been and we must be a meliorist society—a society dedicated to the proposition that we can approach and remedy the great problems before us. The younger generation cannot afford the time to play around with drugs that frequently have the capacity to impair one's mind for a prolonged period of time. It is especially the responsibility of the young to recognize our major problems and not to react with mere angry protest or withdrawal, especially withdrawal into the drug scene. Rather, they must commit themselves by sustained and constructive effort to alleviating these problems. If they do not, if they withdraw into a world of drug-induced pleasure—if they abrogate their responsibilities to themselves and their world—the simple fact is that these gigantic problems will become progressively worse, and one or two decades hence they may be truly insoluble.

3.

Questions and Answers

All of the questions in this chapter have been raised by audiences attending my lectures on drug abuse. The selection includes those questions asked most frequently and those that I believe best illustrate an important point. Some questions, especially on marihuana, are closely related, resulting in some repetition in the answers. In an effort to answer specifically each question, I have let the repetitions stand.

Question: How can you say marihuana is dangerous? Many of my friends have been using it, and none of them has gotten into any trouble.

Answer: This really relates to the difference between an individual's experience and the more extensive data gathered epidemiologically. It is clear that the dangers from use of small amounts of American-type marihuana are limited, and therefore it is very possible that someone with, say, fifty friends or acquaintances who use marihuana will not know any who have had major trouble with it. But someone else with an entirely different group of friends might know one, two, five, or ten out of fifty who have had trouble with marihuana itself or have escalated to other drugs which did harm them. The important point to emphasize is that one can't generalize from one's limited experience. If you are going to make broad and dogmatic statements such as "Marihuana is a harmless drug," you must utilize not only your own experience but all the available evidence you can gather. If one merely limits his information to his own experience, his viewpoint may be decidedly warped. Of course, dosage and regularity of use are important in this context. For example, if a group were composed of experimenters, all smoking irregularly, or even daily at a maximum dose of one to two, it might be that not a single one would have any trouble with the drug. A second group of marihuana users, far more committed to the drug scene, might smoke more extensively. Among these there would be a much higher incidence of loss of goals, the possibility of turning into potheads, difficulty with the thinking process, or simultaneous use of other drugs such as LSD, intravenous amphetamines, or heroin. The individuals in a third group in which marihuana was used might have a preference for stronger forms of cannabis such as hashish or tetrahydrocannabinol, and in this group the adverse reaction rate surely would be substantially higher. Finally, on the other side of the ledger, an antidrug educator, a health counselor, or a school physician will not see those who are experimenting with marihuana and enjoying it, but rather those who have had adverse reactions or have lost control of the drug, so that he might consider marihuana a drug with considerable potential for harm. What it amounts to is that it all depends on the vantage point. The argument "X drug didn't hurt any of my friends" is totally irrelevant to the central question of whether a drug is potentially harmful.

The limitations on personal experience are emphasized beautifully by a recent experience I had in Oklahoma. I gave a talk covering the material in Chapter 2, and following the discussion period a young man came up and angrily berated me for saying THC in appropriate dosage could mimic the LSD experience. I quoted the studies to him, but he adamantly refused to alter his view that THC was always as mild as marihuana. Finally, I asked him how he could be so sure, and he said, "I know because I've used THC myself, and my experience shows you are wrong." Of course what he did not know was that the THC available on the illicit market was unstable, and that he may have thought he was taking a standard dose of THC but, in actuality, he was getting either no THC or only a minuscule amount. Under such conditions, he would naturally think THC was a very mild drug. In this case, his own experience with THC gave him a completely distorted concept of the effects of the drug. It shows how cautious one must be in generalizing from a limited personal experience.

Question: I am still unclear as to how often an occasional or once-a-day marihuana smoker gets into trouble.

Answer: Infrequently. But as I have indicated, depression, despair, panic, paranoia, or a mental break can occur after a single cigarette. Dr. Walter Bromberg of Bellevue Hospital recorded the first seven cases in America in the late 1930s. In a recent article in the *Annals of Internal Medicine,* Dr. William Grossman recorded the case of a healthy young man who ingested bhang, a form of cannabis even milder than marihuana. The young man reported he felt giddy, shaky, and anxious, thought he was going to die, and felt like two people. This lasted only forty-five minutes, but many months later he noted: ". . . even now, that night remains in my mind as the worst and most frightening experience I've ever had."

Doctors J. A. Talbott and J. W. Teague, writing in the *Journal of the American Medical Association* in October, 1969, reported twelve cases of acute, transient psychosis in U.S. soldiers in Vietnam who smoked Vietnamese marihuana, a type about twice as potent as that usually consumed in America.

There are other data on the frequency of unpleasant effects of marihuana. Richard Blum, in *Students and Drugs,* notes that of the college students surveyed, 46 per cent reported ill effects, including:

headache or nausea 21%
emotional upset due to drug 15%

physical distress 11%
troubled thinking 9%
unpleasant hallucinations 8%
loss of self-control 4%
incidents leading to trouble with friends 4%
psychological distress 3%
study problems 2%
bad dreams 2%
car accidents 1%
unfortunate sexual incidents or difficulties 1%

Blum found that among those surveyed, intensive users reported 1.3 different ill effects per person as contrasted to 0.8 per person among less intensive users. Most unpleasant effects reported by Blum and by Dr. David Smith in a similar study, were not severe enough to cause marihuana users to stop smoking. The more severe reactions—panic, depression, mental breaks—affect an estimated 1 per cent of marihuana users.

D. J. Wolk, who reported the marihuana experience at the University of Bridgeport in Connecticut in the *Journal of the American College Health Association,* found that in different groups, up to 20 per cent became frightened or tense after marihuana, and up to 14 per cent felt depressed and unhappy.

An increasing number of investigators and students are finding that the younger the person, the less able he is to control the drug and the more likely it is that even on one or two cigarettes a day he will have difficulties thinking and studying. Marihuana is unpredictable. Some individuals are unaffected, others have a good experience, and still others have untoward effects most of which, for the experimenter, are transient and mild, but occasionally can be more severe.

Question: Wouldn't those who develop a severe mental breakdown after marihuana or LSD have had the same breakdown if they had not used the drug? Don't they have personality problems so severe that lots of things can precipitate a breakdown? If this is true, how can you blame marihuana or LSD?

Answer: It seems true from the marihuana studies of Dr. Doris

Milman, reported in the *Journal of Pediatrics,* and those of Dr. William Grossman, recorded in the *Annals of Internal Medicine,* from my own conversations with physicians in England, and from our experience with LSD at Bellevue Hospital in New York City, that if an individual has substantial underlying abnormality, the use of a mind-altering drug has great potential for making it more severe, or even for inducing mental derangement requiring hospitalization. As a matter of fact, in 1967, 1968, and 1969, physicians and psychiatrists were seeing more and more people with major personality aberrations (but who were functioning in society at least to a degree) who took LSD in the hope of ameliorating the personality problems they themselves recognized. There is not one whit of evidence to suggest that LSD benefited any of them. Quite the contrary. Many of these people got so much worse that they had to be hospitalized, often for very long periods of time. The evidence strongly suggests that the more severe one's personality problem is, the more likely is one to have an adverse reaction from marihuana, LSD, or any similar psychedelic agent. It is, of course, true that such patients might have a severe breakdown with a variety of stimuli, including job or family stresses but, surely, the last thing one wants to do is give such a person a drug that will make his mental abnormality worse. In such cases, the drugs can surely be accused of precipitating a mental breakdown that otherwise might not have occurred. On the other side of the coin, a perfectly normal individual who is under the influence of a psychedelic drug can have a mental breakdown requiring hospitalization, even if he uses it in moderation. This is not infrequent with LSD, occurs occasionally with potent forms of cannabis, such as ganga or hashish, and is reported, albeit rarely, with American-type marihuana.

Question: What is black hashish?

Answer: Black hashish, a cannabis product, was first described in London. It has been alleged that it is unusually dark in color because it is adulterated with opium. In point of fact, black hashish was investigated chemically by the London police and, at least as of the beginning of 1970, there was no evidence that it was mixed with opium.

Question: Does marihuana cause brain damage?

Answer: There have been some reports, primarily from Greece, suggesting that cannabis products can cause permanent damage to brain cells. Careful analysis of these reports and an on-the-spot assessment by a member of the Narcotic Addiction Control Commission from New York State suggest that the individuals surveyed suffer from deterioration in personality and psychological functioning, but not from specific damage to brain cells. Supposedly there are new animal studies showing brain damage, but this seems to be rumor rather than fact.

Question: Is marihuana addictive?

Answer: Addiction is defined as physiological dependence. This means that if a person uses a drug daily and then abruptly discontinues use, he will experience withdrawal symptoms such as nausea, vomiting, chills, fever, or abdominal pain. Opiates such as morphine and heroin are addicting. Marihuana is not. It may be psychologically habituating, so that the user who is removed from his supply will have a great desire to obtain more and will go to extraordinary lengths to get either marihuana or a similar agent. If, however, this is prohibited and he must go without, he can readily do so. The question brings up another important point about marihuana. This is that the proponents of marihuana puncture the myths surrounding the drug and then attempt to make the derivative assumption that because the myths are incorrect, the drug is harmless. Thus, they say marihuana is alleged to be addictive, but it is not. It is alleged to cause violence and criminal activities, but there is no documentation to support this. Since it is clear that these allegations are entirely untrue, then it is equally clear that marihuana is an innocuous drug, say its proponents. Surely it must be evident that the conclusion is a *non sequitur*. It is unfortunate that many opponents of marihuana have deliberately or ignorantly made outlandish and untrue statements relating its use to addiction, aggression, criminality, and sexual aberration. However, the fact that frequently made statements are inaccurate does not permit the conclusion that marihuana is harmless.

Question: You quote articles which indicate that marihuana is a potentially dangerous drug, but an article in the magazine section of the *New York Times* implies that the drug is harmless. How can you reconcile these points of view?

Answer: I have already pointed out the potential dangers of marihuana. The article to which you refer, by Andrew Weil, M.D., Norman Zinberg, M.D., and Judith Nelson, was first published in *Science* December 13, 1968, and later amplified on May 11, 1969, in the *New York Times Magazine.* The investigators are reputable. They set up an experimental study using limited amounts of marihuana. Their total experimental population consisted of nine inexperienced smokers and eight who were chronic users of marihuana. They demonstrated that in this small population marihuana appeared to be a relatively mild drug, although it did impair coordination and thinking in marihuana-inexperienced individuals. And this was dose-related; the more marihuana the subjects took, the greater the impairment of thinking and coordination.

These investigators interviewed prospective participants and selected their groups carefully. They excluded five people who were hyperreactors to nicotine, and may thus have screened out the very persons who might have had an adverse reaction to marihuana. And there is an additional and curious defect in their study. The experiment should have been a double-blind one—one in which neither subject nor the examiner knows what is given. In this study, the experiment was double-blind for the marihuana-naïve individuals but not for the chronic users. The chronic users knew exactly what they were getting, and this makes it necessary to be very cautious in interpreting the conclusion that marihuana causes no impairment of coordination or thinking for habitual users. After all, chronic users are out to *prove* that marihuana is harmless. This means that any valid experiment must be performed "blind," meaning the subject does not know exactly what he is getting. In justifying the failure to do this with chronic users, Dr. Weil said that he would be glad to perform such a study if anyone could show him how to fool a chronic marihuana user with a placebo. Subsequent studies have shown that many habitual marihuana users can be fooled by a placebo. Consequently, Weil and his colleagues should have at least tried a "blind" study of the chronic users.

In any case, the investigators have no more right to generalize from their limited sample of seventeen subjects than a user does from his circle of friends or a physician from several cases of marihuana-induced panic or psychosis.

I don't think the authors really meant to imply that marihuana is a harmless drug. As a matter of fact, Dr. Weil is the author of an article published in the *New Journal of Medicine,* April 30, 1970, entitled "Adverse Reactions to Marihuana." Among the adverse effects listed are depression, panic, and mental breakdown.

Question: How can we know what to do about marihuana before adequate research is performed into its actions and harms?

Answer: The notion that we cannot handle marihuana until much more research is available is pure malarkey. Recent studies showing that it is not an inordinately dangerous drug do nothing more than repeat conclusions of the 3,000-page Indian Hemp Commission report in the early 1890s. It is true that we do not know the physiological ramifications of marihuana but these details are not needed in order to make judgments as to how we should control it. We do need additional research because there is much about marihuana that we do not understand, but we do not need one whit more information to enable us to take a sensible sociological and legal stand.

At regular intervals, prominent individuals, organizations, and newspapers call for a Presidential Commission to evaluate marihuana. Both President Kennedy and President Johnson appointed such commissions, both of which proposed changes in the marihuana laws. We do not really need another Presidential Commission; what we do need is sensible action based on already well-established data; nevertheless, Congress is insisting on another study before completing final revisions of the marihuana statutes.

Question: Has marihuana caused any deaths?

Answer: I know of an instance in which a soldier took Vietnamese marihuana and then shot two of his friends. He had no previous history of major disturbance and apparently had not taken other drugs. Jack Anderson, the newspaper columnist, reported in August, 1970, that there was circumstantial evidence that a group of American troops smoked marihuana and then deliberately shot at our own helicopters, which then returned the fire, killing several of the users.

Other than these, I know of no other deaths from marihuana, but it is inevitable that if any mind-altering drug is used extensively, an occasional person will become temporarily deranged and die or be seriously injured in an accident. The likelihood of tragedy is of course increased if the individual is behind the wheel of a car or has a gun in his possession.

Question: Since prohibition was not successful in regard to alcohol, what makes you think it will work with marihuana?

Answer: The two situations are not entirely similar. In the case of alcohol, a society in which its use had been traditional and legal abruptly attempted to suppress it without providing any legitimate substitute, and the public refused to accept this—a hardly surprising reaction in a pleasure-oriented society. This is completely different from prohibiting the addition of new intoxicants to those already legal. Marihuana is not a legal intoxicant being suppressed; rather, it is an additional intoxicant that could be suppressed, just as the Japanese reduced their stimulant epidemic and Iran controlled its extraordinary opiate problem. If we assumed that suppressing any drug of pleasure would fail as prohibition did with alcohol, then we would have to legitimatize every potentially intoxicating drug, and that would be disastrous. There is no doubt that we can suppress to a very marked degree the illicit use of drugs such as marihuana in the United States. The question is how to do it sensibly and compassionately instead of viciously and inflexibly.

Question: If we continue to prohibit marihuana, won't young people move on to other drugs that are far more dangerous?

Answer: Allegedly this happened during the Nixon administration's Operation Intercept, aimed at interdicting the supply of marihuana from Mexico. It was said that when young people could not get marihuana, they began to use heroin, LSD, mescaline and other more dangerous drugs. However, there has been no solid evidence to document this assumption. If marihuana is not available and stronger types of cannabis such as hashish are available, the user will clearly turn to these more potent forms of marihuana. A knowledgeable Michigan psychologist makes the point that experimenters or drug neophytes who cannot get marihuana because of reduced supply do not suddenly experiment with more dangerous agents. But the confirmed drug user, deprived of his marihuana, is likely to turn to other available drugs even if they are more dangerous. Although this hypothesis needs additional documentation, it makes sense. In any case, the facile statement that if the supply of marihuana is reduced young people will automatically turn to drugs such as LSD and heroin is totally undocumented and, very probably, incorrect.

Question: Do you think the marihuana fad will pass?

Answer: I do indeed. Most illicit drugs in this country grow in popularity for several years and then decline. If we were to legalize marihuana now, this in itself would guarantee that its use would not fade over the next five to ten years. But if we keep it illegal and make the laws sensible and educate honestly, the odds are overwhelming that this particular drug fad will diminish, although it is unlikely it will disappear entirely. If we legalized marihuana, then we would have marihuana and alcohol, and three to five years from now additional illicit drugs would be presented to us by those demanding their legalization. Of course many disagree with this and feel marihuana is here to stay.

Question: Are there medical uses for marihuana, or long-term benefits?

Answer: Cannabis products have been used over the centuries for a variety of reasons, and it is clear that the drug may have sedative or tranquilizing effects, but this potential use of marihuana is not now applicable since many other more effective drugs are available. The benefits claimed by marihuana enthusiasts, including augmented creativity and unusual insights, have in no way been documented. To many users, feeling good is in itself beneficial, and marihuana may make you feel good, but there is no evidence at all that it has lasting beneficial effects on the user. It is true, of course, that the pure active principle of marihuana, tetrahydrocannabinol (THC), has only recently been synthesized, and this substance rather than the impure marihuana could turn out to have medicinal uses. Whether it actually will have any medical value remains to be seen.

Question: How often can experienced marihuana users be fooled by a placebo cigarette that looks and smells like marihuana but has none of its active materials?

Answer: There is no clear answer to this, but in perhaps the best controlled study six of ten chronic marihuana smokers were unable to distinguish between a potent marihuana cigarette and one that had no active material at all. It appears clear that many experienced smokers can tell if the cigarette they are smoking is good marihuana, bad marihuana, or fake, but many equally experienced users just can't distinguish true from ersatz marihuana.

Question: If marihuana were legalized, could you control the dosage and thus reduce its dangers?

Answer: If marihuana were legalized and if the amount of marihuana in a given cigarette was rigidly controlled, this would help in reducing the likelihood of acute adverse effects such as panic or depression, since these are for the most part dose-related. But dosage means not only the potency of a given cigarette but also the total amount used. If marihuana were legalized, you could not prevent an individual from smoking three or four cigarettes in a short period of time. That might be the equivalent of smoking one or two more potent cigarettes. Since adverse effects relate to the total amount of active material smoked, use of several cigarettes at one sitting would increase the likelihood of panic, depression or mental abnormality. And it is well to realize that some persons experience these adverse reactions after smoking one cigarette of only moderate potency. Furthermore, if marihuana were legal, many users would still elect to use the stronger hashish or tetrahydrocannabinol even if the latter two were illegal. And legalization would pose other problems. Many thousands who have not experienced marihuana would use it, and some of those who liked the experience would seek experience not only with more potent forms of the drug but also with such agents as LSD or heroin. Thus legalization of marihuana would increase the numbers of chronic users of the drug, and in so doing would probably increase the number using more powerful and more dangerous mind-altering agents. If marihuana were legalized, there would be age restrictions so that the drug would be forbidden for those under sixteen or seventeen. But if the drug were being used with abandon by older persons and it continued to get ebullient publicity, its use among the very young would increase, and in this age group marihuana can do considerable psychological damage. What it amounts to is that legalization of marihuana is a facile solution that won't solve anything.

Question: If marihuana is laced with opium, will this cause a person to become addicted?

Answer: The amount of opium likely to be included in a marihuana cigarette is quite small, and therefore the addiction potential is very limited indeed. Nevertheless, if a person smoked enough marihuana adulterated with opium, he could become drug-dependent; and if he stopped taking the mixture, he then would have withdrawal manifestations, including abdominal pain, nausea, and vomiting. One additional step would have to be taken before he could become an addict: he would have to recognize, on abrupt discontinuation of the cigarettes, that his physical complaints could be relieved by smoking another one. Knowing that if he were smoking only marihuana this would make no sense, he might then make the correct assumption that his marihuana had been mixed with opium, and once he had recognized that his withdrawal symptoms represented opium deprivation he would indeed be an addict. Thus addiction from opium-laced marihuana cigarettes is possible but unlikely.

Question: Are gangsters involved in the sale of marihuana?

Answer: The drug subculture would like to believe that the distribution and sale of marihuana is all good clean fun. It simply isn't so. Even at the college level there are students who are making substantial profits from drug sales, and the further one gets away from college distribution, the more likely it is that one will come into contact with confirmed criminals. In Israel, for example, there has recently been great interest in the smuggling of hashish, and the Israeli police found that, although most of the smugglers were not hardened criminals, some unequivocally were, and that they represented well-organized Mafia-type organizations. The best estimate at present is that approximately half the importation into the United States is carried out by persons who otherwise do not engage in criminal activity, and about half is carried out by confirmed criminals. In June, 1969, a New York City college student was shot and killed during a large marihuana transaction with organized criminals, and two others were shot to death in Arizona in July, 1970.

Question: Should parents smoke marihuana with their children in an attempt to understand the problem better and thus be able to cope with it more effectively?

Answer: Absolutely not. A parent can educate honestly and communicate adequately without ever using marihuana himself. If a father does sit down and smoke it with his son, he is exhibiting his own contempt for regulations and laws, and this will not be lost on the boy. After all, if his father will not obey the laws in regard to marihuana, why should he? It is true that for a short while it may give father and son a feeling of togetherness, but this will pass and the youngster will be left with a loss of respect for his father and further evidence that the laws are not worth obeying.

Question: Isn't it hypocritical to allow alcohol and prohibit marihuana?

Answer: Superficially it does appear we are being hypocritical. Ours is an incredibly intoxicated society, and we condone, even enthusiastically support, much of our drug taking. One need only look at a current coffee advertisement saying that if your husband drinks a certain brand in the morning, he will go bounding off to the office full of oomph. What really is being said is that he will be under the influence of our legal stimulant, caffeine. In addition, pills such as Viv, Vivarin, or Verve are advertised as helping one get through the day or evening; in each the active ingredient is caffeine. And we still permit outlandish advertising for our other drug escapes, tobacco and alcohol. Then why not marihuana? Surely the answer is that you cannot regard marihuana by itself or in a vacuum. The question is not how bad marihuana is, but whether we already have too many drug escape mechanisms. We cannot keep adding intoxicants indefinitely and still function as a society. If we add marihuana, where do we stop? I personally think that we have enough intoxicants and we should add a new one only if it is entirely safe. Under any other circumstances we should substitute for one of our current legal intoxicants, not add. The question is the overall status of our society and its intoxicants, not merely the parochial problem of marihuana.

Question: I am curious about marihuana. Why shouldn't I try it just once?

Answer: There are three reasons: First, even one cigarette has some potential toxicity. Second, although detection and arrest are very unlikely, it could be catastrophic if the one-time user were caught. Third, by using the drug even once, a person indicates he accepts the concept that the marihuana laws are not worth obeying. The laws may indeed be bad, but willfully breaking them only contributes to a climate of lawlessness. It is well enough to say, "I'm not hurting anyone else," but this rationalization is not satisfactory. The fact of the matter is that if enough people decide to break laws at will, we shall have not democracy but anarchy.

The argument about the necessity for not flouting the laws may appear to have little appeal, but it must be pursued. In a country increasingly concerned about the consequences of lawlessness, this argument is likely to become progressively more effective.

Question: Isn't all the fuss about marihuana laws superfluous? The majority of young people soon will be smoking pot, and when they assume leadership roles a few years from now, one of the first things they will do is legalize marihuana.

Answer: I do think that as young persons mature, the nationwide experience with marihuana will lead to a more realistic attitude. But I would expect the laws to be made more sensible in a few years, not by marihuana users, but rather by the old gloomy establishment. As for the idea that in future years marihuana-experienced legislators will go further and legalize marihuana, I think it is unlikely. It is well to remember that the majority of marihuana users voluntarily discontinue use before leaving college, and even though increasing numbers do continue use, they are still a small minority of all college graduates. There is at present little reason to anticipate a major change; it will take several years, however, to make a final judgment of what happens to those entering college with their drug habits already established. The odds are that as they mature, as they see the consequences of chronic heavy drug use, as they accept positions of responsibility, their attitudes toward legalization will grow progressively more negative. At the very least one cannot assume they will unequivocally legalize marihuana.

Question: Why not just legalize marihuana, proscribe the other illicit agents, and be done with all this silliness?

Answer: Would it were that easy, but all the evidence is that legitimatizing marihuana would not alleviate our problem. We are in a kicks-oriented, pleasure-seeking society in which drugs of all sorts, legal and illegal, are readily available. Simply legalizing marihuana is not going to stop people from seeking other drug kicks. Multiple drug use is getting to be the norm, and Erich Goode's data suggest strongly that the more you smoke marihuana, the more likely it is you will opt for other agents such as LSD, tetrahydrocannabinol, other euphoriants or hallucinogens, or even heroin. To legalize marihuana, hoping that all other drugs would go away, would be a simplistic solution; it just wouldn't work.

Question: Is marihuana more potent when smoked or ingested?

Answer: Amazingly, there is no agreement even on this. Andrew Weil, Norman Zinberg, and Judith Nelsen, writing in *Science,* December 13, 1968, suggest that the drug is more potent when swallowed, but the available data appear to contradict this. Dr. Harris Isbell and his colleagues studied tetrahydrocannabinol, the active principle in marihuana, and writing in *Psychopharmacologia* in 1967, showed the drug was more potent when smoked. Drs. Reese Jones and George Stone of the Langley Porter Neuropsychiatric Institute in San Francisco, using typical crude marihuana, confirmed Isbell's findings. Thus, at present, the weight of evidence suggests marihuana is more potent if smoked. The reports of greater potency by swallowing the drug are probably related to a much larger dose than is ordinarily used in cigarettes.

Dr. David Smith of the Haight-Ashbury Medical Clinic makes another important point about smoking versus ingestion. If a person smokes marihuana and begins to have an unpleasant reaction he can promptly stop smoking, thus helping to control the side effects. But if the marihuana has been swallowed and an unpleasant reaction takes place, the user cannot control the amount getting into his system, so that the unpleasant effects may be far more prolonged.

Question: Has there not recently been a study disproving the dangers of driving under the influence of marihuana?

Answer: Heretofore virtually every study has shown distortions of time perception as well as impaired reaction time and coordination for complex motor activities. But in the May 16, 1969, issue of *Science,* Alfred Crancer, Jr., and his colleagues compared marihuana and alcohol and reported that marihuana produced no significant driving impairment in simulated driving tests. Unfortunately, the study was badly controlled. The subjects were experienced marihuana users who were obviously biased. Furthermore, the subjects determined the extent of their own high, the only objective observation being a recording of the pulse rate, a notoriously unreliable parameter. Curiously, the data on pulse rate changes are not even given in the report; we are merely told the results were significant. As a matter of fact, the study was set up so loosely that the subjects could even have taken something to increase their heart rate and merely pretended to smoke the marihuana. Alcohol, on the other hand, was given in the equivalent of seven ounces of 86-proof liquor to a 150-pound man, an enormous dose. It is no wonder the alcohol effects were greater. If they insisted on using that much alcohol, they should have had the marihuana group smoke three to four cigarettes at one sitting.

The study is both unsatisfactory and uninterpretable. Preliminary results from a California group are said to support Crancer's study in a much better controlled investigation. Even if this turns out to be so, the results in a laboratory on a small number of individuals cannot be uncritically applied to the marihuana-using population on the highways. No matter what the laboratory investigators say, a significant number of marihuana users under the influence of the drug will drive erratically; to think otherwise is sheer idiocy. I think anyone with a grain of common sense would not want any individual intoxicated by alcohol, marihuana, LSD, amphetamines, opiates, or barbiturates behind the wheel of an automobile. One of the major arguments against legalization of marihuana is that there is no proven chemical test to detect it in blood, urine, or breath. That means that if one drives under the influence of marihuana and injures another person, proving marihuana as the probable cause and punishing the individual for injuring another while driving intoxicated would be very difficult. Until such chemical tests are available, I believe legalization of marihuana is undesirable.

Question: Would you compare alcohol and marihuana in regard to escalation to other drugs?

Answer: For reasons that are not entirely clear, there appears at present to be little escalation from alcohol to other drugs. There are major differences between the effects of progressively greater amounts of alcohol and of marihuana. The individual moderately intoxicated by alcohol who continues to drink experiences nervous system depression from the drug, with resultant stupor or coma accompanied by profound incoordination and often by vomiting. On the other hand, if one increases the dosage of the active principle of marihuana, tetrahydrocannabinol, the experience may be intensified and even made qualitatively different. In other words, increasing the amount of marihuana, hashish, or pure tetrahydrocannabinol will give a greater high, will increase the intensity of the sensory experience, and can even cause hallucinations similar to those with mescaline or LSD. There is, then, a built-in proclivity for some marihuana users to move on to more potent forms of marihuana or to true hallucinogens. Furthermore, marihuana, unlike alcohol, is a basic component of the current drug fad that appeals to young people, and as such it is far more likely to lead the youthful user into experimentation with multiple drugs. All the recent studies point to this pattern of drug abuse among marihuana users.

Question: Why not legalize marihuana until we know whether it is dangerous?

Answer: This possibility was posed by the student body president of a New York State college in September, 1969. The proposal is immature and silly. If it were adopted, we would then legitimize every new drug until the dangers were known instead of evaluating it before general release, and there would be literally thousands of thalidomide-type tragedies. Besides, we know enough about marihuana to state that if smoked in moderation, it has some limited dangers. With additional research all we are likely to find is that there are some as yet unknown adverse effects. After all, only very recently have studies shown that marihuana extracts can cause fetal abnormalities in rabbits and hamsters. There may be a lot of subtle dangers from marihuana about which we know nothing.

Question: If a young person comes to you and asks about using marihuana or legalizing it, what arguments do you use? Please list them.

Answer: You can't give a simple answer to that question. My arguments are these:

(1) Marihuana can produce adverse effects—panic, depression, paranoia, possibly psychosis—even in moderate dosage.

(2) In some cases it does lead to use of more potent and dangerous drugs. No experimenter can guarantee that he will not escalate to other agents.

(3) It is no big deal. Its effects are of short duration and not particularly spectacular and many users, if put to the test, cannot even distinguish a conventional marihuana cigarette from a placebo that looks and smells like marihuana but contains none at all.

(4) It is illegal. If the user is unfortunate enough to be caught, it can be disastrous for him. The risk is just too great for such a minor-league drug.

(5) Many members of the generation now in its teens and early

twenties complain about the bad example the older generation sets, but the example they themselves set for those from seven to sixteen when they use marihuana and other illegal drugs is equally bad.

(6) In regard to legalization, the question does not concern only marihuana or marihuana versus alcohol, but rather how many intoxicants we can add to our society and still have it function. To put it another way, if we legalize marihuana, where do we stop?

(7) Young people cannot demand more and more responsibility and influence and at the same time demonstrate by use of illicit drugs their contempt for authority and the democratic processes, as well as their inability to establish priorities and discipline themselves.

Question: Do you think our society will be severely damaged if marihuana is legalized?

Answer: Probably not. I suspect we could tolerate marihuana. My main argument is that before legalizing the drug we had better take a hard, honest look at it and at the issues. To do so we must (1) accept the fact that there are some inherent dangers in marihuana use for some people, (2) realize that the problem is not marihuana versus no marihuana, but multiple drug use among young people, and (3) regard marihuana in the bigger context of where we as a society are going in regard to intoxicants and mind-altering agents. Then and only then can we make a meaningful decision on legalization. In other words, if we are going to legalize the drug, let us at least do it after a realistic appraisal of the facts and the important issues.

Question: Does marihuana cause real hallucinations?

Answer: Infrequently. In one survey by Dr. Martin Keeler reported in *Diseases of the Nervous System* in 1968, six out of fifty-six users of marihuana reported hallucinations. These occurred primarily after heavy use. Ordinarily, marihuana and hashish used in conventional amounts do not induce hallucinations.

Question: Can you have flashbacks after use of marihuana, and if so, how long can they last?

Answer: Recurrence of unpleasant feelings after marihuana has been reported. I have recently been told of two cases with recurrences lasting for as long as six months after discontinuing use, but this is unusual. For the most part, the episodes of recurrence end after two to twenty-eight days.

Question: You insist that marihuana is frequently the starting point for escalation to more dangerous drugs, but isn't it also true that those who use heroin and LSD also started with mother's milk, green peas, and Pepsi-Cola? Could one say that these lead to LSD or heroin?

Answer: It is often said that there is no relationship between marihuana and other drugs, but it just is not true. As I have indicated, marihuana does not compel anyone to go on to anything else, but the more one uses it, the more one is involved in the drug scene and the more likely it is that one will choose to escalate to more dangerous agents. Studies done on LSD when it was popular and readily available indicated that if an individual started with mother's milk, green peas, and Pepsi-Cola, he would not be likely to get to LSD unless to that threesome he added marihuana. To put it another way, in today's society marihuana involvement leads to multiple drug use, whereas mother's milk, soft drinks, tobacco, and alcohol do not propel people into use of agents such as LSD and heroin.

Dr. R. C. Pillard, writing in *The New England Journal of Medicine* in August, 1970, put it most precisely. He said, "In short no one has failed to find a statistical relation between marihuana and use of other drugs."

The evidence on escalation from marihuana to other drugs rests on three types of information. First there is concomitant use; that is, use of marihuana plus other drugs at the same time. The data show clearly that the more marihuana used, the more likely more dangerous drugs such as LSD or intravenous speed will be used.

The studies of Erich Goode which I have quoted are confirmed by David Popoff in the April issue of *Psychology Today*. He found that of those using marihuana once a month 31 per cent tried LSD as contrasted to 58 per cent of those who used marihuana weekly and 77 per cent of those who used it daily. Of those who did not use marihuana, 99 per cent did not use LSD.

Second, there is chronological evidence. School studies show that the curve of marihuana use goes up before the curve of drugs such as LSD. In the San Mateo, California, study about 20 per cent of the students had used marihuana by the eighth grade, but LSD use did not reach 10 per cent until the ninth grade. In these large-scale studies marihuana appeared to come first.

Third, there are sequential studies indicating that 80 to 95 per cent of heroin users first used marihuana. Similar results have been found with LSD. Richard Blum noted that the chances were 6 to 1 that an LSD user smoked marihuana before trying LSD. Recently, a carefully controlled but small study in Australia by D. Silberman and J. Levy showed that marihuana users were far more likely than matched controls to use multiple illicit drugs.

To my way of thinking, there is in 1971 no way around the conclusion that marihuana leads to other drugs. Even those disputing this in regard to heroin usually concede that escalation from marihuana to LSD is a valid phenomenon and that those with personality problems frequently move from marihuana to other illegal drugs.

Question: Could the adverse effects ascribed to marihuana be due to adulterants?

Answer: This is an important point. However, the adverse effects reported with marihuana were well described before it became the thing to add DMT, scopolamine, and other substances to it. Consequently, adulterants cannot ordinarily be implicated.

Question: Is it not true that marihuana users often start with alcohol?

Answer: Yes. Blum's studies show they tend to experiment with both tobacco and alcohol, but this is a manifestation of general experimentation and curiosity. The confirmed alcohol user does not escalate to marihuana, LSD, or mescaline, but the confirmed marihuana user very often escalates to LSD or mescaline.

Question: You keep knocking marihuana. Why don't you just admit the Establishment doesn't like it because it is fun and because it's the kids' drug?

Answer: Of course it is a fun drug for a lot of people. All I want to do is place it in proper perspective so that based on the facts, we can make sensible decisions about it.

Question: With marihuana, how much of the effect is personality and how much the drug?

Answer: At low dosage, most of the effects are due to the personality and emotional state of the user. At very high dosage the drug itself predominates. At intermediate dosage, and this is the situation in most cases, the effects are a combination of the user's personality and the drug.

Question: If a person uses marihuana occasionally or regularly, can you give percentages that tell what is likely to happen to him?

Answer: Not precisely, but one can make reasonable estimates. For the occasional user: about 1 to 3 per cent will have a significant adverse effect such as panic or depression; perhaps 60 per cent will voluntarily stop using marihuana after up to three years; about 15 to 20 per cent will continue irregular use for prolonged periods without any difficulties; and about 15 to 20 per cent will move on to LSD, speed, heroin, etc. The last estimate is based on a review of fourteen epidemiological studies; in these, among those using marihuana one or more times, the escalation rate to more serious drugs ranged from 8 to 40 per cent and averaged 19.2 per cent.

For regular users, taking the drug at least three times weekly, the data are more vague. I would think the outcome might be as follows: 1 to 3 per cent will become potheads; perhaps 20 to 40 per cent will move on to more dangerous drugs; 20 to 40 per cent will continue regular use without escalation or any other difficulty; and 25 to 40 per cent will discontinue use voluntarily after various periods of time.

Another way of looking at this is that marihuana is safe for perhaps 75 per cent of users; for perhaps 25 per cent it can be potentially dangerous because of acute adverse effects, chronic effects (such as becoming a pothead) or escalation to more dangerous drugs.

Question: LSD is a chemical produced in a laboratory. What if I use organic, naturally occurring hallucinogens such as peyote buttons or psilocybin from "the sacred mushroom"? Are not these far safer?

Answer: Absolutely not. There is no significant difference between using impure peyote and using chemically synthesized mescaline or between using impure mushrooms and using synthetic psilocybin. The only difference is one of dosage. If you use peyote buttons, you are likely to get less active materials than if you take mescaline, the active principle in peyote.

Question: If you take LSD and then become pregnant, what harm will this do to the child if you have discontinued use prior to conception?

Answer: Dr. Kurt Hirschhorn of Mount Sinai Hospital in New York City reported the following in *Hospital Practice* in February, 1969: If a woman took LSD, stopped, and then became pregnant, the chances that her child would inherit genetic defects were intermediate between the normal non-LSD user and a woman who took LSD during the early part of her pregnancy. In other words, there was some risk, but it is not nearly as great as it would have been had she continued taking LSD during the pregnancy itself. And of course the whole area of genetic damage is still unsettled.

There are preliminary studies suggesting that if a woman takes LSD, stops the drug, and then becomes pregnant, her chances of having a spontaneous abortion are somewhat increased.

Question: If a man takes LSD and has chromosomal abnormalities, can he pass them on to his children?

Answer: Since the changes found in blood cells can also be found experimentally in reproductive tissues, it is possible that the man can pass the defects on to his children, but at present there is no direct evidence that this is so. Clearly, a great deal more evidence will have to be gathered before any definitive statement can be made.

Question: If a woman takes LSD and then has a blood test which does not show any chromosomal damage, can she still pass the abnormalities on to her children?

Answer: If no abnormalities are found in the blood cells themselves, the chances of defects in the reproductive tissues are so minuscule that this possibility can be virtually ignored. Thus if a person uses LSD and is concerned about genetic damage, a blood test should be completely reassuring.

Question: Can you get addicted to LSD or other hallucinogens?

Answer: The hallucinogens, much like marihuana, may be habituating to the extent that one can develop psychological dependence on them, but they are not addicting; that is, the body does not develop physical dependence upon them. Consequently they can be discontinued abruptly without causing important physical manifestations. Far and away the most important addicting drugs are the true narcotics, such as opium, morphine, Demerol, Dilaudid, methadone, and heroin. Codeine is also a narcotic, but it is extremely hard to get truly addicted to this drug. Although most people consider the amphetamines only habituating, a small number of people who take them by vein become truly addicted; on abrupt withdrawal they experience incredible tremulousness and abdominal pain. This may also be true of cocaine. The other group that may cause addiction is the sedatives, or barbiturates. As a matter of fact, those addicted to barbiturates such as phenobarbital, Amytal, or Seconal have more difficulty with withdrawal than the overwhelming majority of those addicted to heroin. The tranquilizers, so popular in our society, have on rare occasions produced true addiction, but for the most part dependence on these drugs is psychological and not physical.

Question: Can good LSD trips return in the same manner that bad ones can?

Answer: Yes. Both the good and the bad aspects can recur, but the tendency is for the unpleasant aspects of the original trip to dominate during the recurrences. For the most part, the recurrences are short-lived, lasting at most only a few minutes, but they can be more prolonged and severe; several suicides and severe accidents have resulted from them.

Question: What are the current uses of LSD?

Answer: Early studies suggested that LSD might be beneficial in persons with sexual deviancy, but this was found to be incorrect. Currently there are four potential uses for LSD: First, it may be beneficial in some patients with severe chronic alcoholism. But here lies a perfect example of early unrestrained enthusiasm. At first LSD was said to be a cure for alcoholism. Now, two careful articles, one by Dr. Leo Hollister and his colleagues and the other by Dr. Arnold Ludwig and his coworkers, both published in the *American Journal of Psychiatry,* indicate that LSD is no more effective than other treatment modalities for alcoholism. It would appear that the enthusiasm for LSD in the treatment of alcoholism will not be sustained. Second, there is a small number of studies suggesting that the drug may be helpful in the treatment of childhood schizophrenia when everything else has failed. Certainly, if other remedies are ineffective in treating this dreadful disease, LSD is worth trying. Third, if used very carefully by competent psychiatrists trained in its administration, LSD may be beneficial in the treatment of certain neuroses, especially those associated with phobias and compulsions. It must be stressed that LSD is useful here only if given under rigidly controlled circumstances. If given by therapists untrained in its use or by laymen or if self-administered, it will only make the psychiatric problem worse. Finally, there are several studies suggesting that LSD may be beneficial to patients dying of inexorable disease associated with pain. Although the numbers treated are small, it would appear that after taking LSD, approximately half the patients have a strikingly diminished need for pain-killing narcotics and that another half, not necessarily the same ones, may undergo profound personality changes, thus achieving tranquillity even in the face of death. This area deserves much more clinical exploration and in the long run will probably represent the most important medical use for LSD and similar mind-altering agents.

Question: Could LSD's alleged genetic harm be due to adulterants?

Answer: This may be the answer to the entire controversy. Some of the studies showing genetic damage appear to be well controlled; so do some of the studies showing no damage. It may well be that the amount of damage is directly related to the type and amount of adulterant mixed with LSD. It may also be that the damage is not from LSD alone, but rather from LSD acting in concert with a variety of other drugs; most of the street LSD users studied also admitted using other mind-altering drugs.

Question: What are the effects of LSD taken without knowing it?

Answer: A person who takes LSD without knowing he has taken it is likely to experience ego disintegration, that is, to feel he is losing his mind and yet have no idea he has ingested a drug which can produce this. The result is likely to be overwhelming. There may be panic that lasts for hours, days, weeks, or months. Furthermore, the individual may become so disorganized that he inadvertently does something to hurt himself. He may even have an acute mental breakdown requiring hospitalization. It is a monstrous offense to give anyone LSD without his knowledge, and this crime should be punished very severely.

Question: Does LSD cause so much trouble for those who take it because it brings out feelings and truths with which they cannot cope?

Answer: In some cases, yes. If a person takes LSD in indiscriminate circumstances without careful supervision by a trained psychiatrist or therapist and if he is not prepared to deal with the repressed emotions and thoughts that are released by LSD, then this kind of unexpected confrontation can easily result in panic, in intense feelings of persecution, or in an acute mental break requiring hospitalization.

Question: How long can your judgment be warped after LSD?

Answer: Some authorities believe judgment may be impaired for many months. Recently I was asked by the federal government whether a flying license should be withheld after LSD use and if so for how long. I answered that the combination of possibly defective judgment and recurrence of the hallucinations should preclude licensing for a minimum of two years after the last LSD use.

Question: Can LSD cause long-term problems other than chromosome damage?

Answer: The big question is whether many or at least some of those who take LSD one or more times are ever the same. After all, an LSD trip can return two years later, and the drug may induce long-standing mental derangement. It may also change the user in more subtle but equally important ways. Users may lose ambition and goals, have their judgment impaired, be more susceptible to outside influences. Nobody knows whether such changes can be permanent, but for some people they may well be. Those who use LSD often allege the importance of individuality, personal integrity, and freedom but, paradoxically, the use of the drug may rob them of these. To put it another way, after LSD they may never again be an independent "I" but rather be an "I plus LSD," and not nearly so personally free and independent as they think.

Question: Many of my friends use LSD and have never had severe trouble from it. How does this fit in with your statements about its dangers?

Answer: It may be your friends are very lucky. More likely, what they buy as LSD may be so adulterated that they are getting very little LSD. As I have indicated, if you buy 500 micrograms of LSD you may in actuality be getting 1, 10, or 20 micrograms of active material. Your friends may still feel they are getting a big kick, but in this case the kick is probably due to a lot of suggestion and very little hallucinogen.

Question: If the LSD taken is not adulterated, can I still use it repeatedly without mental or physical damage?

Answer: Of course. Some people have used LSD hundreds of times without obvious damage. The point is that you can suffer a severe breakdown or panic on the first trip or the fiftieth. Nobody can give exact figures, but it is clear that a large percentage of repeated users run into severe mental trouble and some may develop chromosome damage. Some who take LSD many times and appear to have no ill effects may suffer more subtle personality damage that the drug prevents them from recognizing. To sum it up, some people who take LSD repeatedly will get away with it, but many others will not.

Question: Does methadone work?

Answer: Methadone is used to treat heroin addiction. It is a synthetic narcotic that it taken by mouth to block the action of heroin. It is important to emphasize that people maintained on methadone remain addicted, but because they are able to take the drug in simple fashion once daily, they are not compelled to spend their entire lives in criminal activities to obtain heroin; thus they are potentially amenable to rehabilitation. The best-known and most extensive program of methadone maintenance has been conducted in New York City under the aegis of Beth Israel Hospital. As of June, 1970, about 3,000 people had been admitted to this program and its affiliates. Of those who were followed for at least one year, about three-quarters remained in the program. Of these, two-thirds were either employed or in school, and the number of arrests was about one-quarter of that expected in a general heroin population.

The advocates of methadone say that it is no longer an experimental program but a proven one and should be applied to the population in general. But unbiased observers urge caution. In May, 1969, the New York State Council on Drug Addiction released a thorough report on the methadone program. It noted that methadone was without doubt beneficial for some individuals but pointed out that those in the program were volunteers, and of those who volunteered a considerable percentage were rejected for one reason or another. Furthermore, once accepted, an individual had to wait six to eighteen months to be admitted to the treatment part of the program. Thus, by selecting volunteers, the methadone program is approaching only those who are motivated, and this motivation is further tested by having the individual wait for a substantial time before he actually begins therapy. Additionally, the average age of those in the methadone program in New York City has been thirty-three years. These people have been addicted for a long time, and one would ordinarily think they would be most difficult to cure, but it is well known that many addicts after the age of thirty grow out of the habit spontaneously without any specific treatment. Any treatment program in which the average age of the addicts is over thirty must be interpreted extremely cautiously because of the real possibility that many of the subjects would recover with a variety of treatment approaches or even with no therapy at all. A significant number of those who are maintained on methadone and give up use of heroin still have an innate need for drug intoxication, and as a result many of them turn to drugs such as amphetamines or cocaine and some rapidly develop a major problem with alcohol.

Further evidence of the selectivity of the program may be found in a report by Marvin Perkins and Harriet Bloch in the April, 1970, issue of the *American Journal of Psychiatry*. Regarding the people accepted into the methadone program, they noted: "More white patients than nonwhite were admitted; and admitted patients were more often employed, were less criminally involved, used fewer barbiturates and had proportionately fewer alcohol and psychiatric problems than non-accepted applicants."

These criticisms do not mean that methadone maintenance is ineffective or undesirable. It very clearly is beneficial for certain heroin users who are likely to be in the older age group and who are well motivated. However, there are no data yet to suggest that methadone is effective for young, unmotivated individuals. The question, then, is what percentage of the addict population is well-motivated. The answer would appear to be somewhere between 20 and 40 per cent. This is supported by the experience of the Addiction Research and Treatment Corporation in Brooklyn, New York. This is a methadone program in which volunteers are switched from heroin to methadone while living at home and attending the clinic; they are never hospitalized. The clinics are situated in the midst of the heroin-inundated Bedford-Stuyvesant district of Brooklyn, so that the methadone is readily accessible to the street addict, and the program is well publicized. The first addict was treated in the fall of 1969, and by March, 1970, 176 addicts were enrolled. Their average age was thirty-six years, and those operating the program noted that the young street addict in that community was just not willing to give up heroin for methadone, whereas older addicts were eager to give up their heroin habit.

Motivation does seem to be the key. Some programs are now admitting addicts with virtually no waiting period and very little selectivity. Yet the results are as good as those reported by the Beth Israel group presumably because they are still volunteers and are motivated. Even the young appear to respond if motivated for cure; an analysis of the New York Beth Israel program by its extramural evaluation committee showed that the smaller number of persons in their early twenties did as well as the larger number of older addicts.

Thus, at the present time, methadone appears to be effective for the minority of the addict population. Indeed, the data available suggest that it may effect recovery in only 10 to 20 per cent of the total addict population. It will be important to determine how effective the drug might be in those who are young and ill motivated. Until we have that kind of information, the precise role of methadone in the treatment of addiction will remain unclear.

Although methadone does appear to be beyond the purely experimental stage, the idea of allowing physicians to dispense methadone in their office practices is potentially dangerous. At the College of Medicine and Dentistry of New Jersey we are now seeing methadone addicts who are getting enormous amounts of drugs from several liberally prescribing doctors, and they are so heavily addicted they are much harder to withdraw than the heroin addicts. If methadone were permitted for office practice, overprescribing would be inevitable. Besides, methadone *per se* never cured anybody. It is methadone plus other rehabilitative efforts that can help some addicts, and the practicing physician ordinarily cannot devote the time to the individual addict to assure a comprehensive approach. Methadone does help some addicts and its use should be expanded, but only under a rigidly controlled clinic situation. And it is well to remember that just because one methadone program works well does not guarantee that other methadone programs will function as effectively.

A recent report by Dr. Thomas Bewley of the Tooting Bec Hospital in London emphasizes the desirability of not permitting methadone to be used indiscriminately. Bewley analyzed the urine of 100 heroin addicts being treated by methadone or heroin maintenance in a London clinic. In sixty, the urine reflected exactly what the physicians had given them; in thirty-one others, additional drugs, such as stimulants or sedatives that had not been prescribed, were found (these were drug buyers). In 9 of the 100, despite the fact they were given heroin or methadone, neither was found in the urine (these presumably were sellers). Obviously, if methadone were widely prescribed without adequate controls, some individuals would be taking additional drugs and others would be selling their legally prescribed methadone. This has already happened in poorly conducted methadone programs in both the United States and Canada.

Question: Are those taking methadone really normal?

Answer: They often are, but the methadone advocates imply, and sometimes explicitly state, that everybody is normal while taking methadone. This just isn't so. In one carefully planned New York series, two of fifty-five individuals could not even tolerate methadone because it caused marked nausea. Some reported "nodding" (behaving in a lethargic manner) while on the drug, and others were depressed enough to require mild stimulants just to get them through the day. Loss of sexual drive and impotence were commonly reported, although not so frequently as with heroin. Thus methadone does not necessarily make the addict normal. And it can provide a kick similar to heroin if the individual is not fully addicted. In Baltimore, easily obtained prescriptions encouraged many young people to switch from heroin to methadone; others started initially with methadone and reported a very satisfactory high. Indeed, some of them insist they would rather use methadone than heroin because they think methadone produces a greater, more pleasant high.

But it is true that most addicts receiving methadone therapeutically get no high, have normal reflexes, and frequently can function adequately in society.

Question: Do Synanon and Daytop work?

Answer: Synanon is a non-medically oriented therapeutic community in which abrasive group therapy is used to treat heroin addicts. Daytop is a therapeutic community similar to Synanon, but it provides far more extensive medical and psychiatric guidance. Additionally, Synanon's major objective is to withdraw individuals from society for long periods of time or perhaps even permanently and have them live in Synanon communities. Daytop has its people live in the Daytop community for a one- to two-year period, after which they gradually return to the outside community. Synanon is so rigid in its approach and so harsh to the individual that it only appeals to a few addicts who are willing to exist in this kind of subservience to the group. Synanon has never accepted any valid form of extramural scrutiny, and thus one can only make estimates about its results. It would appear that of those who volunteer for the program about half leave without completing treatment. Since the approach appeals only to a small percentage of the addict population, with a particular form of motivation, it is clear that Synanon is not the ultimate answer, although it may be a reasonable approach for certain individuals. In assessing Synanon's results, it is also well to recognize that some of those admitted to the program are not heroin users while others have major personality problems in which heroin plays only a relatively small part.

It is far too early to make any judgments about Daytop. It is obviously a reputable and well-motivated program. As of January, 1970, approximately 120 persons had been certified as having completed the inpatient phase of Daytop's program, and of these about two-thirds were employed in anti-addiction programs. That is, they had changed from professional addicts to professional anti-addicts. There is nothing wrong with this; many such individuals are needed. But the final test of the program will come when it is known what percentage of treated individuals have been successfully rehabilitated and have returned as functioning members of the community—not necessarily involved in the drug addiction field. There are many other therapeutic communities treating heroin users such as Odyssey, Genesis, Phoenix, Samaritan, and Renaissance houses. Each claims good results, but none has undergone adequate evaluation, and none has returned a significant number of drug-free individuals to the community.

Question: Why not just give out heroin or methadone to keep the addicts happy and thus prevent crime?

Answer: There is no evidence that just giving out drugs will rehabilitate anyone. Surely that is the important lesson of the British experience. Furthermore, in every country in which narcotics have been given out freely, the receivers have expanded the drug subculture by giving away some of the drug and selling some. This could be avoided by administering the drug only from special clinics once a day, but there are other problems in just giving out drugs in the hope of reducing crime. Since most heroin users are not truly addicted and many are merely experimenters, many would go to physicians or clinics and be erroneously labeled as addicts. They would then be given the heroin or methadone, and eventually that treatment would make them actual addicts. Thus society would be in the position of turning nonaddicted users into full addicts. This would be morally indefensible unless you could show that maintenance by itself would truly rehabilitate, and so far nobody has been able to substantiate such a claim. The Beth Israel methadone maintenance program in New York City has had considerable success because an intricate and very impressive rehabilitative effort is part of the program. Furthermore, simply giving out heroin or methadone wouldn't necessarily eliminate criminal drug selling. After all, if the illicit heroin were readily imported and the profits remained gigantic, then the sellers might well constantly search for new markets among young neophytes.

The first obligation of society is to attempt to cure the addict by one of a variety of programs. Admittedly, if this is impossible, then giving out the drug may well have merit, but it should only be done in a rigidly structured situation in which free administration is accompanied by vigorous attempts at rehabilitation.

Question: What is OD?

Answer: OD stands for overdose, and it is the leading cause of death in those who take heroin by vein. In New York City in 1970, approximately 1,000 people died of acute narcotism, most of them from overdose, making OD the leading cause of death in the fifteen- to thirty-five-year-old age group in the city. (The same was true in 1967, 1968 and 1969.) OD occurs whenever an individual gets more heroin than his body is accustomed to. This results in respiratory depression and acute congestion in the lungs, which can kill so rapidly that the needle will still be left in the vein. It appears to be occurring more and more often because there are more people experimenting with heroin and because the adulteration of the drug is so unpredictable that nobody taking heroin has any idea of the exact dose he is using. For example, many individuals who use heroin daily or several times a day may be getting such adulterated stuff that they are not physically dependent on the drug, nor is their body fully acclimated to it. If someone like this should then unknowingly obtain purer heroin, injection of the usual amount can result in fatal overdose. This is not, of course, the only serious medical complication of heroin abuse. Others include hepatitis, a potentially serious liver infection; endocarditis, an infection of the heart valves which is usually fatal in these patients; tetanus, or lockjaw, which is almost invariably a very severe disease; inflammation of the veins; and infection of the skin. All these complications result from the use of unsterilized needles that are contaminated with a variety of microorganisms.

Question: How long can a person take heroin without becoming addicted?

Answer: This depends on the person and the strength of the heroin used. Most of the heroin distributed today is far less potent than the heroin of a decade ago. Most packets contain only 3 to 15 milligrams of heroin, and frequently the heroin content is less than 3 milligrams. As a result, it gets progressively harder to become addicted. In fact, many habitual heroin users are labeled "needle addicts," in that they are psychologically dependent on the injection itself but are not physically addicted. Because of this, it is now easy to withdraw the majority of heavy heroin users from their drug. Even those using six to eight bags a day (a $30- to $40-a-day habit) often can be rapidly withdrawn without a substitute narcotic, by using mild tranquilizers during withdrawal. Thus heroin users may take impure heroin daily over a long period of time without actually becoming addicted. In addition, many individuals are intermittent or weekend users. They can take the drug for months or even many years without ever becoming truly addicted.

Question: Why do heroin addicts appear to grow out of their narcotic needs in their mid-thirties or early forties?

Answer: Nobody knows the answer to that, but it does appear clear that many do grow out of their heroin habit. In one study, over 80 per cent of those who started on heroin in their teens were voluntarily abstinent 20 years later. Although the overall proportion who grow out of heroin addiction is far less than 80 per cent, a significant percentage does. One intriguing explanation is that the need for heroin diminishes as the sexual drive decreases. According to this theory, the teen-age heroin user, without realizing it, may be using the drug in part to alleviate feelings of sexual inadequacy or sexual aggression. If the sexual drive is reduced as the user reaches his thirties or early forties, his need for heroin may subside.

Question: What is the current status of the British system for treating addicts?

Answer: The so-called British system, conceived in 1925, was an approach to the use of heroin and cocaine. A physician was permitted to maintain a drug user on heroin and/or cocaine if he had been unable to withdraw the patient and felt that the drug-taking was necessary for the normal functioning of the individual. It has widely been assumed that this program was undertaken to solve England's drug problem. Nothing could be more incorrect. In point of fact, England had no drug problem at the time the program was established and remained relatively drug-free until the early 1960s. Since then there has been a profound increase in drug abuse in England. Between 1960 and 1969, the total number of heroin addicts increased about tenfold, and among those in younger age groups the number increased about 2,000 per cent. This is hardly surprising. Until recently, young people could readily obtain drugs legally from a few doctors who were noted for their indiscriminate prescribing (one practitioner was literally prescribing drugs in the subways). The English drug user would obtain his drug legally, spend his time in the local pub, and avoid work when possible. Because many of these people had no fixed address they could not receive welfare, so to obtain money for food and shelter they sold part of their drug supply to neophytes who were not heavy users and therefore were theoretically not eligible for maintenance by physicians. Because the drugs have been so freely available in England, the English addict tends to be far more heavily addicted than his American counterpart. Another major difference between the English and American drug scenes is that, in England, use of any drug tends to taper off when the individual reaches his mid-twenties—considerably earlier than in America. By mid–1967 English authorities were alarmed by the country's astounding increase in drug addiction, and in April, 1968, the British system was abandoned. Instead, heroin and cocaine users were compelled to receive their drugs from specialized clinics. In one clinic, between April, 1968, and April, 1969, this system resulted in a 100 per cent decrease in the total amount of opiate administered to the clinic population. But unfortunately there is still no effective rehabilitation program, and until one is established it seems unlikely that England can successfully cope with its fast-growing problem.

The English experienced an additional problem as a consequence of some physicians administering intravenous methamphetamine (Methedrine) in an attempt to wean heroin users off the drug. They sometimes did accomplish this, but the addicts became amphetamine habitués. The amphetamine problem grew alarmingly over a brief period of time, and in the fall of 1968 the free prescribing of this drug was also abandoned; it too must be given to habitués under the aegis of specialized clinics or hospitals. I feel the lesson to be learned from the English experience is this: Giving out these drugs will only increase the problem markedly unless maintenance is rigidly controlled and is accompanied by intensive attempts at rehabilitation. In England, among those who received their drugs from physicians, the death rate was twenty-eight and the suicide rate fifty times the expected rate. It is well to remember that a large number of people are clamoring for the United States to allow free prescribing of methadone and thus adopt the so-called British system as a panacea at the very time the British have abandoned it as a failure.

Question: New York State is spending a veritable fortune on its civil commitment program for heroin users. Has it actually been successful?

Answer: The New York State program has been in effect for about three years. During that period it has handled some 7,000 addicts. There is no doubt that it is expensive, now costing over 80 million dollars a year, but there are major advantages to it. Addicts may join the program voluntarily, they may request it after arrest on a drug-related charge but before trial, or they may be referred after conviction. Additionally, they can involuntarily be committed to the program without having committed a crime. Involuntary committal can be initiated by any person who knows the addict well, but in practice it has been limited to the addict's relatives or to those living with him. Once legally committed to the program, the addict is under supervision for a minimum of three years, approximately nine months of which are spent in an institution where he is offered group therapy, vocational training, counseling, and education.

This program is well funded, flexible, and potentially valuable, but thus far its success has been limited. The reason appears to be that no one has yet learned how to inculcate motivation into these highly unmotivated individuals, whose main objective often is to get out of the program and back on the street where they can obtain more drugs. There is no doubt that a modicum of success will result from the program, but it is my own conviction that it will not be a huge success until a far more vigorous effort is made to instill motivation. If that can be achieved, the recovery rate should be very great indeed, but until then it is likely that the long-term effective rehabilitation rate will be around 30 to 40 per cent. If nothing else, the New York State program illustrates that it is much easier to treat addicts if they are volunteers, motivated for cure. Unfortunately this is not the case with most of the young men who get into the state program.

The program itself is now under bitter attack. This is unfortunate and destructive. Governor Nelson Rockefeller formulated the program and should receive praise for it, not condemnation. Because of his imagination, it will now be possible to determine just how many addicts who are young and ill-motivated can be rehabilitated. Never before had the manpower and money essential to mounting a comprehensive program been allocated. The Governor's program, which has been implemented reasonably well, will not magically cause addiction to disappear; neither will anything else. But the program does provide us with the tools to answer the basic question of the potential for cure among youthful addicts. When we know what this potential is, it will be possible to formulate the most practical and economical approach to the heroin-dependent individuals.

It is obvious from what I have said that in evaluating the success in the treatment of heroin addicts, one must carefully distinguish between programs catering to volunteers and programs, such as the New York State program, that deal primarily with those committed involuntarily.

Question: Are heroin addicts violent?

Answer: Until 1969 we always carefully pointed out that the heroin user would steal, forge, become a prostitute, or sell narcotics to keep up his or her own heroin supply, but was not violent.

Heroin users were responsible for perhaps 20 to 30 per cent of crimes against property in New York City but, if anything, were responsible for fewer crimes against persons than non–heroin users in the same age group. Now that is changing. More and more heroin users are armed, and increasingly involved in muggings and other crimes against people; occasionally the violence results in homicide. Thus the heroin addict participates in the growing violence within our society.

Question: Shouldn't the law enforcement people just get out of the area of drug use? After all, isn't what an individual puts into his own body his own business as long as he doesn't hurt anyone else?

Answer: It would be very simple if an individual just took the drug himself and paid careful attention to educational material outlining the potential dangers, but unfortunately it doesn't happen that way. Those who use drugs such as LSD or Methedrine or marihuana or even heroin almost invariably try to turn others on, and they will do so in any way they can regardless of how much misinformation and intellectual dishonesty there is in their proselytizing. In this sense, almost all chronic users of illicit intoxicating drugs are pushers. So it isn't simply a matter of users taking drugs themselves and then going about their business.

Furthermore, we have learned from our vast experience with drugs and from tragedies such as that of thalidomide that the lay public is not likely to have all the available information at its fingertips. You can't expect someone who has been told STP is a fun kick to spend his time fully exploring the available literature to assess its potential dangers. That's why we have a medical profession in charge of prescribing drugs and why we have a Food and Drug Administration to protect us against potentially dangerous agents. Also, the user and frequently the seller have no idea precisely what's in their pills, capsules, or injections. Under these conditions it is absolutely imperative that society control drugs; it would be outrageously irresponsible to let potentially dangerous pleasure-giving drugs be dispensed without adequate protection for the user.

The philosophy "What I put into my own body is my business" has been in large part responsible for the fantastic drug problem among the very young. People of college age insist on setting their own rules about drugs. Then, with the inadvertent help of the media, they let the world know of the so-called glories of drug intoxication. Having seen this example, the nine- to sixteen-year-olds are emulating their elders; but being unsophisticated and immature, they are incapable of discriminating among the various drugs available and are using anything and everything, sometimes with tragic results. Even when they stick to milder agents such as marihuana, they cannot handle them with impunity. Suddenly those with the philosophy "What I put into my body is my own business" are avowing enormous concern over the welter of drugs being used by the very young. But their belated concern cannot free them from blame: those of college age who used drugs illicitly and urged others to join the fun bear a heavy burden of responsibility for the emerging catastrophic drug abuse problem among the very young.

Question: Do drugs lead to campus rebellion?

Answer: It is true that those involved in raucous campus rebellion are more likely to be drug users than others on the campus. This is in part one-upmanship. Not long ago on a television show I debated an articulate young man from a midwestern college who was an admitted marihuana smoker. After the show he went to great pains to point out to me that he was not dependent on marihuana, that he was functioning well, that his main concern was the campus protest movement, and that he could stop smoking marihuana at any time without missing it a bit. I said it was perfectly obvious from talking to him not only that he was not dependent on marihuana but that he didn't particularly have any relish for it. I asked him why he didn't just stop using it. He said that in radical causes one always had to keep inventing actions which showed one was actively flouting the conventions, regulations, or laws of the Establishment, or else one lost credibility in the protest movement. One way of continuously indicating his contempt for the Establishment was open use of marihuana, and he kept it up just to prove to his fellow protestors that he was indeed actively anti-Establishment. Thus anti-Vietnam protestors and those engaged in disruptive campus activities are more likely to use drugs, especially marihuana; but there is no evidence that use of the drugs leads to rebellious activities.

Question: Is drug use associated with Communist activities on campus?

Answer: There are several studies indicating that illicit drug users are more likely to lean left politically, and a significant number are found in radical political movements. However, political radicals are walking a tightrope. On the one hand, they are in rebellion against society and welcome marihuana use as evidence of this. On the other hand, they fully recognize that involvement in the drug scene and effective political activism are incompatible. After all, if you are spending your time taking drugs, you don't have time to be a clear-minded, committed political radical. The rejection of heavy drug use by activists is nothing new. In the mid–1950s the toughest opponents of heroin use in New York City were the fighting youth gangs. Their attitude simply was, "If you're on the stuff, you're no good to us in a fight." Today more and more radical student groups are urging their members to avoid the drug scene. In any case, as with campus rebellion, there is no evidence that drugs such as LSD or marihuana lead to radical political activity.

Question: What is nutmeg?

Answer: Nutmeg is basically a stimulant whose active ingredient is related to adrenalin. It has been used for centuries, especially in India, and it is sometimes used in the United States as a substitute for marihuana. If one to several teaspoons or tablespoons are ingested, there may be substantial stimulation and occasional hallucinations. Nutmeg has never become very popular, because of unpleasant feelings of disassociation, dry mouth, palpitations, and discomfiture in breathing. The face may become extremely red; fear of impending death has been described, as well as abdominal pain, swelling of the eyelids, lowered blood pressure and, in one case, sudden death. Nutmeg is unpleasant enough that extensive use by young people in this country is not predicted.

Question: How do hallucinogens work on the body?

Answer: This is not known. From the best studies, done with LSD, it is known that concentrations of a naturally occurring body substance called serotonin change dramatically after the drug is taken. In one study in animals, behavior changed after LSD at the same time that the amount of serotonin within the animal's brain cells increased dramatically. However, the exact underlying mechanisms of the hallucinations are not known. One can say that the chemical changes occur simultaneously with the behavioral changes, but this does not imply cause and effect. The establishment of the exact mechanisms involved will be a major advance in the field of psychiatry.

Question: What is the danger in sniffing glue?

Answer: Glue sniffing has produced substantial judgmental defects that have at times caused severe and even fatal accidents. Glue is also capable of killing an individual in four other ways: First, he may be sniffing it with his head placed in a plastic bag, lose consciousness while his head is still in the bag, and suffocate. Second, on rare occasions there may be acute swelling of the brain, which can be fatal. Third, some of the glues have a base that can injure bone marrow, with resulting anemia, infection, and bleeding. This, too, occurs rarely. Fourth, there may be sudden lethal changes in heart rhythm. Over the last few years, glue sniffing has led to a small number of deaths in the United States. Chronic glue sniffing may cause severe psychological deterioration, and some believe it can actually cause brain damage. A recent report suggests that it may be associated with liver and chromosomal damage, but the evidence for both of these is at present tenuous. What it amounts to is that occasional experimentation is ordinarily not associated with any permanent damage, but there are potential dangers for the experimenter and the dangers are increased for chronic users.

Question: Are small amounts of amphetamines harmful?

Answer: The usual dose of oral amphetamine is 5 to 15 milligrams a day and that of phenmetrazine (Preludin) 25 milligrams three to four times a day. Taken in this fashion, under a doctor's direction, there are few risks, the most important being (with these drugs or any other central stimulants) judgmental defects. Thus persons under the influence of these drugs may make serious mistakes when driving automobiles or may write bizarre answers in school examinations. The severe dangers of stimulant use are usually associated with injection or ingestion of very large amounts.

Question: You have listed delusions of persecution and brain damage as the major dangers of amphetamine stimulants. Are there others?

Answer: Severe adverse reactions to large amounts of amphetamines, such as Methedrine, taken in gigantic dose by mouth or by vein, include potentially very dangerous abnormalities of the heartbeat, convulsions, and fantastic increases in blood pressure which may result in paralysis or brain hemorrhage. Additionally, in a modest number of cases sudden death has been reported, sometimes associated with fever of up to 107 or 108 degrees. The heavy intravenous user of Methedrine also may become astoundingly emaciated and as a consequence very susceptible to severe infections.

In July 1970, Drs. Myron Ginsberg, Marc Hertzman and Wolfgang Schmidt-Nowara reported the case of a twenty-one-year-old man who ingested a large amount of amphetamine and then experienced fever of 108 degrees, kidney failure and diffuse hemorrhages. A group of physicians from Los Angeles, California, published a small series in the *New England Journal of Medicine* of Methedrine users who developed severe, often lethal, blood vessel inflammation. This startling finding could be due to the Methedrine itself but it is just as likely that the blood vessel damage is due to some adulterant in the Methedrine. In regard to the brain damage, Dr. David Smith of the Haight-Ashbury Medical Clinic believes that in many cases the apparent brain damage improves after a prolonged period of abstinence. In other cases, of course, it persists and probably is permanent.

Question: What is catnip?

Answer: Catnip contains a great variety of constituents. When smoked in cigarettes, it can produce striking mentation changes. Four cases of catnip use were reported in the *Journal of the American Medical Association* in February 1969 by Drs. Basil Jackson and Alan Reed. For the most part, catnip intoxication mimics marihuana intoxication. However, in one of the cases reported, the reaction appeared more like that seen after LSD. It seems very likely that catnip intoxication is a dose-related phenomenon. If small amounts are taken, the reaction will indeed be mild and marihuana-like; if the dosage is greater, an LSD-like reaction will occur. The nature and extent of adverse reactions to catnip have not yet been fully established.

Question: Do psilocybin and dimethyltryptamine act like LSD?

Answer: Psilocybin, which is obtained from the sacred Mexican mushroom, and dimethyltryptamine (DMT), which can be readily synthesized and is found naturally in Latin America, are potent hallucinogens that are chemically dissimilar to LSD but have similar actions, although neither is as potent as LSD. With psilocybin the time course of the trip is very much like that of LSD, whereas dimethyltryptamine, which can be smoked or injected, generally produces a briefer two- to four-hour experience starting about thirty minutes after administration. Many of those who have taken DMT claim that the experience is actually more powerful than that observed with LSD and often more unpleasant, frequently resulting in severe panic reactions. This may well explain the fact that DMT has not gained measurably in popularity over the last three years. LSD-like flashbacks, or recurrences, can occur with DMT.

Question: Some studies show that STP is not very dangerous. Is this true?

Answer: A careful study by Dr. Leo Hollister and his colleagues, published in *Science,* has shown that pure STP is a moderately potent hallucinogen and does not produce mania, breathing difficulties, etc. But this has not been the experience with street STP. This disparity may possibly be due to the addition to street STP of adulterants such as atropine.

Question: Do any drugs other than LSD have the potential for producing chromosomal damage?

Answer: In answering this question it is important to emphasize that drugs can cause chromosomal damage or damage to the fetus without chromosomal abnormality. In one study, psilocybin has been found to produce chromosome damage, but much more information is needed. Mescaline, dimethyltryptamine, and marihuana have not been shown to cause chromosomal damage. Claims of chromosome damage in marihuana users have been made by a New Jersey investigator, but his data are contradicted by indirect evidence in humans by Dr. Kurt Hirschhorn of New York's Mount Sinai Hospital and by studies in rats by Patricia Martin, published February 15, 1969, in the British journal *Lancet.* Mescaline has produced fetal abnormalities in hamsters. Recently, William Geber and L. C. Schramm showed that marihuana extracts given to pregnant animals caused fetal malformations in hamsters and rabbits; these studies confirmed earlier ones on mice and rats. However, when pure tetrahydrocannabinol, the active principle in marihuana, was used no such fetal abnormalities were found, suggesting that the fetal damage was caused by non-mind-altering substances in the crude marihuana. Studies by Juhana Idanpaan-Heikkila and his colleagues show that marihuana, if given to a pregnant animal, will pass through the placenta; so marihuana smoked during pregnancy conceivably could have an adverse effect on the offspring. Studies by Dr. Vincent Lynch of St. Johns University in New York City strengthened this possibility. He reported in October 1970 that pregnant mice that breathed marihuana smoke during pregnancy had a high incidence of offspring with cleft palates and defective jaws.

Obviously much more research is needed before any definitive judgment can be made but it is fair to say that at present there is no evidence in man to suggest that marihuana damages either chromosomes or the fetus.

Question: Can you get the same effect from oral amphetamines as you can get from intravenous amphetamines?

Answer: In order to get the same effect with oral stimulants, the dosage must be substantially greater. Thus if you are modestly stimulated when a certain dosage of the drug is administered by mouth, you will be enormously stimulated if the same dosage is injected intravenously.

Question: What are DET, bufotenine, MDA, and MMDA?

Answer: Bufotenine is related to dimethyltryptamine (DMT) and was once thought to be a potent hallucinogen, but it probably is not a hallucinogen at all. DET is diethyltryptamine and is similar to DMT. MDA and MMDA are amphetamine derivatives; neither can predictably induce hallucinations in man. MDA is a mood elevator and augments perceptions. The trip is usually primarily introspective. It has become transiently popular in various areas of the country, particularly on the West Coast. There is some evidence it can induce serious, even fatal, cardiac irregularities. Dr. Keith Richards and his colleagues at the University of Rochester School of Medicine in New York State have recently observed two cases of severe MDA toxicity, the manifestations including high fever, muscle spasm, and convulsions. Chemical analyses showed the material ingested was pure MDA.

Question: What is HOG?

Answer: HOG was particularly popular in the summer of 1968. It apparently is a veterinary anesthetic (phencyclidine hydrochloride) that ordinarily produces a "twilight" feeling of free-floating dissociation. The drug accentuates underlying personality problems and can produce marked agitation, severe panic, depression, stupor, coma, and convulsions. The drug is usually mixed with parsley and smoked. Also known as PCP, it is sometimes mixed with oregano and sold as "Angel Dust." Increasingly, what is sold as THC, mescaline, or LSD is partially or totally phencyclidine. For example, Drs. Alan Reed, Jr., and Andrew W. Kane reported in December, 1970, that they had analyzed five varieties of mescaline sold in the Midwest; one of these was actually LSD and the other four were phencyclidine.

Question: Can one detect drug use easily?

Answer: It really depends on the drug. With heroin you look for needle marks and constricted pupils as well as behavioral changes characterized by sleepiness or nodding. With drugs such as atropine, Asthmador, and STP (street variety), visual and auditory hallucinations are often accompanied by a deep red skin color, fever, and dilated pupils. The central stimulants produce marked agitation and at times tremor, but it is hard to ascribe these specifically to a drug unless the user gives this information. It is even harder to detect marihuana use. Pupillary dilation ordinarily does not occur, and the behavioral changes may be subtle. For the most part, any time an individual has an abrupt and unexplained change in personality or a change in academic achievement, the possibility of drug use should be suspected. When a very neat individual suddenly becomes extraordinarily slovenly and there are no other evident reasons for this, drug use may be the cause. But there is no easy answer to this question. A New York physician has demanded for years that all students be regularly examined for needle marks, but this would not pick up the many heroin experimenters who do not have needle tracks, nor would it pick up the hallucinogen or pill users. It might help detect a few addicts, but most of these rapidly become school dropouts anyway and are lost to routine scrutiny.

It is well to remember that the manifestations of drug abuse are often mimicked by normal adolescent behavior. Parents and teachers have to be very careful not to overinterpret changes in dress or behavior. If they are not careful, they will be accusing young people of drug abuse who do not use drugs or whose use is ephemeral and relatively insignificant.

Question: Do you advocate routine urine or saliva tests in high schools?

Answer: This was proposed in New Jersey and Long Island in the summer of 1969. I personally feel there are enormous dangers inherent in this. In most jurisdictions, drug use is not a crime, whereas possession of the drug is. In these places, urine or saliva testing is an invasion of privacy similar to wiretapping and bugging. In New Jersey one municipality accepted saliva testing without even knowing that the proposed tests were unproven and probably worthless. The urine tests will not pick up marihuana, glue, or LSD, and they cannot distinguish between legitimate amphetamine or barbiturate use and abuse. Furthermore, there is very frequently the possibility of laboratory error. Such detection tests applied widely by school administrations would promote paranoia and might really disrupt the educational process. The main danger is the possibility of misuse of the tests by school officials, politicians, or the local police. But such tests could be enormously helpful in analyzing the prevalence of drug abuse and could be used to determine educational needs relating to drugs and the impact of educational efforts. I would think such studies should be conducted only by public health and medical officials and the information should be used only for epidemiologic and educational purposes, with guarantees of anonymity for the individual students. Thus civil liberties would be protected and the data still gathered. Also, chemical urine tests should be available to parents requesting them and to school health officials who deem them necessary for academic or psychological evaluation of a given child.

Question: What is cyclazocine, and what are its uses?

Answer: Cyclazocine is one of the synthetic drugs related to the opiates. It is a narcotic antagonist and is administered to heroin addicts so that they will not be able to get a high from heroin. Thus it is used in the same manner that methadone is used, but unlike methadone it is ordinarily nonaddicting (it does have some addiction potential but this is very small). How effective cyclazocine is in the treatment of narcotic addiction is as yet unknown. Some addicts refuse to use it because after its administration they have difficulties in coordination and find themselves in a disjointed, unpleasant mental state. A newer drug, naloxone, is similar to cyclazocine; its efficacy in treating addiction is equally unclear.

Question: Which is the worst drug to get off once you have started?

Answer: Of course, the traditional answer is heroin, because it is addicting, but at present it is actually very easy to get most individuals off heroin. Many users are psychologically and not physically addicted, and even for those who have true addiction, withdrawal with methadone is quite easy.

The drugs that are hardest to wean users from are the barbiturates and the central nervous system stimulants. Barbiturate addiction is severe indeed, and abrupt discontinuation may result in convulsions and death; withdrawal often has to be performed over a period of several weeks and with extreme caution. The stimulants can usually be stopped fairly promptly, but the problem here is that those who become acclimated to intravenous use of these drugs remember their stimulating high and have a strong tendency to go right back to them as soon as they are permitted to do so. Consequently, the feeling in Sweden, where this is a major problem, is that psychological dependence on these drugs is so strong that once a person is habituated to them, it is harder to keep him drug-free than it would be if he were habituated or addicted to any other agent, including sedatives, tranquilizers, hallucinogens, or even heroin.

Question: You continuously point out that interest in athletics will keep people from getting involved with drugs. Isn't this inconsistent with the stories indicating that drug use is rampant among our best amateur and professional athletes?

Answer: It is true that stimulant use appears to be widespread among professional athletes, especially football players. One of my colleagues watched a 250-pound lineman gulp a whole handful of stimulants just before game time. This is reprehensible. This is a terrible example, and potentially dangerous. Amphetamines in large doses can cause high blood pressure, heart irregularities, and even sudden death. Bicycle distance racers have died from a combination of amphetamine use and heat exhaustion. If this keeps up, I would urge that immediately after professional football and basketball games a certain number of players, chosen at random, be compelled to give a urine specimen for testing for stimulant drugs. If any are found, the player should be suspended and the game forfeited. It is now popular to disparage athletic competition, but those who have participated know that often such competition is enormously valuable in helping the individual mature and in training him to cope with the problems of everyday life. If it is not overdone, involvement in sports is still one of the best antidotes for drug use, and perversion of the basic concept of competitive athletics by athletes using drugs to augment their performance should be dealt with vigorously.

Question: Are there any drugs on the horizon which might be safe and provide mild intoxication?

Answer: None has yet been introduced, but there are several used around the world whose adverse effects appear to be minimal and which do appear to have the capacity for mild intoxication. These include khat, which is used predominantly in North Africa, and kava and betel, both of which are used in the South Pacific. Additional investigation into these three drugs is warranted.

Question: Are any of the drugs you've discussed aphrodisiacs?

Answer: Virtually all the pleasure-giving drugs being urged on young people are advertised as potent aphrodisiacs. This has been said of cannabis products, LSD, and even the opiates. Marihuana may reduce inhibitions, and this may lead to sexual activity, but there is no evidence to suggest that the drug per se augments sexual ability. All the true narcotics, including heroin, morphine, and opium, are potent sexual depressants. LSD, mescaline, and dimethyltryptamine are definitely not aphrodisiacs. LSD may produce hallucinations with all sorts of erotic overtones, but the user is ordinarily so wrapped up in his own trip that he never gets around to physical sexual gratification. The small number who attempt to have sex during an LSD trip often find themselves incapable of performing. Sedatives and tranquilizers depress sexual activity. But there are two drugs used illicitly that might be considered aphrodisiacs. The first is amyl nitrite: if it is inhaled during intercourse, it may prolong the climax. The other drug with aphrodisiac potential is methamphetamine taken by vein. Taken by mouth, the central stimulants, including the amphetamines, reduce inhibitions and energize, so that if the individual is engaged in sexual activity, interest is likely to be sustained for very long periods of time; but there is no evidence that orally administered amphetamines significantly augment performance. On the other hand, about half of those who use methamphetamine by vein and subsequently have sex insist that not only is interest maintained but performance is markedly improved. It is also worth emphasizing that those who use Methedrine intravenously for a substantial period of time find that although they may continue having sexual activities, they enjoy them progressively less. Eventually the men become impotent, and the women may find that even after discontinuing the drug they achieve no satisfaction from sex for a period of weeks or even months.

Question: Is mescaline harmful?

Answer: Since LSD has reached a plateau in popularity there has been more use of mescaline, although it has not by any means reached the epidemic proportions that LSD did. It is absolutely impossible at present to assess the potential harms of this drug. Experimentally one can substitute mescaline for LSD if the differences in potency of the drugs are considered; that is, a great deal more mescaline must be administered to get an LSD-like effect. And there are other differences, both in the hallucinations and in some of the untoward effects, but these are relatively minor. The only group in which enough mescaline has been used to enable some judgment is the native American Indians. The use of the drug as peyote by certain American Indian tribes is entirely legal. (The dried peyote buttons, obtained from a cactus, contain a variety of alkaloids, the most potent of which clearly is mescaline.) However, the studies of peyote use among native American Indians have been primarily sociological and anthropological and have not adequately explored the question of potential medical harm. All that can be said now is that if mescaline use becomes more prevalent among our young people, it is likely that the undesirable effects will mimic those noted with LSD. It is also well to remember that much of what is sold as mescaline actually has no mescaline in it at all.

Question: The people I know who use drugs say they know the people who sell them the drugs and have complete confidence in them. How does this square with your statement that you can't trust the seller?

Answer: When a user tells me he trusts his supplier to give him pure and potent drugs, I ask him how can he be so sure. A recent study in New Jersey showed that not one of thirteen street samples of mescaline actually had any mescaline. What was sold as tetrahydrocannabinol had no active material in it. LSD is frequently 10 per cent LSD and 90 per cent adulterants. Heroin is always adulterated. Even marihuana may be laced with DMT, scopolamine, or opium; or what sells for marihuana may be primarily beet root, oregano, or alfalfa. The fact is that the user cannot be sure of the contents of any mind-altering drug obtained from his friendly and supposedly trustworthy supplier. More often than not the supplier himself really doesn't know the content of the materials he dispenses. Studies in Canada and the United States have shown 20 to 40 per cent of street samples to contain, not the substance the seller claimed for them, but something else; and even if the sample contained the right drug, the dosage was extraordinarily variable. Thus Dr. Stanley Krippner examined twelve street samples of what was sold as 250 micrograms of LSD. His study was reported in *Science* May 8, 1970. Only two samples had 150 or more micrograms of LSD; the others contained either no LSD or small amounts incapable of inducing mentation changes; in some samples there was more STP (a very dangerous agent) than LSD. Other studies by the Federal Bureau of Narcotics and Dangerous Drugs indicate that 20 per cent of alleged marihuana samples confiscated contain no marihuana at all.

Question: If I suspect my child is using drugs, should I call the police?

Answer: Whenever drug abuse descends on a community, this question is put to me by concerned parents. If the child is a suspected or even a known user the answer is almost invariably no. Reporting one's children to the police antagonizes the youngsters, prevents an effective dialogue, and, if the police are not understanding, may result in an attempt to stop further drug use by scare tactics on their part. Some young people have been haled before the courts or subjected to public abuse because their parents called in the police. Self-education and communication have a far greater chance of improving the situation, especially if the law officers know little about drugs and have a hard-nosed, inflexible attitude. This doesn't mean that scare tactics by the police will uniformly fail. Sometimes they succeed, but often the disastrous ramifications as far as the family is concerned far outweigh any possible benefits. On the other hand, if the parents know who the pushers are, they should be reported to the police. The problem for parents with a child who is selling drugs is more complex; but even here, if the child is a seller of only small amounts and is a user also, calling the police is usually not the thing to do. It is, after all, very difficult for parents to call the law down on their own children.

Question: How can you explain the upsurge of heroin use in affluent communities?

Answer: I can't, except to say that it can produce a feeling of pleasurable lassitude and that this alone, in a society dedicated to pleasure, is enough to put a drug in the repertoire of many users. Nevertheless, the sudden popularity of heroin in affluent communities caught most of the experts by surprise. We had been anticipating a rapid rise in use of stimulants rather than depressants such as heroin.

Question: Why is it we see so much drug abuse in America today?

Answer: Perhaps the point to stress is that drug abuse is at present the final common behavioral pathway for a host of motivating forces. We are, of course, a drug-oriented society and one dedicated to pleasure and the relief of mental or physical pain by drugs. And drugs are now the "in" thing for young people. As a result of these factors acting in concert, young people with different personalities and divergent motivations may still end up on similar drugs. Thus one may be depressed, another anxious, another out for kicks, another rebelling, another lonely, and still another suffering the pangs of normal adolescence. Despite such differences, each may adopt the same behavioral pattern, namely the use of a specific drug.

Question: What makes young people stop using drugs?

Answer: This is a crucial question because we know that most users of drugs stop taking them on their own after a period of months or even several years. Some people stop because of a traumatic experience. One young man told me he stopped because somebody he was close to burst into tears when she found he used drugs. This upset him so much that he promptly stopped using LSD. A teen-aged girl stopped heavy drug use because she was arrested and spent a few days in a women's detention home. Seeing the other prisoners and being stripped and searched rectally and vaginally for drugs were enough to put an abrupt stop to her drug use. Others suffer unpleasant trips or almost get killed in drug-induced accidents. And still others are influenced by watching friends suffer terrible trips.

But even more important than trauma is the acquisition of identity and maturity. When young people feel more secure, when they feel better about themselves, the need for drugs diminishes. They may say, "I've been through drugs and now I don't need them." But what they really mean is, "I feel more content about myself as a person."

Still others have their curiosity answered or, having experimented because of peer group pressure, stop after just limited use. Much more information is needed on why people discontinue drug use. In one study by Drs. George Mizner, James Barter and Paul Werme, 23 per cent of users of amphetamines who halted use of that drug did so because of fear of physical or mental harm, and this was true of 42 per cent of LSD users. While 16 per cent of marihuana users who stopped did so because of fear of the law, only 9 per cent did so because of anxiety about physical or mental harms. However, 62 per cent of amphetamine users, 60 per cent of marihuana users, and 38 per cent of LSD users stopped for reasons other than those listed on the questionnaire.

Question: Would you comment on the treatment of heroin overdose by a heroin user's friends?

Answer: It is frequently barbaric. They inject milk or salt directly into the vein or sometimes pack the genitalia in ice. It is now popular to treat heroin overdose by injecting Methedrine and, conversely, to treat an unpleasant Methedrine high by injecting heroin. The complication rate of such treatment is enormous. The one thing drug users do for heroin overdose that makes sense is to slap the individual around and keep him walking and awake. We can show experimentally that if we give mice heroin and force them to keep walking, they will survive a given dose, whereas mice given the same dose and permitted to lie down and go to sleep will die.

Question: Why is it that in a given environment some people succumb to drugs, and often others in exactly the same environment never turn to drugs?

Answer: That is the $64,000 question and nobody knows the answer. If one accepts the notion that currently drug abuse is the common pathway for expressing a variety of psychological abnormalities, it is understandable that a compulsive neurotic, a psychotic, a person suffering from depression, a severely anxious person, and an unusually immature individual all may end up on drugs. And we do know that parents who use drugs to excess tend to breed children who readily turn to illicit drugs. But that doesn't really answer the question, for we do not know why one person in a given environment experiments with drugs, another becomes deeply involved in the drug scene, and a third avoids drug use entirely even though superficially all three appear similar. Presumably there are important personality differences, but these have not been adequately defined; most studies have concentrated on the personalities of those who already have turned to drugs and have not contrasted the drug users with non-drug-using persons in an identical milieu. What is needed is a careful prospective study started in grade school before drug use starts; by following a large number of young people over a period of years, judgments could be made about why certain individuals turn to drugs and others do not.

Question: Is treatment of drug abuse dependent on an evaluation of motivation?

Answer: Absolutely, and yet one must not make a fetish of the motivational approach. It may not work for the experimenter, the moderate marihuana smoker, or the heroin addict in a deprived community. But assessment of the motivation of affluent teenagers who are involved with multiple drugs is critical. If there are major personality defects, if loneliness is an important factor, or if either anxiety or depression propels the young person to drug use, then treatment of the underlying problem is the key. If boredom is a major cause, then the remedy may be surprisingly simple, namely involvement in exciting and constructive activities. Unfortunately, over and over again we see parents look only at the drug use and ignore the basic issues, such as readily perceptible depression; that's an invitation to disaster.

Question: You keep talking about drugs and their dangers. We all know about the dangers. Why don't you focus on the social conditions in our society which lead young people to use drugs? After all, look at what faces those of us in the younger generation —hypocrisy of the older generation, an immoral war in Vietnam, and a military-industrial complex which is ruining our environment, just to name a few.

Answer: It is easy to blame drug use on the population explosion, the Vietnam war, or environmental pollution, but there is absolutely no evidence that any of these major problems facing our society contribute substantially to drug abuse, at least for the overwhelming majority of young drug users. If young people use the generation gap or the hypocrisy of society to justify their drug use, then they are doing themselves a disservice. Furthermore, they can hardly extol the positive aspects of the drug experience on the one hand and on the other insist they are using drugs for totally negative reasons. And if they point to the troubles of the world as a reason for withdrawal and drug use, they in essence are admitting their unwillingness to commit themselves to helping solve the major problems. It is therefore vital to refuse to accept facile generalizations about world problems as reasons for drug use. Instead, we must point out to young people that the 1970s may be the decade of decision. If they withdraw and fail to make a significant dent in life-threatening areas such as the population boom, pollution, urban deterioration, and the arms race, then the 1980s may indeed be an era in which the problems are so overwhelming and seemingly insoluble that many young people will with considerable justification be taking drugs as an expression of despair and withdrawal from what appears to be a dying society.

Question: How easy is it to manufacture STP and LSD?

Answer: STP is an amphetamine derivative which is not difficult to synthesize. LSD is very easy to make chemically if you have lysergic acid itself, which is obtained from a fungus. But to make the lysergic acid is extremely difficult and takes a sophisticated chemist.

Question: What is Odyssey House? Does it work?

Answer: Odyssey House is a therapeutic community based in New York that is operated with at least a modicum of psychiatric guidance. It has reported very good results but has not yet been carefully evaluated and has returned only a few rehabilitated addicts to the community.

Odyssey, like every other therapeutic community, has a very large early failure rate; in different therapeutic communities from 50 to over 80 per cent of those volunteering for the program leave without completing treatment. Most break away in the first few months, and the vast majority of those not completing treatment promptly go back to drugs.

If the therapeutic community can hold an individual for at least three months, he is much less likely to leave without completing treatment. So the first few months are crucial. The high dropout rate during this period is so distressing that consideration is being given to administering methadone or even heroin to those who appear to need it so that they will stay around long enough to be caught up in the charisma of the program. Once that happens, the danger of dropping out is minimized.

Question: Could there be a chemical reason for escalation from marihuana to heroin, LSD, or other drugs?

Answer: There is a strong possibility that all emotional behavior has a biochemical basis. Escalation might well be related to definable biochemical mechanisms, or it could all be psychological, without a clear-cut biochemical basis. At present we just don't know the answer to that important question.

Question: Is it true that use of marihuana is epidemic in Vietnam?

Answer: Yes, but the precise number of soldiers using it is not known. One survey puts it at about 30 per cent, but it may be considerably higher. More disturbing is the growing evidence that significant numbers are using more dangerous drugs and the evidence that some are using marihuana in the battle areas and in the front lines. Under those conditions marihuana-induced tragedies will be inescapable. In 1970 in Vietnam there were between 30 and 100 deaths due to use of drugs such as heroin.

Question: Is drug abuse in our society due to all the drug advertising on television?

Answer: I am sure that irresponsible advertising contributes to the problem, but I think if all the advertising were made responsible, it would not solve nor even markedly ameliorate our drug problem. The advertising industry is often focused on by politicians or others because it is visible, is culpable to some extent, and allows us to blame somebody else rather than accept that the major causes of drug abuse lie within the family, our educational system, and the nature of the society we have created for ourselves.

Question: What do you say when young persons in your audience ask you how you can make any judgments about these drugs if you have not tried them yourself? Have you tried drugs experimentally?

Answer: I have not personally used any of the illicit drugs such as marihuana, LSD, or heroin, but surely a person does not have to be a drug user to try to educate against drug abuse. This would be as silly as saying somebody had to have tuberculosis before he could effectively treat it. No one actually needs to take LSD to warn others about its extraordinary dangers. When LSD first became popular, LSD cultists said we couldn't tell them anything about the drug if we hadn't tried it ourselves. In answer, we said that we had no intention of arguing with them about the magnificent hallucinations and the wonderful colors; all we wanted to do was warn them of the potential harms we knew of on the basis of our experiences at Bellevue Hospital and across the country. Obviously, no member of the drug subculture would insist with a straight face that one had to take heroin in order to tell others about its dangers.

In regard to marihuana, we do not deny that it makes people feel good. We don't have to use the drug to accept this premise and, after all, this really is all the drug subculture is telling us. As educators, it is our job to tell potential users that although they may get pleasure from the drug, they also may get no effect at all; that they can have the same feeling merely by thinking they are smoking marihuana; that it does have certain dangers even if taken in moderation; and that taken chronically or to excess it has very substantial dangers. To perform this kind of educational function, one doesn't need to take the drug; indeed, there is a growing body of opinion that claims that once you are a heavy or chronic user of even a moderately potent agent or even an occasional user of a very potent agent, the drug experience so warps your judgment that you cannot view that drug dispassionately or with intellectual honesty.

Question: In the past you have blamed the hippies for a major share of the drug problem. Is this still your position?

Answer: In my book *The Drug Scene* I did castigate the formal hippie movement of the 1960s, because although it was allegedly a love movement, it was in fact a drug movement. As of 1971 the formal movement no longer exists. Many people are now using the word hippie in derogatory fashion referring to a variety of individuals they don't particularly like; long hair, slightly unkempt beards, sloppy attire, a certain life style are sufficient for pejorative designation as a hippie. Since there is no longer a formal hippie movement and since the term is being used indiscriminately for denigrating purposes, I think it would be best to drop it from our lexicon.

Question: Is it true that repeated marihuana users show reverse tolerance in that they can get high on less marihuana than they required originally?

Answer: Yes, that is so for some users but not for others. For a long time we thought that so called reverse tolerance was psychological in nature. However, in the December 18, 1970, issue of *Science* Louis Lemberger and his colleagues show that marihuana metabolites can be found in the body for more than a week after administration of the drug. Reverse tolerance might be explained by persistence of marihuana breakdown products in various tissues.

Question: Is nitrous oxide used for pleasure purposes?

Answer: Yes, to some extent. Nitrous oxide is, of course, the dentists' laughing gas. Ordinarily except for judgmental defects no harm results but there are a few cases of use of nitrous oxide in a closed environment, resulting in exhaustion of the oxygen and subsequent suffocation.

Question: If you put marihuana in the food without a person's knowledge will it produce a pleasant high?

Answer: Probably not. The effects of marihuana depend on the mental set at the time and awareness that the user is taking a mind-altering drug. Marihuana given in that fashion might induce vague feelings of intoxication but euphoria would be unlikely. After all, marihuana was used in cough medicines and all sorts of folk medicines for many years and euphoria apparently did not accompany such medicinal use.

Question: If a woman uses drugs up until the time of delivery will the baby bc drug dependent?

Answer: If the woman is on heroin, the baby may be born addicted. Approximately half of these babies will develop symptoms of withdrawal a few hours after birth. If this is not recognized and treated, the infant can get severely ill or may even die.

Treatment consists of administration of an opiate or a drug such as chlorpromazine (Thorazine) and it may take up to eight weeks before the infant is fully recovered. If a woman uses barbiturates very heavily until delivery, there is reason to believe the baby may be dependent but there is very little information pertaining to this.

Question: What is the difference between hard narcotics and hard drugs in general?

Answer: The term "hard" drugs usually means heroin and the term "soft" drugs anything else. I have heard people refer to hard narcotics, but I don't know what that means, since there is no drug that can be called a soft narcotic. In point of fact, the terms hard and soft have no meaning and should be dropped. Instead we should talk of less dangerous drugs such as marihuana and more dangerous drugs, such as LSD, cocaine, etc.

Question: Can you predict who will go on to become a multiple-drug user or lose control of a drug such as marihuana?

Answer: In some cases you can. A person who is using drugs because of underlying personality problems, such as depression or severe anxiety, is often virtually incapable of avoiding multiple-drug use or excessive use of a single drug. In other cases, however, the users slowly slide from marihuana to multiple-drug use without any evidence of severe underlying personality abnormality.

Question: Are the lyrics in popular music responsible for the severity of the drug scene?

Answer: In 1968 many of the songs and popular groups extolled drugs. I am sure they contributed to the severity of the drug scene. By the years 1970–1971 drugs have diffused so extensively throughout our society that lyrics appear to have far less influence. Furthermore, songs themselves don't start drug epidemics unless a segment of society is ready to accept the drug. In 1933, for example, *International House,* a funny W. C. Fields movie, featured a song that focused on marihuana, but that song had no apparent deleterious influence on the large number of very young persons who saw and enjoyed the picture.

Question: Why is it so hard to cure heroin addiction?

Answer: In part, this relates to difficulties in instilling motivation into young, unmotivated persons who for the most part are immature and non-goal directed. But it is a lot more complex than that. Once a person is dependent on heroin, he may well have a biochemical urge to return to the drug. If you addict rats and then withdraw them from the drug, they will manifest subtle changes in body physiology for the entire next year. Furthermore, if you then offer them plain water or water with an opium preparation, they will preferentially drink the opiate-containing water for one and a half years after being taken off morphine. Thus the discouraging cure rate among young heroin addicts may be due to a combination of an immature personality, availability of heroin, a depressing environment, lack of motivation and a strong, psychological and/or physical urge to return to the drug.

Question: If you feel the peer group is important in getting young people involved in drugs, how do you cope with peer pressure?

Answer: There is no easy answer to that. There are three basic ways to deal with a peer group that is functioning in undesirable ways. First, you can provide it with external leadership to give it a constructive orientation. Second, you can infiltrate a pro-drug peer group with young persons acceptable to the group who are openly antidrug and will attempt to change the attitude of the peer group. Third, the family should try to provide the child with enough inner strength that he can resist the urging of the peer group to participate in behavior such as drug use.

Question: If you tell young people marihuana is a fun drug, aren't you encouraging its use?

Answer: Perhaps that is a danger, but it's much more dangerous to lie to them by implying anything else. If you don't tell the truth about the drug to start with, they won't hear anything else you say. And then what good are your educational efforts? I admit marihuana can be fun if they will admit it's no big deal. Then we can start from there to look at potential dangers and the possibilities of legalizing the drug.

Question: What right have you to compare alcohol and marihuana? Alcohol is legal and by equating the two you are encouraging use of marihuana which is illegal.

Answer: The comparison is strictly from the public-health point of view. Granted one is legal and the other illegal and granted we have the right to limit the number of legal intoxicants, nevertheless, from the public-health point of view the risk is similar. Of those using alcohol about 10 per cent become alcoholics and another 10 per cent get in trouble from alcohol without becoming alcoholics.

In regard to marihuana, if you add the approximate 1 per cent experiencing acute adverse effects, the 1 to 3 per cent suffering difficulties from repeated use and the 20 per cent escalating to more dangerous drugs, it becomes clear the potential risk from the public-health point of view is about the same.

Question: You have listed for us as reasons for drug use a reaction to the frustrations of everyday life and academic pressures. Aren't people like you just giving the kids a rationalization for taking harmful drugs?

Answer: I think the point is valid. But there is no getting around the fact that some persons who cannot cope with frustrations react to these frustrations by taking illicit drugs. As I pointed out such a reaction pattern is neither constructive nor effective. But there is no denying its existence. I do think the concept of frustration leading to drug abuse is overdone. More and more you hear the statement that young people are taking drugs in frustration at not being able to control their lives. To me that is a perfect example of facile rationalization and self-delusion to justify a certain behavior pattern. Furthermore, there is thus far no acceptable study showing that lack of control over one's life leads directly to drug abuse.

As far as relief from academic pressures is concerned, this too can be overdone as a reason for drug use. Nevertheless, academic pressures are increasingly great for some young people. Handling these pressures by drug use is, of course, highly undesirable. On the other hand, taking drugs as transient relief from the constant pressures may be illegal but depending on the drug and the individual, it may be harmful, harmless or in terms of needed relaxations even mildly beneficial.

Question: You have indicated repeatedly that marihuana use is associated with escalation to other drugs. Do you really think if marihuana disappeared, young persons would not use LSD, speed or heroin?

Answer: No, I did not mean to imply that. Right now the evidence is that repeated marihuana use is associated with progression to stronger drugs among a significant percentage of the marihuana users. Marihuana introduces the individual to the drug scene; if he were not so introduced the assumption is that many would never get to more powerful and dangerous agents. But marihuana is only one link in the chain that results in use of very dangerous drugs.

If marihuana were eliminated, I believe that many would never get from alcohol-tobacco experimentation to, say, LSD. Others undoubtedly would find other intermediate drugs and still end up on LSD, speed or heroin and still others would, as some do now, go directly to LSD or heroin. And of course the concept of marihuana being a stepping stone to more potent agents for some people applies only through 1971. The drug scene changes with great rapidity; the situation might be entirely different in 1972 or 1973. By then a much larger percentage might move from legal drugs directly to LSD or similar agents. Indeed, among certain groups there was a growing tendency during 1970 to go directly to heroin without the marihuana step; nevertheless even in these groups the clear majority still start with marihuana before heroin use.

4.

A Program for Parents

Everyone working in the area of illicit drug use has been approached time and again by parents who ask, "What do I do if I suspect or know that my child is using drugs?" The following approach appears to me to be realistic. It is not guaranteed to solve the problem, but then there is no easy solution. What every parent needs is an approach that will not aggravate the situation but may do a lot of good.

1 Don't panic. Panic is perhaps the most common reaction of parents—even before they have tried to evaluate the severity of the problem. Nothing could be less effective. The panic is understandable, for parents see drug abuse as presenting a catastrophic situation. The parent who panics usually conveys the impression that the young person's life is ruined or that he is a "dope fiend." The notion "How could you do this to me after all I have done for you?" is implicit or sometimes explicit. But if a young person has experimented only with marihuana and has not been caught, surely he will find it hard to accept the idea that what he has done has exerted a permanently harmful effect on his future life. Similarly, most young people are not likely to be impressed with the argument that illicit drug use proves they are ungrateful to their parents. And the use of the tainted word "dope" can be a disaster. It is an imprecise term that covers the whole drug field, and it carries such implied opprobrium that it almost inevitably arouses in the young person negative feelings that make further communication almost impossible.

Often a parent's panic turns into rage. I know of instance after instance in which parents have physically or verbally manhandled their children because of suspected or known drug use. In some cases they literally have forced the youngsters out of the home. Beating them, berating them, or implying that their drug use injures the parents' psyche or status just won't work, and kicking the kids out only guarantees that they will turn to their drug-using friends for solace. Thus the most important first step is to stay calm. The situation may not be nearly as bad as you think, and in any case your job as parent is to recognize a potentially disastrous situation and then do something to make it better. Panic or rage will only make it worse.

Equally ineffective are those parents who react with monumental insouciance. They say, "All young people are doing it, so why worry?" This is the kind of parent who dawdles until his child is in real trouble. At least in some cases, panic or rage shows the youngster you care; indifference implies not sophistication but lack of love, and can push some young people into further drug use if only to make you show you care.

Another frequent reaction of parents is self-castigation and despairing introspection. "Where did we go wrong?" they repeatedly ask each other, themselves, and outsiders. A certain amount of self-appraisal is of course salutary, but it is often carried to self-defeating extremes. Obviously the parents are to blame in some cases, but plenty of children who are devoted to their parents and do not feel their parents have failed them are playing around with drugs out of curiosity or peer group pressure. The first thing an outside consultant often has to do is convince the parents that there is no basis for bitter self-criticism and that there may well be nothing specific in the parent-child relationship that propelled the youngster to drug abuse. I would warn parents that, as I have said before, drug use within the family should not be considered a police problem. It should be handled within the family if possible with outside counseling and/or medical help.

The idea that reporting to the police will scare the child away from drugs is usually invalid; furthermore, it will alienate the youngster and may get him into unnecessary trouble with the law. Even if the state has a law saying you must report if you have knowledge of a crime, such laws are not implemented and the parent can get around them easily because of deceptions in the illicit market.

If a young person admits drug use or even shows you his alleged supply, you cannot be sure he has actually taken a drug or that what you see is what it is supposed to be. The effects he has felt may be purely psychological and what you see may be fake—and this applies to marihuana, LSD, cocaine, or any other drug being used illegally today.

I ordinarily do not advocate circumventing laws, but reporting your children to the police is rarely an effective approach to drug use. In some areas the police say they should be told so that the youngster can get rehabilitation and treatment. If such is needed, that is the parents' responsibility, and should not be delegated to the police.

If a young person is a pusher then the decision is more difficult. If after assiduous attempts at controlling the problem he will not stop selling drugs, the health of the family and/or the community may mandate involvement of the police. But this should be a last resort. For the intransigent user, a last resort, if all else fails, may be, in some cases, exclusion from the household. This should be utilized very infrequently, but I have seen families literally destroyed by one user who refused help, would not stop drug use, and set a terrible example for younger siblings. If that happens, the health of the rest of the family must be considered paramount. I would hate to see people use the foregoing statement to reject their drug-using children. Last resort means exactly that—only when all else fails—and then only after appropriate outside consultation.

2 *Educate yourself.* In our bewildering society, it is often difficult to deal with a drug problem within one's own family even if one is knowledgeable about drugs. And if one is ignorant, the situation is impossible. Those who know a little about drugs are likely to make sweeping generalizations based on established prejudices or misinformation. These inexact generalizations can run so counter to a young person's own view of drugs that an inflexible polemic can begin between parent and child, precluding effective dialogue. Young people may scoff at the older generation, but they do respect knowledge. With facts at your command you may be able to penetrate a youngster's frequently infuriating veneer of indifference to you and his superciliousness about drugs, based on his conviction that he knows more than you do. How then do you, a parent, obtain this knowledge?

Few parents can cope with the encyclopedic information that exists about the farrago of drugs used by young people. But most parents can acquire a modicum of expertise with relative ease. Listening to a lecture, reading newspaper or magazine reports, or attending a one-day workshop will not suffice. Instead, the parent would do well to carefully read several books that thoroughly cover the current American drug scene (See Bibliography). The books must be both comprehensive and dispassionate. If the author is a zealot either for or against drugs, the book is likely to be so full of bias that it will not provide the reader with the data necessary to handle the problem in his own family. What one really wants is impartial information about the effects of the individual drugs, the potential and actual dangers, the popular fads, and the legal restraints. Once this information is acquired, it must be carefully considered and formulated into a cohesive viewpoint. This is as important as getting the basic information itself. You must know the facts and then organize them so that you can approach your children articulately, accurately, and persuasively.

3 *Learn to communicate.* It seems almost superfluous to sug-

gest that it is impossible to handle this problem unless there is adequate communication between parent and child. But communication between generations has indeed broken down in our society. In part, the astounding technological and scientific advances of the past thirty years and the gigantic problems they have created have quickened the pace of our lives and disrupted the fabric of our society, thus intensifying the generation gap normal to all societies. But surely the complexity of life should not be used as a rationalization for failure to establish dialogue between parents and children. Also, the communication gap can exist in both directions. I recently gave a lecture in Connecticut at which the sponsors had questions written on cards so that I could select those I felt were most important for the limited question-and-answer period. About half-way through the cards I came to one that took me aback. It said, "My parents think I use drugs. I do not. How can I convince them I am not a drug user?" It would be hard to formulate a more poignant or articulate expression of a major communication gap between parent and child. This young person's plea also illustrates that where there is no communication, there is likely to be no trust.

Many parents seem to assume that there need be no significant dialogue until a problem arises, at which point they can say in essence, "Here is a problem, now let's communicate about it." This, of course, is preposterous. If there had been no free and easy communication before, it is unlikely that it can be set up effectively without resentment when a parent suddenly suspects that drugs may have entered the life of his youngster. As Richard Blum's studies of students in California indicate, users of illicit drugs frequently feel alienated from their parents. Clearly, a parent has to make a conscientious effort to communicate with his children about their feelings, problems, hang-ups, and fears. Ideally, such communication should start as soon as the child can talk. This means discussing not only those things that concern and worry him but also those that make him feel good. This is particularly important in speaking of drugs. If your child is convinced there will be valid communication with you only about those things that are worrisome or make him feel bad, then it may well be that he will not even think of discussing with you the early phases of his use of agents such as marihuana, which may, after all, only make him feel good.

There is another dividend to communicating with young people about drugs. As Dr. Helen Nowlis has noted, drugs are so much a part of youthful rebellion and the entire adolescent scene that if you can communicate in this particular area, it is much easier to discuss the rest of the problems which plague young people in those emotionally turbulent years.

To sum up, parental knowledge and sophistication about drugs is not enough. Without communication, the knowledge is useless: the parent knows precisely what he would like to tell his child about drugs, but it doesn't do a bit of good. Knowledge and good communication will not in themselves guarantee the child will not use drugs. But at the very least, they make it likely the child will be willing to come to you with questions about drugs, knowing that the answers will be forthright and factual. This in itself will be a major deterrent.

4 *Evaluate the problem.* Parents have to determine exactly how serious their child's drug problem is. There is no correct approach that covers all cases. After all, there is a world of difference between the youngster who tries marihuana at a party to avoid being called chicken by his peers, or even the one who smokes the drug on one to five occasions, and the user who centers his life around it.

This assessment of the severity of the problem is enormously important. As an example, I receive many calls from frantic parents whose children are using heroin every few days but clearly are not addicted. The parents always ask where the youngster should be referred for treatment. The answer is that no advice can be meaningful until somebody has found out how severe the underlying personality problem is. In many cases the drug use itself is a secondary factor and treatment should focus on the fundamental psychological difficulty. In other cases drug use may be the primary factor or the cause of personality disturbances; here treatment can be directed at the drugs or at the life style of the individual.

Let me illustrate this with a case referred to me recently from a suburban community. The parents of a young man asked me to talk with their son because he was a heroin addict who was stealing from them and in trouble with the law. They obviously regarded him as a reprehensible ingrate. When I asked him what drugs he took he said sedatives, marihuana, and heroin. Now each of these has the capacity to alleviate anxiety. After further dialogue it became very apparent that he suffered from an overwhelming identity crisis that had led to severe depression, and this was turned into tension and anxiety. He took drugs to relieve the anxiety. He was indeed addicted to heroin but in a sense he had no heroin problem. His problem was depression; it was this that needed treatment. To focus on the heroin without treating the depression would have been a tremendous mistake.

In evaluating a child's drug problem, one must first find out whether he is deeply involved (a chronic user) or his experimentation is ephemeral (a transient user). Then one has to consider the kind of drug being used and the root of administration. There are in general four possibilities: (1) transient experimentation with mild drugs, (2) transient experimentation with serious drugs, (3) chronic use of mild drugs, and (4) chronic use of serious drugs. The mild category includes marihuana, codeine, glue, cough medicines, stimulant aerosols, nutmeg, catnip, and small amounts of sedatives, tranquilizers, or stimulants taken by mouth. The serious category includes LSD, mescaline, cocaine, opium, morphine, heroin, Methedrine, STP, Asthmador, dimethyltryptamine, and any other drug administered by needle. Sedatives, tranquilizers, or stimulants would also be included in the serious group if very large amounts were ingested. This differentiation does not imply that the user never gets severe toxic effects from experimenting with some of the drugs listed in the mild category. But by and large, serious medical or psychiatric complications from transient experimentation with the milder drugs are infrequent.

At the same time one is evaluating the drug involved and the extent of its use, one has to make a judgment about the personality and emotional health of the user. It is a fallacy to think that drug use per se indicates a diseased personality. In point of fact, the clear majority of drug abuse consists of a fundamentally healthy personality's transient experimentation with pills or marihuana primarily because his peers are doing it or he is curious. At the other extreme, certain people who are alienated or unhappy literally are driven to take drugs because of overwhelming misery. For them, even experimentation must be viewed with considerable alarm. They are virtually incapable of stopping at mere experimentation, and almost ineluctably move on to chronic use of serious agents. Many psychiatrists experienced in treating young users of illicit drugs are convinced that those who become drug-dependent often have an underlying personality pattern of pervasive depression. Thus a severly depressed person who experiments with marihuana is far more likely to end up becoming marihuana-dependent—a so-called pothead. Similarly, experimentation with heroin by such an individual is far more likely to result in addiction, and experimentation with LSD will far more often result in his becoming a so-called acid-head. Many people who are severely depressed or alienated or suffer from major mental abnormalities such as schizophrenia have taken a potpourri of drugs in the hope of improving their personalities. Of course, under these circumstances whatever the drug taken the personality problem will not lessen and may be seriously aggravated.

The need to determine the presence and severity of underlying personality problems adds an additional variable to those already mentioned. This then doubles the number of potential combinations to eight, the paired variables being: experimental versus chronic use, mild versus potentially dangerous drugs, and healthy versus unhealthy personality. These are listed in the following table.

Assessing Severity of the Problem

Type of Drug	Mild (1)	Severe (2)
Kind of Use	Transient (1)	Chronic (2)
Personality	Healthy (1)	Unhealthy (3)

3–4 Total Score = Mild to Moderate Problem
5 Total Score = Problem of Intermediate Severity
6–7 Total Score = Severe Problem

If one assigns the number 1 to experimental use, mild drugs, and healthy personality, the number 2 to chronic use and dangerous drugs, and the number 3 to an unhealthy personality, it is possible to make a rough guess as to just how bad a given situation is. It should be noted that more weight is placed on the personality pattern than on the type of drug being used. At the least worrisome end of the spectrum, a basically healthy individual experimenting with mild drugs would receive a total score of 3. In contrast, a person with substantial underlying personality problems who chronically uses more dangerous drugs would have a total score of 7. A reasonable rule of thumb is that a score of 3 or 4 is of far less concern than a score of 6 or 7. A score of 5 should also be of deep concern because it means either that a basically healthy person has become dangerously and chronically involved with drugs or that a fundamentally unhealthy personality has initiated a pattern of drug use that is likely to progress.

Another way of evaluating drug use is to look, not at the drug itself, but at what it means to the user. All too often this factor is ignored, but it really must complement any assessment of the problem. Inexplicably, most parents will not spend the time and energy needed to learn the motives of their drug-using children, even though comprehension of these motives is likely to be the starting point for effective communication and remedial action. The approach to a youngster who is using drugs because of curiosity, peer group pressure, or for kicks must be profoundly different from the approach to one who has a sick personality or one who is using drugs in an attempt to cope with an identity crisis, or the emotional turbulence of normal adolescence.

At a recent conference in England of British and American drug experts, we discussed the following categorization of drug users, which appears to have some merit:

(A) Experimenters, including the rebellious and the curious.

(B) Recreational users. These are more than transient experimenters but are not perpetual users. The best example is the college student who smokes marihuana on weekends or at parties or even two or three times weekly, but is in no way committed to the drug scene, and can stop any time it appears necessary. Large numbers of drug users in the United States would fall into this category. Recreational users may have trouble from the drugs they use, but most confine their use to milder agents, and the majority suffers no major medical or psychiatric complications.

(C) Those who use drugs because of the normal emotional turbulence of adolescence. Growing up is not easy. The search for identity, the loneliness, the sexual confusion, and the emotional chaos may cause perfectly normal youngsters to use drugs. They should be distinguished from rebellious or curious experimenters and from purely pleasure-oriented recreational users. A particular danger for such young people is that they will establish a permanent pattern of turning to drugs in trying to cope with emotional stress.

(D) Users from depressed areas. This would include the ghetto-dwelling heroin user. These individuals often have inadequate personalities and take drugs in part as a rebellion against an environment from which they see no ready escape. Clearly, some of their inability to cope with their depressing milieu is related to their own inadequacies, but it is also related to despair at being locked into a life of poor education, dilapidated housing, filthy streets, and relentless poverty.

(E) Users with major underlying personality problems. For them, drug use is one symptom of psychological derangement among many, and the drug is of less consequence than the derangement.

(F) Users for whom the drugs per se are a problem. This is a rapidly growing group in the United States. This type of user may have had mild to moderate personality dysfunction, but he has no major psychiatric problems. He tends to experiment with milder drugs, such as marihuana, and gradually drifts into severe multidrug use. By the time he comes to anyone's attention, he has acquired major personality difficulties due specifically to the drugs. This is a group conveniently ignored by those who say, "Forget the specific drugs used; what is important are the alienation and the lack of communication that led to drug use." This statement may be valid for some experimenters, but for many chronic users there is no way of avoiding the fact that the drugs have become the major problem. This can be true of the marihuana user, although it is far more often true of users of amphetamines, heroin, or LSD.

It may well be that the parents of a drug user, because of personal emotional involvement or something else, simply can't assess the problem well. In such cases parents should be encouraged to seek outside help. It's not easy to say who exactly should provide that help. If a psychiatrist who is knowledgeable about drugs and relates well to young people is available, he probably can best make the crucial judgment of the youngster's underlying personality. And he, better than anyone else, can determine how much of the observed behavior relates to personality aberration and how much to the effects of drugs. This is often quite a difficult judgment requiring an enormous amount of experience and expertise. Referral to a psychiatrist is not necessarily a panacea. Some psychiatrists know very little about drugs, and others are so restricted by their own emotional problems that it is hard for them to render an effective judgment for others. If an experienced and trusted psychiatrist is not available, then the person most competent to make the necessary judgment is likely to be the family physician or an internist. But here again the helper may not be particularly helpful, and it may be necessary for the parents to turn to a clergyman, psychologist, or even a close friend they feel is understanding and perceptive. In one manner or another it is usually possible to obtain outside help. Frequently, it is extraordinarily difficult for the parents to come to the initial recognition that they cannot make the judgment themselves. It may be that their lines of communication are not good enough to bring in adequate information, or that they are too close to the situation to think impartially, or that they do not have the expertise to separate drug effects from underlying personality abnormalities. In any of these cases, they must recognize that the problem cannot be handled intramurally and that it is appropriate and indeed highly desirable to go outside the family unit for help. If a parent questions the validity of his own conclusions the least bit, a consultation should be obtained. This may be important for an additional reason: Often the situation is so discouraging that the despairing parents blame themselves, often incorrectly, and then allow the child's drug use to literally tear the family apart. Sometimes bickering and strife between husband and wife threaten to break up the family unit. This can be halted by an impartial extramural consultation.

5 *Be able to follow through.* Once it is decided that a drug problem exists, something has to be done about it immediately. If the evaluation score is 3 or 4, parents can feel relatively reassured, for they are dealing with a healthy personality and either experimentation or chronic use of a milder agent. And loneliness, curiosity, peer group pressures, or normal adolescent emotional confusion may be the youngster's motivation. Under these circumstances, patient understanding and continuous communication may be all that is needed. Many people insist on approaching what amounts to a peccadillo with a host of vigorous remedies; this is therapeutic overkill, and it often tends to make the situation worse. A high school or college student who tries marihuana once or even several times very likely does not need referral to a psychiatrist, a psychologist, or a physician, nor does he need group

therapy. What he really needs is for somebody—parent, counselor, or friend—to sit down with him and try to convince him as unemotionally as possible that it's foolish to play around with marihuana, a minor-league drug that in our society has major-league legal consequences. Obviously, whoever takes this job on must not only be armed with knowledge but also share it with absolute honesty. Exaggeration or distortion merely defeats the educational effort.

If the drug problem is very severe, the user should be referred for intensive treatment. Under such circumstances, there are three avenues open to the parents: First, if the major drug involved is an opiate such as heroin, there are quite a few rehabilitative programs available. These include outpatient, non-psychiatrically oriented therapeutic groups such as Encounter or Greenwich House in New York City, residential therapeutic communities for volunteers such as Synanon, Daytop, and Odyssey House, drug maintenance programs such as those in which methadone is used, and voluntary or involuntary civil commitment programs such as the massive ones now available in New York State and California. Clearly there are many approaches to heroin addiction; to some extent a program can be chosen by considering the need and personal makeup of the user. Importantly, though, this wide array of rehabilitative programs applies only to the user of heroin-like drugs. No similar programs exist for heavy users of amphetamines, barbiturates, hallucinogens, or marihuana. Furthermore, there is no reason to believe that heavy users of the non-narcotic drugs respond to most of the programs directed against heroin abuse.

Second, if the drug in question is in the non-opiate category (marihuana, LSD, etc.), a parent can refer his youngster to voluntary groups that attempt to restructure the attitudes of an individual against use of any illicit drug. Encounter, for example, falls into this category too. These groups are interested in young people who abuse drugs of any type; their therapeutic goal is the constructive functioning of the drug-free individual. Various religious groups have similar though somewhat differently structured programs. Actually there are few such groups available; those that do exist often do not speak to the needs of the individual user, and their efficacy remains unproven. Nevertheless, they may offer the best available hope for cure, and there is no doubt that they markedly benefit some people.

The third avenue open to parents is referral to a health service or psychiatrist. For the individual with marked depression, alienation, or other severe underlying personality defects, this is undoubtedly the best recourse. And even if he has no such problem, the student user may readily accept referral, especially if the health service or psychiatrist is known to be sympathetic and experienced in the drug field.

But whatever route is chosen, whatever technique is adopted, the clear obligation of the parent is to follow through and continue doing so as long as is necessary, no matter how discouraging and painful the path may be.

I am always asked what a parent should do if the child refuses help. There is no simple answer. If the drug is heroin he can be civilly committed involuntarily in some states and if he is deranged he can be forced to accept psychiatric care. But this applies to a minority who refuse aid; for the majority the parents must patiently try to get the child to accept evaluation and treatment on a voluntary basis. Most drug users who actually need help agree to go to a clinic, voluntary group, psychiatrist, or counseling service for initial evaluation although many of them will not commit themselves to an extended treatment program. It may require a great deal of effort on the part of the parents to find a treatment approach the child will accept. Unfortunately, the treatment resources in many communities are completely inadequate, thus limiting the options for parents and drug-dependent children.

6 *Prevention of the problem.* It is much easier to deal with drug abuse in its early, unorganized phases or to prevent it entirely than to reverse an established pattern. There are five major points to be considered here: First, it is necessary to continuously educate one's children about drugs. This means that the parent

must first educate himself and then try hard to keep up to date by reading, attending lectures, and workshops. The vogue in drug fads changes every few months, and education acquired in 1970 is archaic by 1971, at least to some degree. However, once one acquires a basic foundation of knowledge about drugs, it is fairly easy to add new information. Thus a parent can keep abreast of the drug scene and pass on what he learns to his children.

Second, parents must set a good example. "There is nothing so infectious as example," said La Rochefoucauld, and certainly in the field of drug abuse this maxim is precisely correct. If a child sees a parent drinking too much or taking pills, capsules, or injections for every ill, whether the medicaments are needed or not, is it any wonder that he will succumb to the lure of the drug proselytizers? A parent who feels tense and takes a tranquilizer or feels slightly depressed and takes a mild stimulant is, after all, taking medication in order to feel good or at least better. Whatever the objection may be to young people's using drugs illicitly, most drugs are taken because they have the potential to make the user feel good. In this country more than 125 million prescriptions for sedatives and tranquilizers and an additional 25 million for stimulants are written by physicians each year. It is a safe estimate that well over half of these are not needed in the first place, and often the medication is self-administered at some subsequent date not under the direct advice of a physician. If parents use drugs indiscriminately, they should not be surprised if their children use drugs promiscuously and also perhaps illicitly. As a matter of fact, ample studies show that pill-taking parents tend to breed pill-taking children. I suspect that the best thing a parent could do would be to go to the medicine cabinet and immediately throw out about 90 per cent of the medicaments in it, and then to promise himself not to take any medication unless absolutely necessary. Once such a behavior pattern is established in parents and the attitude is imparted to their children, the drug problem among young people in this country will inevitably decline.

Third, parents must deal fully with problems and unresolved issues that crop up in parent-child relationships. This is an important point; Richard Blum in his book *Students and Drugs* emphasized that those youngsters who become illicit drug users report a greater frequency of problems and unresolved issues in their relationships with their parents. Most parents tend to dismiss problems or only partially solve them. To do so is to create an emotionally unstable child. All issues, especially the ones that appear of utmost importance to the child, should be completely resolved. It may take only a few moments or it may take weeks or months of vigorous effort, but the dividend in terms of a stable, confident child is enormous, especially since such a child is less likely to use dangerous or illegal drugs.

In this context, I should like to stress how important a role a child's healthy identification with a parent plays in the prevention of drug abuse. Whether or not someone will be susceptible to drugs may be determined very early in his life by the quality of this identification. Recently we visited a family in which the father is absent a good deal, taken away by his work. The father is implacably opposed to drugs. Both parents had been worried about the effect of the father's absence on their nine-year-old son. As we were sitting down to dinner one evening, I noticed that one of the boy's textbooks was covered with pictures of his father as a young athlete. I remarked on this, and the mother answered, "Oh, John wouldn't admit it, but he admires his father enormously." Of course it is possible that the boy was using the pictures as a substitute for a father who is seldom there, but nevertheless it was obvious that there existed a positive identification between father and son. When this emotionally secure boy is offered drugs, as inevitably he will be, the odds are overwhelming that he will reject them on the basis of this strong relationship with a father who is very much opposed to them. If, perchance, the boy does decide to go along with the crowd and try drugs, it's almost certain that his use of them will be transient and limited to the milder agents.

Fourth, and perhaps most important, parents should conscientiously try to get their children involved in constructive, intriguing, and exciting activities. This is an absolute must if we are going to turn our children away from drugs. Over and over again I see young users who appear to have no goals and are committed to nothing. They say, in one way or another, "I'm not really interested in anything." In general, parents should not mandate involvement of their children in a particular project, but they should search out and offer opportunities for involvement, letting the children select for themselves. It is virtually a catechism that a young person involved in healthy activities is far less likely to become deeply committed to the drug scene than one who is not. This does not mean that an involved youngster will not use drugs—he may indeed, but the likelihood is that his use will be ephemeral and confined to the milder agents, and he will therefore be amenable to sympathetic parental or outside guidance. Noninvolvement and boredom in energetic and naturally intemperate young people promote drug use.

To my way of thinking it is perfectly reasonable to offer the six- to fourteen-year-old child several opportunities for involvement and allow him to select which of these he or she wants, and to encourage the child to substitute programs of his own if he isn't interested in those that are being offered; but the one choice the child should not have is to reject all the opportunities.

To be successful here, a parent must set an example by participating in society himself. If he concentrates solely on either making money or enjoying his leisure and this materialistic way of life is rejected by his child, what is the child left with? And the parent's participation must be serious; there are far too many hand-clapping bench-sitters who applaud potential solutions to the ills of society but do nothing to bring them about. Parents must move from intellectual support to active commitment in attacking society's problems. Their honest participation will naturally induce similar action on the part of the child, and this in turn will reduce the chances of his becoming enmeshed in the drug scene.

One word of caution must be added. Even if parents set a good example and even if the child is offered plenty of opportunities for commitment, a considerable number will reject any constructive involvement. They suffer from what I have called internal boredom and have a deep-seated inability to get interested in anything constructive on a continuing basis. For these individuals drug use is likely to be a problem until therapy ameliorates the inner boredom.

Fifth, parents should not be conned into accepting facile rationalizations, such as the generation gap, for legitimizing a child's misbehavior in regard to drugs. Statements such as "You have your alcohol, I have my intoxicants," or "What I use is my own affair if I don't hurt others," or "Your generation made a mess of things, so don't tell us what to do," should be met firmly and rejected as simplistic and superficial; if anything, they should be allowed to be only a starting point for a detailed discussion. Nor should parents permit a child to use the threat of drug use to manipulate them. The child is actually saying, "If you don't do what I want, I'll use drugs." This type of reaction, which I see with increasing frequency, may be an attempt by the young person to achieve power, but more often it is clear evidence of immaturity and insecurity, and it should be met on those terms. To allow oneself to be so manipulated is a disservice to both oneself and one's child.

A related problem is that parents and educators tend to accept uncritically whatever the younger generation writes and says. But the young people themselves will usually admit that much of what their spokesmen are saying is a put-on, and they regard as ludicrous the older generation's serious reaction to so many sweeping pronouncements.

There is more that parents can do in the area of prevention. They can demand of their communities and schools effective preventive educational programs. For the most part, community programs have either been ignored or left to zealots who hold biased views of the drug problem. This can result in approaches that do far more harm than good. Instead, educational programs must be comprehensive and unbiased; and they must have financial support so that teachers can take in-depth courses on drugs and be paid extra for serving as special counselors for students, and so that appropriate movies, books, and pamphlets can be obtained.

Parents can also try to get legislators, councilmen, and governmental executives to defuse the drug problem by making our laws sensible and constructive.

And before sending their children to a secondary school or college, parents should investigate it. Interviews with administrators and the children's conversations with students already enrolled should establish whether there is a significant drug problem and what, if anything, the school administration is doing to cope with it. If the administration is indifferent, deliberately ignoring the problem, or actively helping it grow, parents might do well to send their children elsewhere; since peer group pressures are one major cause of drug abuse, if these can be avoided by choosing an educational institution with care, it is wise to do so.

Finally, parents should be very careful about trying to become detection experts. They should not watch their children like hawks after prey. Parents are told that sloppy dress, bleary eyes, an excessive taste for sweets, excess giggling all suggest drug use. These manifestations in the overwhelming majority of young persons indicate nothing of the kind. One expert from New York City, a physician, even told parents on a television program that the cardinal sign of marihuana use is dilated pupils. This caused many parents to stare at their children's pupils in the hope of detecting early marihuana smoking. That irresponsible physician might have also told parents that if you examine pupils in a dim light they automatically dilate in normal persons. Besides the evidence now clearly shows marihuana in ordinary doses does *not* dilate the pupil.

Parents should be knowledgeable about drugs, aware of the manifestations of use, and aware that unexplained emotional or behavioral changes might be due to drug use. But they had better not be excessively suspicious or unnecessarily zealous in attempts at detecting drug use; the penalty for such overreaction may be alienation, rebellion and consequent drug use.

5.

An Approach to Education

Everyone agrees that education is the best approach to ending drug abuse, but this agreement has not been strongly or effectively implemented. There are many reasons why this is so. The inefficiency of central bureaucracies and the failure to appropriate adequate moneys are two of the main ones.

The bureaucracy factor can be illustrated in New York, a state that has been consistently in the forefront of rehabilitation efforts in regard to heroin addiction. In the spring of 1968, several organizations simultaneously decided to investigate the antidrug program available for New York City students. This appeared to be a particularly good time, since the data clearly showed that there was a fast-growing drug problem among both the young who remained in school and those who dropped out. Meetings were held with high-level representatives of the New York City Board of Education. The board representatives said emphatically and correctly that antidrug education was mandated by the new statewide curriculum. They pointed out that every school had available to it brochures about drug problems, teaching aids, and written information describing what students were to be taught in this important area. Then the board was asked precisely what the schools were teaching and the answer, which I must say sounded somewhat incredible, was a repetition of the central hegemony's mandate stating what was supposed to be taught, and another statement regarding all the materials available. When they were pressed, it became abundantly clear that these top-level representatives of the school system had no idea what was being taught in the schools. They thought that their function, as members of the central bureaucracy in a nondecentralized school system, was to tell the schools and principals what should be taught and what materials were available, but to go no further. They had no idea whether any of their materials and commands were actually being translated into specific courses for the students. Yet when questioned, they could state glibly and honestly that the schools had a major antidrug program. They did indeed have one, if a major drug program consists of merely handing out a batch of materials about what ought to be taught. Curiously, the board did not really think it feasible to find out from the schools what actually was being taught, even though it readily acknowledged that in some schools, despite the mandate, there might be no antidrug teaching and in others the course might well be given by a hygiene instructor or athletic instructor or some other individual who in fact knew nothing about drugs.

What this informal discussion with the New York City school board revealed is buttressed by an experience of the city's own official Addiction Services Agency. On February 26, 1968, a letter was sent to superintendents and principals of 250 intermediate, junior high, and high schools, signed by the superintendent of schools and the commissioner of the Addiction Services Agency, informing them that trained personnel in the agency were prepared to assist in developing drug prevention programs for their schools. The letter stipulated that the school had to initiate the request and set up an ad hoc committee, after which the agency would give a course on attitudinal skills and assign a resource person to the school as coordinator.

The response was appalling. Fifty of the schools replied asking for help, but only eight actually established ad hoc committees, and only four completed the training course. Four out of two hundred and fifty at a time when the New York City problem was growing at a very rapid rate!

Lack of interest on the part of the schools is by no means confined to New York. Richard Blum and his colleagues in California had a similar experience. As they noted in *Students and Drugs,* "We invited on behalf of our local council on drug abuse thirty-three superintendents to discuss the problem and the arrangements for a survey of prevalence. These superintendents represented an estimated 102,766 students. Of those invited, thirty-one responded positively and said they would attend a meeting. Only seventeen showed up for the meeting. Of those, five actually expressed some interest in finding out what their students were doing and thinking about drugs. In the final analysis only two schools cooperated although two others did sponsor a drug education program arising out of our discussions."

The problem in regard to expenditures is equally distressing. For example, the New York State Legislature allocated some 46 million dollars during the 1969–1970 fiscal year to implement Governor Rockefeller's pioneering and commendable effort to rehabilitate heroin users through civil commitment. Included in that appropriation was about 1 million dollars for education, representing about a 60 per cent reduction from the amount requested. The preliminary figures released by the New York State Narcotic Control Commission and other civil commitment programs indicate that the cure rate among the civilly committed will not be astoundingly high. Indeed, if the rate reaches 50 per cent it will be very encouraging. Thus the experts acknowledge and the available data confirm that to rehabilitate established addicts is extraordinarily difficult. Logic would seem to dictate that the most effective approach to addiction is to prevent it rather than treat it. The Narcotic Addiction Control Commission justifiably spends a fortune in attempts to control and rehabilitate the committed addicts, but spends a relatively meager sum on preventive education, and even that limited amount is cut extensively by the Legislature. Although educational funds at the state level in New York have been inadequate, New York State has committed far more than any other state or municipality; indeed moneys have been virtually nonexistent in other areas, including New York City, which has the largest concentration of addicts in the United States. I might add that in early 1970 Governor Nelson Rockefeller became alarmed that educational funds were inadequate and provided substantial sums for education by executive fiat.

The Federal government has likewise not met its educational commitments. It has spent approximately one million dollars in an educational campaign under the able direction of Dr. Sidney Cohen of the National Institute of Mental Health, but this is a minimal amount when compared to the gigantic need. Until late 1969, low priority was accorded antidrug education; indeed, the administration gave no support to congressional bills which would have provided up to 10 million dollars a year solely for education. Then, in late 1969, priorities did begin to change. Fifteen million dollars was found for an attack on the drug problem, several million of which was available for educational programs. And both the administration and Congress appear now to realize that a lot of money must be committed to education if the drug explosion is to be contained.

The conventional approach to drug education by most schools, colleges, and communities combines half-day to two-day workshops with movies and lectures by authorities in the field. It is my own conviction that these alone have not done and cannot do the job. People listening to a series of speakers cannot take away enough valid information to conduct educational campaigns of their own. The organizers of the workshop usually attempt to have somebody from law enforcement, a medical man, somebody involved in rehabilitation, interested community representatives, and sometimes ex-addicts. Not infrequently, in order to make the workshop exciting and attract a large audience, they deliberately have people with controversial or conflicting views. This in itself is to be commended, but all too often what happens is that the protagonists spend so much of their time squabbling over petty points that the audience cannot but be confused. It is now the custom to have one or more general sessions and then break up the workshop into smaller groups for intensive discussions. But these small groups tend to turn into repetitive bull sessions in which the amount of information imparted to the audience is negligible and the content often biased; and because there is no major input from the workshop participants themselves, the remarks and points of view are not carefully assessed. Indeed, I think this is the major defect in workshops. Because their format is not particularly attractive and they are not remunerative, many of the best educators in the antidrug field pass them by, preferring to deliver single lectures to generally larger numbers of people. Thus the workshop conveners are often faced with a shortage of skilled and articulate educators and have to pick far less effective ones. The audience contributes virtually nothing of its own intellectual capacity; it merely sits, absorbing a small amount of what is being said.

With the talks and seminars sometimes come brochures or other handouts that tend to be so cut-and-dried they are merely glanced at and discarded or placed in a file cabinet. If the workshop lasts into the afternoon or evening, audience fatigue grows geometrically and the workshop becomes progressively duller. I don't want to deny the potential value of workshops, but by themselves they can serve only to get people interested in education about drug abuse. They cannot impart enough information, cannot equip people to educate effectively in this area, and must not be the mainstay of our educational efforts. The one- to two-hour workshop conducted weekly for six to eight weeks is a better format, but can also only excite interest and be a starting point.

Often these workshops are intended to show teachers how to detect drug use. But teachers should not expect to be the drug detection experts. All they need to know is that an abrupt decline in scholastic ability, inappropriate behavior, inordinate sleepiness, or any undesirable behavioral change that cannot be readily explained could be due to drugs: Obviously there might be many non-drug explanations and ordinarily the decision as to etiology of the behavior pattern should be made by the medical or counseling services, not by the teachers. The teacher's role should be to consider the possibility of drug abuse and to refer the student to the appropriate diagnostic service.

The criticisms I have made in regard to workshops also apply to the single lecture. These may last from 40 minutes to 1½ hours. Many of the speakers either are not particularly articulate or lack the charisma needed to communicate with a passive audience. Even those with a certain flamboyance and verve can get across only the general outlines of a point of view and a program in the limited time available. It all comes across too quickly, in kaleidoscopic fashion. Frequently, for example, people come up to me after lectures and say something like this: "You know, I enjoyed your talk, but I found that you mentioned data I thought were very significant and I would start to think over what you had said. While I was trying to sort all this out, you would go on to something else, and then everything would get a bit jumbled." This makes a great deal of sense. There is an enormous amount to discuss, and I, like many other speakers, use a rapid-fire delivery in order to cover as much as possible. This inevitably means that even the attentive listener is hearing too much too quickly to sort it out well. The best he can do is take notes assiduously and rapidly, hoping that these will be accurate and he will be able to refer to them in more leisurely fashion later. Of course a question-and-answer period helps; indeed, perhaps the most one can anticipate from a single lecture is to excite the listeners' interest, provide them with a broad outline of the problem and with realistic approaches to it and then, through the question-and-answer period, make sure that as many questions as possible are answered. As with the conventional workshop, the big defect in the lecture system is the lack of input from the audience. I have taken to requesting that sponsors urge audiences to read some of the pertinent literature prior to my lectures, but ordinarily these requests are unavailing, and the audience comes without having really prepared itself for the evening's discussion.

As for motion pictures, some are archaic and consequently ineffective, and others are just badly made. But there are some that are up to date and well put together, including *The Seekers* (M. Solin, Benchmark Films, Inc.); *Marijuana* (Bailey Films, Inc.); *LSD: Insight or Insanity* (Bailey Films, Inc.); *LSD–25* (Professional Arts, Inc.); *Trip to Nowhere* (U.S. Navy); *The Distant Drummer* (National Institute of Mental Health); *Grooving* (M. Solin, Benchmark Films, Inc.); *The Losers* (Carousel Films, Inc.); *The Speed Scene* (Bailey Films, Inc.); *Not Me* (New Jersey Community Action Training Institute); and *Monday* (Robert Appelbe Prod., Ltd.).

There are other satisfactory films, but those listed appear to me to be especially good. Additional new films will be available in 1971, but the point to stress is that films, like workshops and lectures, are only a supplemental aid in attacking the drug problem. In themselves they can neither educate teachers and parents nor keep significant numbers of young people from experimenting with drugs.

If we assume then, that motion pictures, pamphlets, brochures, workshops, and lectures help an educational program but are not in themselves predictably effective, what are the mainstays of such a program? It appears to me that there are two vital interrelated components: First, if a person undertakes self-education or enrolls in a course, he must become knowledgeable about existing literature on drugs. To many, this substantial intellectual effort may appear to be a formidable, even an impossible task. But it really isn't. Actually, reading only a small number of appropriate books and articles will provide a solid foundation. Most books on drugs published in the United States are vague or biased or cover only a minute part of the problem. Furthermore, some of the best books are now only of historical value. A reader should approach the literature at a practical level, first to get a feel of what the drug scene is all about, and second to acquire enough information that he will know more than the young people he is trying to reach.

A bibliography current as of February, 1971, is included. It should be eminently satisfactory both for the neophyte and for the individual who already has a little knowledge. It is divided into three categories: highly recommended books; books that could be considered supplemental reading for those who have finished the books in the first group and for those inclined to read voraciously in the drug field; and a number of important articles in either popular or medical magazines, plus a few reasonably comprehensive paperback monographs.

Very simply, you cannot deal with the drug problem through ignorance, and the needed knowledge is not acquired by osmosis, by sitting back watching a screen, or by listening to an allegedly knowledgeable man giving a lecture. For a start, all that is required is the ability to read and the willingness to spend time exploring the existing literature.

Second, it seems abundantly clear that courses will have to be established in order to teach the teachers. This will of course require a monumental effort, but a most worthwhile one. For those playing a major educational role, self-education through reading is not nearly enough. That reading must be incorporated into courses which would include lectures, seminars, field visits to various drug programs, critical discussions regarding the available data, careful analyses of the important controversies, and special instruction in the art of communication. The last is of immense importance. No matter how much knowledge is assimilated, if an individual cannot effectively communicate it, what good is it? Schools and colleges should send to these courses individuals who are articulate and persuasive and have shown that they are accepted by students. Also, they must be willing to read extensively and invest a great deal of intellectual effort. (Reading lists should be mandatory.) I would recommend that each be required, as part of his training, to formulate a talk for students and then give it before either his colleagues or an appropriate student body. The talk should be followed by an intensive question-and-answer period that the speaker alone would be expected to handle. Then his speech and his handling of the question-and-answer period should be critically analyzed by both his colleagues and those responsible for teaching the course.

Many educators stress sensitivity and attitudinal-change training as part of any course. Put in simple terms, this means making sure that the participants learn to listen to young people, to empathize with them, and to understand their motivation for drug use. An inflexible, pejorative approach to drug use is decried, and the ability to project oneself into a given situation so as to comprehend it from the young person's vantage point is emphasized. In part, the notion is that you can't deal with drug use in young people until you have been compelled to look inward at your own anxieties, anger, and hang-ups and then have relearned how to communicate with others.

The popularity of sensitivity training as an approach is reflected in two articles that appeared on March 7 and 9, 1970, in the *New York Times*. At Junior High School No. 52 in New York City, the scene of the drug-induced death of a fourteen-year-old boy, the entire teaching staff underwent sensitivity training and encounter sessions described as "a series of wrenching group dynamics sessions." Said one teacher, "We found out some of us had hostilities toward one another. There was a lot of shouting yesterday." One article noted that "the theory behind the program is that teachers must be made aware of inconsistencies in their own personalities and moral preachings before they can win the confidence of students. This is done by sessions of self-examination and criticism by other members of the group. The core of the nine-hour program was an encounter session in which the participants were confronted with the disparity between their pretensions and the reality others find in them. Although the participants were asked not to say things that only wound others, the sessions were usually heated. Hostilities and buried attitudes about such matters as race often came to the surface."

Sensitivity training means different things to different people.

The current vogue is an outgrowth of the so-called T-groups popularized in the 1930s for the study of group dynamics. Today sensitivity training is often synonymous with confrontation sessions, frequently led by individuals with little expertise. As noted in a symposium in the *American Journal of Psychiatry* in December, 1969, group leaders must have an "intellectual grasp of the principles of group dynamics and training and experience in mental health work." They infrequently do.

The encounters can be traumatic to the participants, while confrontation alone, with its emotional and psychological self-stripping, does not provide an individual with the means to handle drug abuse in the schools. It can be psychologically dangerous for the participating teacher who is learning confrontation tactics, and it can be profoundly harmful to young people in emotional crises who are asked to take part in encounters either because of drug use or as a preventive measure. Indeed, it was pointed out in the *American Journal of Psychiatry* symposium that confrontation sessions should not include individuals in emotional turmoil. This would exclude most of those seriously involved in drug abuse, as well as a large segment of the "normal" adolescent community.

In some areas teachers are given a few hours of so-called sensitivity training and then are expected to "rap" with groups of young people about their identity, sex, and drug problems. This is an invitation to disaster. The meetings tend to turn into unproductive, superficial bull sessions, and the teacher, lacking any real knowledge, may be open to ready manipulation by the more sophisticated of the students. But if sensitivity training is obtained from adequately trained individuals and is combined with acquisition of real knowledge about drugs, it should enable the teacher to provide individual counseling and educational programs on drugs and also to act as an ombudsman for the students. I would note that the teachers taking the course I am proposing should really need very little sensitivity training, since they would be selected on the basis of being interested in and relating well to young persons.

It has been said recently that attitudinal-change, sensitivity-training, and confrontation sessions, workshops, and courses will be the next major epidemic to hit the United States. This is an easy technique to use, requiring little formal training; anybody with a few hours' experience can conduct such sessions. But it is a hard technique to use correctly and requires an enormous amount of insight, caution, and expertise. It may work in therapeutic communities treating drug addicts, but even this is not yet known, nor is it known how often the technique is psychologically harmful to the addict. As an educational technique either for teachers or for teacher-student sessions it is completely untested, and the statements in support of it consist of public panegyrics, not carefully documented follow-up studies.

I am well aware that my reservations about attitudinal-change, sensitivity-training, confrontation, and encounter sessions run counter to the prevailing trend in both education and rehabilitation. More and more educators are convinced the purpose of education is to teach people how to feel; I remain convinced that the major purpose of education is to teach young people how to think. Recently one of the major exponents of this approach labeled my approach "archaic and traditional." I know he also meant, by implication, ineffective. Maybe so, but I do know teachers we train in the "archaic and traditional" fashion will know a lot more about the drug scene than they did before and that they will not themselves be hurt by our courses, nor will they be given the tools to perhaps hurt others emotionally. I have seen enough young persons, teachers and students, thrown into emotional turmoil by encounter sessions to urge that we proceed with caution and with some built-in evaluation to make at least some judgment about how many persons are helped, how many are unaffected, and how many are harmed.

There are many ways of designing a formal course for those who have a major role to play in drug education. In some instances, the course could be given at night for an appropriate period of time; in other instances it would seem desirable to offer a two- to six-week course during which those enrolled would spend five or six days a week full-time either at a home base or on field trips. In such intensive courses it would be quite easy to include lectures and seminars by experts representing different experiences and emphasizing disparate approaches to the problem. It would be well, for example, to spend several days each studying the effects of the opiates, stimulants, and hallucinogens—discussing pharmacology, complications, prevalence, epidemiology, and rehabilitation. Indeed, it is crucial to do so. One of the difficulties with present preventive educational efforts is that there is an astounding lag between the fast-changing drug problems and the educational approaches to them. Our Federal, state, and local educational efforts are directed primarily against heroin, yet this is only a small part of the overall drug problem. Far more important is young people's growing inclination to experiment with a host of mind-altering agents. Just as important as the heroin problem is abuse of euphoriants, stimulants, and hallucinogens. For the nonopiate problem there are *no* known effective rehabilitation programs, although there are some in the inchoate phases that report good results. Some individual users may benefit from psychiatric therapy, but most experimental and even most chronic users of stimulants, euphoriants, and hallucinogens do not need and will not respond to formal psychotherapy. This being the case, the most effective potential recourse is education, both preventive and remedial. Courses must therefore be balanced and comprehensive.

A substantial number of the sessions should be devoted to an analysis of the reasons for drug use and the most effective ways of approaching young people, and a great deal of time should be given to small group dialogue and to discussion of important articles in the literature. One of the major purposes of these courses should be to break down long-held stereotypes that allow people to continue to believe that LSD–marihuana users are basically escapist "hippies" and heroin users blacks or Puerto Ricans with little education or ambition.

In many of the courses it will be desirable or necessary because of legislative mandate for the teachers to compose workshop curriculum formats to use themselves in educating other teachers in their school districts. A sample workshop curriculum is provided in the outline below:

I. Terminology, general approach, outline of problem
II. Reasons for and theories behind drug use
III. Society as a whole, school as a whole—alcohol, tobacco—pleasure, escapism—multiple drug use—economics and laws
IV. Pharmacology and effects—drugs, dosage, actions, pleasure effects, untoward effects
V. Pharmacology and effects (continued)—physiology
VI. Marihuana, a general approach to facts and dangers—intoxicants and the future of our society
VII. Approaches to drug users—rehabilitation with drugs, without drugs
VIII. Alternatives to drug use—avoiding boredom, peer group involvement
IX. Role of teachers—counseling, detection, confidentiality, relations with community

At the New Jersey College of Medicine and Dentistry we have just completed a legislatively mandated three-week course for 108 school teachers in New Jersey. Since this was one of the first such courses in the country we were able to gather an extraordinary guest faculty from around the country. Our own faculty who spent full time on the course included Dr. Edward A. Wolfson, director of the Division of Drug Abuse, and Dr. Stanley Einstein, an internationally known authority and the editor of the *International Journal of the Addictions*. Both are excellent teachers.

Several observations seem pertinent:

1. Even with a substantial faculty, the course size should not exceed fifty to sixty teachers.

2. Teacher selection is crucial. Departments of education and school superintendents cannot usually be depended upon to select the best teachers. I would personally favor letting the students nominate several teachers they would like to see become the

school's *in situ* expert and then let the school superintendent select one or more of these teachers.

3. A three-week course is no panacea. Some teachers will learn a great deal; others will not. Some will be able to conduct reasonably good workshops for their fellow teachers; others will not.

4. Teachers will not become authorities on drugs in three weeks, but they can learn enough to function as local experts if they continue to read, keep up to date, and accept the fact that for the first few months they will not feel comfortable in dealing with inquisitive and persistent students. If they persist at it, all the data will eventually fall into place and they will feel comfortable in their roles, confident that they really do know more than the students.

5. It is silly to assume that we can train a core group of teachers in a few weeks and they in turn will train other teachers so that all teachers become drug experts. It just won't work, and it isn't necessary. Perhaps after taking a course and working at the drug problem in a teacher-student situation for two or three years a given teacher will be ready to train other teachers—but not after a course of a few weeks' duration. The most that can be expected is that the teacher will function effectively in relation to students and that he can conduct superficial workshops designed to excite the interest of other teachers and perhaps convince them that they had better re-examine their attitudes and stereotypes in regard to drug abuse. And that is all that is really required.

6. We had all better try to evaluate our educational efforts carefully because no one knows what the best or most effective educational approach is or whether our educational efforts will do any good at all.

7. If we do adopt this intensive short-course technique as national policy, money will have to be spent to get adequate numbers of drug experts involved in giving such courses. At present there are just too few authoritative persons. Drug abuse is now so popular and so many good educators are becoming involved that over the next few years this problem should diminish.

Another approach, still in an early phase, has been adopted by

New York State under the direction of Dr. John Sinacore. An attempt is being made to have colleges and universities establish special study courses on drugs for those who plan to teach in the health science field. The idea is to establish a teaching cadre of those who have majored in the pharmacological, physiological, sociological, and psychological aspects of drugs, including those drugs used for pleasure. These individuals have to complete formal courses lasting at least one year preparatory to entering the teaching profession as specialists in the health science field. Courses will be given during the academic year or over several summers. This type of program is ambitious. It would unquestionably turn out teachers with an extraordinary depth of drug knowledge. The major disadvantages are that such programs have gotten off the ground slowly, funding is inadequate, a great many colleges and universities are remarkably uninterested, and the number of persons willing to commit themselves to this type of study program is small. Nevertheless, this type of program is potentially the most effective answer to the drug abuse problem. Dr. Sinacore hopes to have 2,500 teachers trained over the next five years.

In the interim, and in other states with less ambitious programs, the shorter, more intensive courses (be they evening sessions or two- to six-week courses) appear to be a sensible compromise between workshops on the one hand and a lengthy curriculum designed to produce health science educators on the other. If the technique of the short intensive course is used, it is imperative that those giving the course assume the responsibility for keeping those who have completed it up to date on important new aspects of the drug scene once they have returned to their school or community. At the New Jersey College of Medicine and Dentistry, we plan to send updating information approximately every three months to everyone who has completed the college's course. In this way, those who return to their communities to assume front-line positions in the fight against drug abuse will have a sound base of knowledge regularly augmented by new information.

After completing a course, most participants should be able to return to their communities more knowledgeable about drugs than the young people who are using them. They can exert immense educational influence by being available to answer factually and dispassionately all questions raised by young persons or others. And they can serve in four other ways: First, they can organize local courses to give others the very information they have recently acquired. Second, they can serve in a major capacity as a component of the counseling services available to young people involved with potentially dangerous drugs. This will be feasible only if the individuals who have completed the course display enough factual information to command the respect of young people who heretofore have arrogantly made the flip assertion that none of the teachers in school knew nearly as much as they themselves did. This hurdle passed, the specially trained teachers may find that young people are willing to place trust and confidence in them. To achieve this, they will have to learn to listen sympathetically without making immediate value judgments, to become impartial but interested advisers. Third, the individuals who have acquired considerable knowledge about epidemiologic methods can serve as school or community epidemiologists in regard to drugs, obtaining data on the prevalence of drug use, the various drugs employed, the complications noted, and community attitudes toward use. The specially trained teachers can thus become the public health arm of those who have organized the course and who almost invariably will be eager to gather as much statistical data as possible on the amount of drug use in individual communities.

Fourth, the trained teacher can play a major role in formulating curricula. The nature of the courses will vary, depending on the individual schools, the local resources available, and the rest of the health sciences program. Ordinarily the first year of education should concentrate on drugs in general, leaving specific drugs for the second and subsequent years. Nobody is better equipped to organize this type of preventive education than a teacher who knows about drugs, is informed about the local scene, and relates well enough to young people to recognize the kind of education they need in regard to intoxicating and mind-altering drugs. The curricula must involve the young people in a dialogue and not merely be an instructional monologue.

These courses being designed primarily for teachers, what is the best way of educating parents? I think the clue is input by the parents. Every school should have available educational kits for distribution to every parent of a junior or senior high school student —kits containing factual data, information on handling the problem, and a reading list. Then workshops could be arranged, attendance to be limited to those parents willing to undertake reading assignments. This would compel the kind of intellectual effort that would markedly increase the potential helpfulness of any workshop.

Once teachers are trained and return to their schools, they must not be involved in any activities that can be interpreted as punitive. School administrations often would like to have such counselors report drug users or users who also sell drugs to the administration or the police. I personally feel that drug selling should not be countenanced in the schools, but the counselor cannot be placed in the role of a policeman and still be effective. The trained teacher can act as information source, epidemiologist, adviser, and referral source, but his activities must be kept assiduously separate from the school administration, and the students must know they can discuss their drug use in confidence. Indeed, his main function will really be to help young people make intelligent decisions about drug use.

A word needs to be said about the ex-addict educator. It is currently popular in this country to assume somewhat inanely that he who has used drugs a lot is by definition in a position to educate against their use. This simply is not true. There is nothing about a professional drug abuser that will make him a predictably good professional antidrug educator. Some of those who have become heavily involved with various drugs are superb counselors; they are implicitly trusted by young people and can communicate with them with astounding ease and effectiveness. Others are mediocre as educators, and some are abominable educators whose clumsy efforts to "inform" others are clearly a veneer for an essentially inadequate and narcissistic personality. Additionally, it is popular for the ex-drug user to assume that if he has had one drug problem, for example, heroin, he is capable of effectively educating against any drug abuse. This too is untrue. An individual who has used heroin extensively and then stopped undoubtedly does know quite a lot about the opiates, and his experience with heroin may serve him well in dealing with potential or confirmed heroin users. But there is not necessarily a carry-over to other drugs. Furthermore, many of those who became deeply involved in the drug scene, saw the light, and then devoted themselves to educating others against the use of drugs have a disturbing tendency to put down all other groups involved in antidrug education, particularly those that are dominated by professionals. This antiprofessionalism is destructive. In New York City it has damaged the whole superstructure designed to combat narcotic addiction. The ex-drug user must be evaluated carefully, used with discrimination, and not be permitted to create a climate of distrust, for when this occurs, rehabilitation and education attempts become racked by internecine warfare, and inevitably the major sufferers are the drug users themselves.

This should not be interpreted, though, as an attack on ex-users or their capacities in the fight against drug abuse. Certain ex-users are marvelous educators. In this difficult area there is no single panacea. The educational battle will be won only if professionals, paraprofessionals, laymen, and ex-drug users join in a multifaceted attack.

One of the questions asked by those who are trying to reach young people is: "How effective can I be without knowing and using the slang and lingo of the drug subculture?" I think one's credibility is not increased by using drug slang. The notion that "you have to come down to the kids' level" has subverted much of our educational system. What is important is that your listeners respect you and feel you are genuine, that they believe you are being factual, that they are convinced you are truly interested in them, and that you communicate effectively with them. If they think you are talking down to them or pretending to be one of them by using drug slang, what you can achieve will be impaired. They will reject older people who almost desperately try to give the impression of being a part of the youth movement. To young people such individuals are merely using the young to feed their own egos.

Young people are most sensitive to exaggeration or distortion. Therefore those who accept the responsibility of educating the young must be extremely careful to be impeccably honest. Anything less will almost inevitably lose an audience.

It is important to stress that students reject those they feel are sententious or punitively oriented. In a study conducted by the Michigan Department of Public Health, young people ranked physicians highest as potential educators on drugs. Similar findings were reported by Blum and his associates. In both studies, young people put police at the bottom of the list. Physicians are accepted because they are regarded as best informed and non-punitively oriented. The implications are clear. If teachers and school counselors wish to become accepted in similar fashion, they can do so only by acquiring an image of expertise in the eyes of students. Nothing else will do, and trying to be pals with students or supporting their rebellions is no substitute for acquisition of knowledge.

At what academic level should drug education begin? In the United States we have always been a step behind the times. When the problem spread to our high schools, we were concentrating on the colleges; now that we are concentrating on the high schools, the problem is rampant in junior high and some elementary schools. Even knowing these facts, some groups, especially those of ultraconservative bent, are now demanding that education about illicit drugs be prohibited because it might arouse the curiosity of young people and actually promote drug abuse. It is decidedly too late for this kind of head-in-the-sand reasoning. It has helped to get us into the mess we are now in. Equally silly is the view, "We have no problem here, so let's forget the whole thing." I find that many schools and communities that assure outsiders they have no drug problem actually have plenty of illicit drug use. At present, virtually all young persons will at some time or another be exposed to the blandishments of the drug subculture.

Use in schools is so prevalent that the following approach makes sense:

If a community has a known drug problem, education should be started in the fourth to sixth grades and no later. If drug abuse is epidemic in the community, it is mandatory to offer preventive education to students before the misinformation of their peer group dominates their thinking and makes educative efforts more difficult. The initial educational efforts in the elementary school should be directed to drugs in general, getting to specific agents of abuse at a later date.

If a community has no known drug problem, education should be started in junior high school. Junior highs might well periodically assess their actual status by interviews and questionnaires, since glib statements that little or no drug abuse exists often hide a very substantial problem.

An additional question is where to put drug education. Should it be taught as a separate course by a "narcotics" or "drug coordinator"? To me the answer is no. Drugs are a part of our society, and education about proper and improper use should be an intrinsic part of the health sciences, not a separate entity. Teaching it separately could result in overemphasizing and glorifying the subject. I would think if far better to select a teacher, school counselor, school social worker, or somebody from the health service to become the *in situ* expert, the ombudsman in relation to drugs, on the basis of his interest and ability to relate to young people, and then to incorporate the drug role into his other responsibilities, perhaps lightening these to allow enough time for the duties relating to drug abuse.

As educational efforts intensify, it will be mandatory to try to evaluate the impact of particular programs. Merely to "educate" is not enough, yet this is exactly what will be done as preventive education is adopted by politicians and the public as a panacea. Clearly, many educational attempts will be ineffectual, and some may make the situation worse. Only by continuous monitoring of seminars, workshops, motion pictures, lectures, and courses on a statistically validated basis will we be able to judge which approaches are most rewarding. Such evaluation is not easy, but carefully drawn questionnaires supplemented by interviews should make possible valid judgments concerning which programs should be expanded and which should be replaced.

Our educational institutions themselves deserve a considerable share of the blame for our burgeoning drug problem. They have given students progressively more freedom without demanding commensurate responsibility. As Dewey said: "There can be no stable and balanced development of the mind without the assumption of responsibility." Institutions have revised curricula to provide students with flexibility, but they have not taken measures either to achieve commitment to constructive activities for their students or to prevent boredom. No place is the failure to prevent boredom more evident than in the freshman year, and this often establishes the pattern for the rest of the college years. As high school curricula get more advanced and demanding, more students are entering college knowledgeable and looking for real intellectual excitement. Instead, they often find the courses are repetitive and not nearly so interesting as those in high school. Disenchanted with the academic environment and bored, such students are ideal candidates for drug experimenting. Most institutions now intentionally attempt to reduce competition, apparently forgetting that well-guided competition can mature a person and orient him toward a goal-directed adult life. Lack of competition in an affluent society is an invitation to mediocrity and purposeless activity, which in turn will cause some individuals who lack interest and motivation to turn toward drug experimentation.

As with the family, I believe it makes sense to provide an array of extracurricular activities for young people and then allow each youngster to choose those in which he wishes to get involved, but the school can reasonably insist that the one option not open to him is to choose nothing. Many will object to forced involvement, but to me it makes a great deal of sense if we are to avoid boredom and the kind of withdrawal that invites drug abuse.

The educational institutions have also failed to separate facile student generalizations about relevance and the conditions of society from legitimate and thoughtful comments on education. Worse still, many institutions no longer appear to be seriously trying to instill abiding intellectual curiosity or a commitment to excellence. Perhaps they have forgotten the definition of education favored by Albert Einstein: "Education is that which remains after one has forgotten everything he learned in school."

Each educational institution will also have to take a very hard look at its curriculum to decide whether the courses are providing the interest and excitement necessary to avoid apathy and boredom. Often the formal courses, as well as the extracurricular programs, are so dull and anachronistic that it is hardly surprising the students reject them, and that rejection in itself can create a climate in which drug abuse flourishes.

One final comment about school courses relating to drug abuse: they must be taught by truly knowledgeable persons and they must be constantly absorbing. Dialogues on motivation, analysis of interesting studies, and discussions on the use of drugs by sophisticated and primitive societies throughout history can be enjoyable as well as instructive. One way to assure the course is not turning the students off is to get continual student feedback.

6.

Proposals for Communities and Business Organizations

There are fifteen basic points for every community to consider in planning an attack on drug abuse:

First, the community must not presume that interest means expertise. Many of the New York State narcotic guidance councils are a perfect example. These were created by the Legislature to coordinate local activities. Each local council formulates its own program and each is supported by state funds. Local clergymen, lawyers, and doctors, among others, are being invested by legislative fiat with an expertise they do not usually have. Following brief and inadequate training, they are being given broad responsibility; they help plan school curricula and community programs, deliver talks on drugs, evaluate rehabilitation efforts, and even act as counselors. If a local group is formed to fight drug abuse, it must recognize that its main function should be catalytic. It should bring in experts and arouse community-wide interest, but it should not pose as an expert body unless it has members who are acknowledged authorities. If the drug abuse group can effectively mobilize the entire community, this in itself is an enormous accomplishment.

Second, the community group should take great care in bringing in outside resources. There is a tendency to bring in experts to give talks or workshops and then feel satisfied that an effective campaign has been waged. The community group should carefully evaluate potential speakers and try to eliminate those who deliver emotional diatribes or who use the podium for personal aggrandizement. Similarly, it is important to make sure the speaker or workshop meets the needs of the audience; suburban communities are not very likely to benefit from talks geared to heroin addiction if their problems relate almost exclusively to stimulant or hallucinogen abuse.

Third, an attempt should be made to conduct a survey through anonymous questionnaires and perhaps interviews to determine the prevalence of drug abuse among the young. Help in preparing such surveys can almost always be obtained from nearby educational institutions.

Fourth, young people should be included in any local committee. This does not mean the young people have to be drug users, ex-users or pro-marihuana. Rather, they should be responsible individuals who are representative of the community's younger generation. If persons of high school or college age are not included, the entire program can go astray. I was recently in a community which had made the decision that the best approach to young persons was an uninhibited dialogue led by those oriented toward sensitivity training and confrontation. The experts to be invited had indicated they would not talk specifically about drugs but rather about attitudes, emotions, and society at large. Only after it had been decided to invite the confrontation-oriented group did someone think of asking the young people. When this was finally done, the committee found they didn't want confrontation; they wanted to have authoritative speakers talk factually and unemotionally about the drug scene, this to be followed by an extensive dialogue on the drugs, their potential toxicity, etc. Many communities impose programs on young people without considering the desires of the target audience, and that makes no sense.

Fifth, the local committee should make sure that adequate educational materials are available in the local library and bookstores, and that the specific items are well publicized. A small amount of money should also be set aside for renting or buying contemporary films relating to the drug scene.

Sixth, the community should take the lead in assuring that one or two teachers from each school are given time and funds to take intensive courses on drugs so that they can become the *in situ* experts in their schools. They should insist that the teachers be chosen, not by seniority or specific position in the school, but rather by their ability to relate to young people.

Seventh, the community would do well to try to modify the stereotyped and rigid views held by most local police. Most police still insist that marihuana leads directly to heroin and that once an individual is a heroin user, he always will be. They are unaware that many heroin users never become addicts and that many heroin addicts grow out of their habit after age thirty or thirty-five. Their frequently anachronistic views and intellectual rigidity account in some measure for the fact that the police are not trusted by most young persons and are at the bottom of the list of those whom young persons would like to have as educators about drugs. Since the police must deal so extensively with drug users, they obviously need up-to-date knowledge and a far broader view of drug abuse than their parochial police training gives them. This objective could best be achieved by having at least one member of each local department enroll in an intensive course similar to those designed primarily for educators. Once such a course is completed, the graduates can be assigned the task of fostering better police-youth relationships in the community, for if these can be improved in regard to drugs, it is likely the improvement will spread to other areas in which the police and young people are usually at odds.

Eighth, the community must make it very clear that selling of drugs will not be tolerated. Money should be provided for undercover activities directed specifically against the seller. There is simply no effective way of dealing with the problem if sellers are allowed to pursue their illicit activities. Often the local police do not have the funds needed for even limited undercover activities. A special phone number should be available for reporting pushers directly to the police.

Ninth, the local anti-drug-abuse committee should provide educational kits for every young person and every parent. We are in the process of developing such a kit at the New Jersey College of Medicine and Dentistry. We believe it should contain a group of brochures, each six to eight pages long, and each with a lively cover. Our own brochures will include the following titles:

Motivation behind drug use
Categories of users and manifestations of drug use
Heroin, stimulants and sedatives
Marihuana, hashish and THC
LSD, mescaline and other hallucinogens
Questions and answers—Marihuana and hallucinogen groups
Questions and answers—Heroin, stimulants and sedative groups
Medical and psychiatric complications
The laws
A reasonable approach for parents
Suggested reading list and available resources in the area

Obviously, the brochures on area resources and laws will have to be individualized for each locale; the others can be used for more general distribution.

Tenth, every community must have certain resources available to both parents and youngsters. Two absolutely necessary resources are a hot line and emergency services for drug overdose or bad trips. The hot line should, if possible, be open twenty-four hours a day to provide all sorts of information to both parents and young people, including data on the drugs themselves, evidence on medical and psychological complications, availability of diagnostic and treatment facilities, and information on motivation. It is likely that once a hot line is established, it will be used extensively by virtually all the various age groups in the community. Emergency services are equally important. Young people must know of a local facility to which they can go if they are in trouble from drugs or if their friends need help. In most communities emergency services will be centered in a hospital unit. Because of the expertise required, both the hot line and the emergency services should ordinarily be supervised by the local medical society, provided, of course, the medical personnel there acquire the needed knowledge. In some areas the responsibility may better be given to a medical school which has shown interest in drug abuse.

In recent months hot lines and "crash" services for bad trips have been initiated by a variety of groups, mostly ex-drug users. These should not be accepted uncritically. Often the people running them have little real expertise. Such groups should always work in collaboration with either the medical society or a medical school to ensure that the information and treatment are beneficial, not harmful or inept.

Eleventh, each community should try to get the local medical society to provide trained physicians and/or psychiatrists to whom drug abusers can be referred. All too often there are just not enough doctors in a given area knowledgeable about and interested in the drug scene and in treating the medical or psychiatric complications of abuse.

Twelfth, each community should arrange to have available to it a diagnostic laboratory able to determine the precise chemical analysis of street specimens of drugs. There is nothing more discouraging than for young people to learn that what was bought at $20.00 an ounce is oregano, their LSD is mixed with strychnine, their THC inactive, their mescaline ersatz. This in itself may convince users or potential users of the duplicity of suppliers and the undesirability of becoming involved in the drug scene. These laboratories probably should be established by each state on a regional basis. These studies should be anonymous, and their results should not only be available to those supplying the samples but also should be utilized on the hot lines. Such analysis centers are available in several areas. Preliminary results show the ingenuity of drug users and the need for at least a two-week interval between delivery of the sample and supplying the results of chemical analysis. In Michigan, results were returned within a few days until it became apparent the users were utilizing the results to decide the purity of a given batch they intended to buy. This kind of abuse of the laboratory is inevitable but if there is a two- to three-week delay in reporting results it is far less likely the information will be used in consummating a drug purchase.

Thirteenth, each community should look carefully at its own school curricula and try to ensure they are interesting to students. Boredom created by poor school curricula can be a major reason for drug use.

Fourteenth, either through workshops or courses, school administrators should be given the facts about the drug scene. The administrative staffs of schools and school districts are often inflexible and ignorant about drugs and actively subvert any effort to create a milieu in which the school can help its young people approach drugs in an intelligent and discerning fashion.

Finally—and by far most important—every community must offer viable alternatives to drug use. I recently visited a midwestern state which prided itself on athletic prowess. From the fourth to the eighth grade, extraordinary opportunities were offered for varied athletic activities, with local, city, and statewide competitions at every age level. As might be expected, the majority of the boys were active in athletics and so most of their time after classes was filled. However, from the ninth grade upward the public school facilities were so overcrowded that only those able to compete at a varsity level could continue the active participation they had enjoyed through the eighth grade. For the others there was literally nothing to keep them occupied after school hours. And so they were active, energetic, and bored. Predictably, they began to congregate at local joints and experiment with drugs.

A northeastern community recently voted down a local referendum requesting tax dollars for building additional recreational facilities for its youngsters. And this same community simultaneously is importing experts in drug abuse to help with its fast-growing problem.

If we are to win the battle against drugs, young persons must be protected against the ravages of boredom. Every community should attempt to offer its youth an array of constructive and exciting activities. This, of course, won't solve the problem by itself. It won't reach the youngster whose problem is inner boredom, an inability to take advantage of whatever activities are offered. It won't prevent pushers from inveigling neophytes into using drugs. It won't stop drug use out of curiosity. But alleviation of boredom is a crucial first step; indeed, any community that will not provide the opportunity for young people to get involved in interesting and productive activities deserves a drug problem.

And any program designed as an alternative to drug abuse for the young must have young persons themselves helping to design and direct it; otherwise it will be rejected as purely an Establishment effort.

There are many problems inherent in setting up a comprehensive community program. One is that such programs may be quite expensive. Frequently, communities insist on confining any program to their geographic boundaries. In order to economize, it is often wiser to regionalize at least some of the program so that two or more communities share hot lines, emergency services, and referral sources.

One of the major difficulties facing most communities is where to refer those who need long-term treatment. In most areas there are few facilities; the available ones are ordinarily reserved for heroin abuse, and there are no experts in handling multidrug use by those under eighteen years of age. Individual psychiatric treatment may help some, but there just are not enough good psychiatrists to go around, the treatment is expensive, and it is notoriously ineffective in many cases of drug abuse. Into this vacuum have stepped self-help groups run by ex-drug users. Some of these are good, others are not, and none is currently adequately evaluated. Communities tend to accept these groups uncritically, in part because they are desperate for help. All therapeutic groups should be approached cautiously, and attempts should be made to find out just how effective and knowledgeable any particular group is.

What is really needed is an updated, computerized national registry of both rehabilitation and preventative educational groups so that any community requesting information can get an immediate print-out summarizing what groups are regionally available and what is known about each program—its reliability, techniques, numbers of persons treated, etc. Similarly, a central national source list for books, articles, and motion pictures with brief summaries and critiques of the contents should be available to every local community. The cost to the Federal government would be minuscule when compared to the immense price every community must pay for inadequate educational and rehabilitation programs. The same centralized source could provide updated information on new drug fads, medical complications, etc.

Another type of community now desperately looking for guidelines is the business community. The precise dimensions of the problem are not yet clear, but the amount of drug abuse in industry has grown markedly. The most popular drug is marihuana, but heroin, hallucinogens, and stimulants are also abused. There is no facile answer to the problem, but the following nine points would seem to constitute a reasonable approach:

1. Establish rules and regulations for the firm and follow them. A business has a perfect right to insist that use of mind-altering drugs is undesirable for business purposes and will be considered a valid reason for peremptory dismissal. Clearly this would apply only while the individual is actually on the job. What a person does off the job should, as with sexual behavior, be his own business unless he creates a public spectacle, commits a crime, etc.

2. If drug use or possession is detected, preliminary decisions should be made by the company health officer. If the person is drug-dependent or has psychological problems, the company should aim for rehabilitation and return to employment rather than dismissal. If he is using merely for kicks, the approach should be entirely different; namely, if he can't obey the company rules, he should seek employment elsewhere. The fundamental judgment as to reasons for use and underlying personality problems should be made by the medical service.

3. Sale of drugs within the company should not be tolerated. This is primarily a police matter, and the employees should know it will be treated as such.

4. There should be no rigid approach to the user. Some companies are now implementing a policy under which all detected drug abusers will be referred for rehabilitation or to a mental health unit. This is silly. Most users are doing it for fun and need neither rehabilitation nor psychiatric treatment. Most need to have it made clear to them that drug use on the job is not proper behavior. After all, the company can point out that mind-altering drugs reduce efficiency, diminish thinking power, can cause severe judgment defects, and will make certain people accident-prone.

5. Educational programs within the company should ordinarily be carried out only on a superficial basis. It is well to have the medical officer fully knowledgeable about drug abuse, and the employees might benefit from pamphlets, a closed-circuit TV lecture, and one or two motion pictures; but a massive program would not appear to be warranted.

6. The company must be very cautious about use of urine for drug detection studies. This is probably an invasion of privacy, especially for those whose drug taking was done off the premises, since the drugs will still show in the urine 24 to 72 hours later. And of course marihuana and LSD will not be detected in such tests.

7. The company should be willing to hire ex-drug users or heroin users who are in methadone maintenance therapy. Ordinarily they are not accident-prone and can function perfectly normally. Besides, for companies to discriminate against the ex-drug user or the drug user undergoing rehabilitation makes a mockery of our entire rehabilitation approach. Yet today many jobs both in the public and private sectors are arbitrarily refused to those who have a police record indicating illicit drug use.

8. If an ex-heroin user is on methadone maintenance, or even if he is not, and he tries heroin, the company should not automatically dismiss him. The urge to try heroin again may be overwhelming for former addicts, and may well be biochemically de-

termined. What the company should look for is adequate function. It has every right to ask an ex-heroin user to submit his urine intermittently for analysis to detect opiates. If these are found regularly the employee should, after appropriate warning, be dismissed. But if heroin is detected only occasionally in such an individual, this should be regarded with a great deal of understanding.

9. The company might well conduct an anonymous questionnaire survey to determine how much of a problem it really does have. If this is to be done, the employees must be absolutely assured that it will truly be anonymous.

7.

Rules and Regulations

In my book *The Drug Scene,* I pointed out that schools, colleges, and universities could best approach drug abuse by issuing fair and thoughtful regulations. Many school and college administrations become concerned, compose what appear to be fair regulations, then ignore them. To make a rule and then make it abundantly clear that one has no intention of demanding that it be followed is to encourage students to flout not only that regulation but virtually every other regulation relating to behavior. At other institutions the student-dominated disciplinary committees have either inveigled or intimidated the administration into accepting the intriguing notion that whatever happens behind closed doors in a dormitory is the business of students and not the administration. Initially "whatever happens" referred to sexual behavior, but as soon as the students won their point there, they expanded the permissiveness to include use of marihuana and other illicit drugs. Still other institutions, perhaps the majority, have had no major overt drug problems and approach the possibility by deftly burying their heads in the sand. These institutions take what appears to be a hard line, telling students that they will not tolerate the use of illicit drugs. Having said that, the administration cuts off all effective communication with students and so hasn't a clue as to whether a drug problem exists. It goes about its business, ignoring fragmentary evidence that would suggest that a significant number of students are experimenting with potentially dangerous drugs and that a small number are actually having sizable psychological or academic problems because of drugs.

None of these three approaches makes any sense. What does make sense is the following two-pronged attack: First, the administration should make it absolutely clear that if students use or possess drugs and are caught, the institution will regard this seriously, and although each case will be evaluated individually and flexibly, the student will face possible suspension or outright dismissal. If this mandate is to be effective, it must be quite clear that the administration is trying assiduously to keep abreast of the problem and that it will indeed look for and react rigorously to drug abuse on campus. It should also be made very clear that the institution will not offer sanctuary for the seller—that the user will not face police action, but the seller will ordinarily be dismissed and evidence regarding his pushing of drugs will, at the discretion of the university, be made available to local law enforcement agencies. Furthermore, the administration must inform its students that if it becomes clear that illicit drugs are being sold on campus and law enforcement agencies request placement of undercover agents there, the requests will be granted, as long as undercover activities are directed toward sale rather than possession. In other words, the academic institution must walk a tightrope so that on the one hand it can prevent unwarranted paranoia within its walls, and on the other, it does not permit drug proselytizers to ply their trade with impunity.

Second, if the college or school is going to vigorously oppose drug use, it must provide for referral of drug users to counseling or psychiatric services. Often such services are not available. I have been to many colleges that have relatively stringent regulations about drug use but have inadequate counseling services. The students say there is a substantial drug problem on campus, but they are unwilling to talk to the administration about it because they are afraid the administration's approach will be entirely punitive. What they are looking for is a referral service to which they themselves can go if they are drug users or to which they can refer their colleagues.

A perfect example of this is a college I recently visited on the east coast. The students at the time were engaged in a peaceful and orderly sit-in; among the demands they presented to the administration was one requesting a drug referral service. At this college, one that allegedly had a relatively small drug problem, the administration had stressed that drug use was cause for dismissal. The students felt the administration knew nothing about drugs, was uninterested in the problem, and was punitively oriented; this effectively cut off all communication on the subject. The administration feared a problem but had little inclination to find out the facts or do anything about it unless something catastrophic happened. The students knew there was substantial drug use, including heavy use of marihuana and of the more potent drugs, including LSD and mescaline. One student leader told me he had friends who were smoking quite a lot of marihuana and were not functioning. They were attending classes, but their grades had fallen, their memory for recent events was impaired and, as he put it, "They are just not thinking clearly or accurately." The local health service consisted of one physician, a general practitioner, who felt that anyone using marihuana was commiting a horrendous offense and should be treated harshly. This surely is not an appropriate attitude for a health or counseling service. Indeed, such a physician is just the wrong person to handle drug users experiencing a bad trip. Dr. David Smith of the Haight-Ashbury Medical Clinic tells of such physicians treating patients on bad trips with a combination of appropriate drugs and inappropriate moralizing that only made the adverse reaction worse.

The students desperately wanted at least one drug expert and a counseling service available on an emergency basis at all times. More important, they were adamant that there must be nothing punitive about the service. They wanted it off campus, feeling that it should have no contact with the administration. Lacking expert help, they thought that perhaps the next best thing was to have students who themselves were drug users act as the counseling and referral service. I pointed out to them that their objectives were laudable but I had some reservations about their proposal. Surely those least capable of effective counseling about drugs were the members of the student body who were themselves drug users. Drug users might well be helpful for talking someone down from a bad trip, but counseling is a different story. And even those among their peers who had been users but no longer were should not be entrusted with the important function of counseling unless they had demonstrated some expertise and training. Merely having used the drugs themselves gave them no qualifications to take on this role. Drug users and ex-users usually lack even the rudiments of training that would enable them to carefully distinguish between behavior patterns resulting from drug use itself and behavior patterns representing severe underlying personality disturbance made worse by drug use. Furthermore, it made no sense to have the counseling services off campus. After all, drugs were being used on campus, and if someone had acute problems relating to this use, he ought to be able to go to a health or counseling service in his immediate environment, not several miles away. I also pointed out to them that it was impossible for the administration not to have some liaison with the counseling service; ordinarily the information divulged to the service should remain confidential, but it was crucial that it be available to the administration under certain circumstances. If, for example, a student suddenly started to do badly in his studies, the administration should be able to contact the counseling service to determine if his failure was related to drugs. If so, the administration would be able to take this into account in dealing with the situation. Of course the administration would have to make it crystal clear to the student body that no information obtained through a health or counseling service would be used for punitive purposes. It is obviously impossible to establish a counseling service to which the student goes and confides his drug use, and then have the service inform the administration, which thereafter takes disciplinary action against the student.

Each school really needs an ombudsman on drugs, a drug expert of the type I have previously discussed. In addition, schools should have either a psychiatrist or a specially trained internist (or general practitioner) able to make judgments about the severity of personality aberrations, if any exist, and to act as a treatment and referral source. Obviously the ombudsman and physician could be the same person, but an educator, psychologist, or social worker acting as ombudsman cannot make medical-psychiatric judgments and should have a medically trained colleague serving in that role. Either the ombudsman or the physician could be the counselor.

The counseling must be done by someone who is knowledgeable about drugs, trusted by the students, and sympathetic to the users. It doesn't really matter whether he is a physician, social worker, psychologist, or carefully trained ex-drug user. What is important is that he be willing to listen without making value judgments. He must be so sophisticated about drugs that students accept his expertise without question. If the students don't have faith in the counselor, the service will collapse. Once a counselor is established in the minds of the students as knowledgeable, trustworthy, and sympathetic, drug users will readily discuss their problems with him. Additionally, friends of users who have recognized that drugs are having a bad effect on them will literally demand that they make use of the available service.

Perhaps most important, an effective counseling service gives an administration a great deal of flexibility in dealing with a drug problem. The college of which I write was in trouble because it had strong drug regulations and no effective health or counseling service. All the administration could do was to take disciplinary action. This simply is not satisfactory. An institution must be able to apply alternative solutions depending on the individual situation. If, for example, a student uses LSD because he has personality problems or because after ephemeral experimentation he became drug-dependent, the last thing an educational institution should do is peremptorily dismiss him from school if he is caught using the drugs. The appropriate approach to such a student is obviously to insist that he go to a counseling service and if necessary receive psychiatric help. In most states this is perfectly within the bounds of the law, since it is possession of a drug that is a crime and not its use. To use implies possession of course, but the legal technicality allows institutions to treat drug abusers without raising the specter of legal action. Even in states in which use is a crime, the offense is considered minor, and authorities are perfectly willing to let schools handle medical or psychiatric problems. If, on the other hand, a school has clear evidence of drug abuse by a student who does not need referral to a counseling or treatment service, a student who obviously uses drugs just because he feels like flouting the established regulations, then the administration can, as its regulations indicate, take any disciplinary action up to and including dismissal. Too many colleges make the assumption that matriculation is synonymous with maturity and emotional stability. This clearly is not so. Many students are immature, incapable of making wise decisions about drug use, and many are emotionally unstable and cannot cope with mind-altering drugs. Nor can they resist progressing from experimenting with marihuana to heavy involvement in the drug scene. The academic institution cannot remain insouciant; it must protect immature and unstable students from the potential deleterious effects of drugs.

Although sale of drugs ordinarily should be regarded harshly, even this offense must be treated flexibly. If a student user sells small amounts, the administration might for various reasons wish to treat him as a user rather than a seller.

Currently, many educational institutions are relying more on educational brochures than on the type of program I have outlined. It seems worthwhile, therefore, to stress that no pamphlet, no lecture, no brochure can substitute for fair rules and regulations that are carefully drawn, widely publicized, and vigorously followed.

Although it seems to me that the above is a reasonable approach, it is unfortunately not that easy to implement, for there simply are not enough good counselors or appropriately trained physicians available. And often the university pay scale is so low that it is difficult to attract them. But ordinarily, if an institution tries hard enough it will be able to find someone who will do a reasonably good job as a counselor in the drug field. If it cannot find such an individual, there is usually at least one faculty member with a background such that he can readily absorb the additional training and education necessary for running a counseling service.

One final point. It is important to note that it is worthless to have stern regulations in regard to drugs if a campus is in such turmoil that utter chaos exists. Drug problems cannot be dealt with effectively if students are carrying guns, occupying buildings, beating up the faculty, or marching around hurling invective and obscenities at their teachers and administrators. As Balthasar Gracian noted: "A bad manner spoils everything, even reason and justice." To put it very simply, if a faculty and administration do not control their educational institution, if they are not willing to insist on a milieu in which education can occur, then they cannot regulate any student behavior, including the use of drugs. Furthermore, some of the worst drug offenders are the teachers and professors who openly use drugs, at times with their students. They infect their students with disdain for law and disrespect for their own institution that undoubtedly has rules against illicit drug use. They inculcate in students a pattern of selfish asocial behavior that will remain long after book facts are forgotten. Surely an educational institution cannot encourage lawlessness of this sort. It has a responsibility to instill constructive behavior patterns in its students. There is only one way to treat such irresponsible teachers and professors: unless they have treatable personality problems, they should be summarily dismissed, for they debase and subvert the entire educational process.

8.

The Laws—Proposals for Legislators

Drug laws are so atrocious that there is increasing evidence that those governing marihuana are in actuality promoting its use. Let me cite several examples indicating some of the ridiculous incongruities in our drug laws.

Until late 1968, it was a misdemeanor at the Federal level to sell LSD, and there was no penalty at all attached to mere possession. LSD, of course, is a potent and enormously dangerous hallucinogen. At the same time, under Federal law the possession of marihuana, a euphoriant that barely is powerful enough to get into the hallucinogen category, brought a minimum two-year sentence. I, among many others, had testified at congressional hearings that we believed LSD such a dangerous drug that strict laws were justified. The law finally passed by Congress and signed by the President stipulated that possession of LSD could result in a sentence of up to one year in jail. Upon repeated convictions, this sentence could increase to a maximum of three years; sale was a felony with up to a five-year sentence. What many of us did not realize at the time we testified was that tetrahydrocannabinol would be placed under these laws, resulting in the following bizarre situation: If an individual possessed marihuana and was convicted in Federal court, even if he only had one or two cigarettes, his minimum sentence was two years, with provision for suspension or probation. If, on the other hand, he was convicted of possession of tetrahydrocannabinol, the pure active principle in marihuana and far more potent, the maximum sentence for a first offense was one year in jail. In other words, we were punishing the possessor of the relatively impotent form of tetrahydrocannabinol at least twice as severely as we were punishing the possessor of the pure active material. Furthermore, the penalties for marihuana possession continued to be far more severe than they were for LSD, a much more powerful and dangerous drug. Precisely the same incredible situation existed regarding sale of these drugs. If you sold LSD or tetrahydrocannabinol, you went to jail for at most five years, and it was likely your sentence would be substantially less. If you sold one marihuana cigarette and were convicted for that offense, you went to jail for at least five years.

The inequities in the laws applied equally on the state level. In New Jersey, for example, until 1971 sale of LSD or Methedrine resulted in a modest fine or conceivably up to six months in jail, whereas possession of one marihuana cigarette was a high misdemeanor with a two- to fifteen-year penalty. Consider another example still current. Let us suppose you and I are sitting together in a private home in Massachusetts. You know that I am smoking marihuana, but you yourself have no inclination to smoke. You are merely sitting there thinking how ridiculous it is of me to be risking the penalties by breaking the law. Suddenly the local police break in and arrest me for possession of marihuana. If you're smart, you'll grab my marihuana cigarette and tell the police that you too possess the drug, for in Massachusetts the penalty for possession is a maximum of 3½ years in jail, whereas the penalty for being in a house where marihuana is being used and knowing about its use is a maximum of five years in jail! Five years for knowing the drug is being used even if you don't possess it, don't use it, and have no desire to ever use it; simultaneously, a penalty of only 3½ years for actual possession! To suggest that such a legal structure is unjust is surely a masterpiece of understatement.

In New York State, considered to have some of the best and most sensible drug laws, possession of a small amount of marihuana may result in a sentence of up to one year in jail. Possession of twenty-five marihuana cigarettes may be punished by a sentence of one to seven years in jail, and possession of 100 cigarettes can result in incarceration for one to fifteen years. In this same state, for assault with a deadly weapon you can go to jail for at most fifteen years, and for rape you go to jail for at most twenty-five years. In other words, the mere possession of a substantial amount of marihuana, even if sale is not documented, is legally considered in approximately the same category as aggravated assault or rape. In many other states the same situation exists even if the offender possesses only one or two marihuana cigarettes.

Surely, if we cannot make the distinction between possession of a drug with limited dangers and violent attacks on innocent victims, something is wrong with our legal system and with our society. Of course some would say that it is necessary to consider the harm drugs may do to young people, or the possibility that those using marihuana may go on to something more dangerous. But vicious penalties can hardly be justified on the grounds that someone may possibly use a more dangerous agent sometime in the future. Besides, many sensible individuals intransigently opposed to the legalization of marihuana would point out that the majority of those who try it experiment only ephemerally, and this does not lead to the habitual use of more dangerous drugs or to severe personality deterioration or to a life of degradation and crime. Consequently, laws implying that possession of marihuana is a horrible crime against society are patently ridiculous. Even if an individual possesses a moderate amount of marihuana (say up to fifty cigarettes), we have no right to inflict a severe sentence unless we can document that he is involved in actual sale, and the burden of proof is on society.

The harshness of the marihuana laws is self-defeating. For example, in an affluent community in the state of Michigan a small number of young men and women recently were arrested for sale of several drugs, primarily marihuana. Shortly thereafter I was in the community as a lecturer and was asked what I thought should be done with these young people. I said my own philosophy was that one should be sympathetic and lenient toward users, and that one could have a sensible penalty structure consistent with continuing opposition to legalization of drugs such as marihuana. I indicated I felt that sale, even of a small amount, was a more serious crime, and that if we were to handle the drug problem effectively, those who sell would have to go to jail. I told the audience that no one is compelled to sell marihuana, and this being true we should have very little sympathy for a seller. Since I did not know the details of the law in that state, in closing I asked the audience, "By the way, what is the penalty for sale of marihuana in this state?" I supposed I expected what the answer would be, but even so I was shocked. If a boy who sold marihuana happened to be under the age of seventeen, the most severe penalty he could receive would be assignment to a training school until the age of nineteen. That would apply even if he were one month short of his seventeenth birthday. However, if he had just reached his seventeenth birthday, he could no longer be tried as a juvenile, and the sentence upon conviction for the sale of any amount of marihuana was a twenty-year mandatory minimum. As soon as this had been spelled out, the audience became quiet, and for a few moments my listeners stared silently at me and I stared back at them. Finally, I shook my head and said: "Look, you may as well just forget this whole thing. What judge in his right mind would be willing to sentence a seventeen-year-old boy to twenty years in jail for selling two marihuana cigarettes? After all, if a judge did do such a thing, I just don't think he could face his own family and his own community. What you people ought to do is go to your state capitol and demand that your legislators make the laws sensible." This Michigan community was in a situation typical of many areas of the United States. The members of the community recognized the severity of their drug problem and were determined to stamp it out. Yet as sensible, well-meaning human beings they were not inclined to have their children go to jail for twenty years for small-time dealing in marihuana. They also recognized full well that if the young people were let off entirely, they would return to the community to tell their peers, "You see, we were busted, but so what? They didn't put us away. We're right back out and nothing happened to us, so don't let them tell you you shouldn't use drugs because they are illegal. The laws don't mean a thing; there's no risk."

The atrocious laws have left this community with no middle ground, and this is happening all over the country. Police are frequently very reluctant to arrest people for possession of marihuana because they feel the penalty structure is unrealistic and conviction is unlikely anyway. The district attorneys don't want to prosecute, the juries don't want to convict, and the judges don't want to sentence. It is not because these people are in favor of legalization of marihuana, and it is not because they want to be soft on the drug trade. It is simply that the laws are so harsh they cannot bring themselves to apply them. But despite this disillusionment with the laws, large numbers of young people are being arrested, and some are receiving incredibly harsh sentences. The *Marijuana Review* of January–March, 1969, estimates that 250,000 to 300,000 persons were arrested for marihuana violations in the United States in 1968—50,000 of them in California. At times bail has been set at an incredible $20,000 to $40,000 for mere possession. The incongruity of this is illustrated by a recent arrest of a major distributor of heroin who was caught with over 10 million dollars' worth of the drug in his possession. Bail was set at $10,000. Alleged murderers have been set free for less than

$20,000 bail. In Texas a few years ago a young woman was given fifteen years for possession of *one* marihuana cigarette, and recently in another southern state possession of a small amount resulted in a twenty-year sentence. In the latter case, to compound the irrationality of this penalty, the pusher was given a lighter sentence. In other cases sellers of tiny amounts of marihuana have been sentenced to up to fifty years in jail. As a matter of fact, some states are trying to make the sale of marihuana to a minor potentially punishable by death. Just imagine if a twenty-one-year-old college student in such a state sold two marihuana cigarettes to a seventeen-year-old freshman; if the law were passed, he could be put death.

In addition, we play games with the laws governing our society. Thus it is that in most states if an individual is arrested for a felony drug offense, the charge is usually reduced to a misdemeanor. Consider New York State. At present if a young man is arrested with 25 to 100 marihuana cigarettes in his possession but is not caught selling them, he can almost be certain that this felony charge will be reduced to a misdemeanor, and he can feel quite confident that he will receive a short suspended sentence. In the state of New Jersey, the charge of possession of marihuana has been frequently reduced from a high misdemeanor carrying a potential two- to fifteen-year sentence to a disorderly-person offense carrying a fine or at most a very short jail sentence.

A retrospective analysis of 3,813 narcotic arrests in New York in 1965 was made by the New York State Joint Legislative Committee on Crime. The results are revealing:

(1) A person charged with felony sale of narcotics received a sentence of five years or more in only one case out of twenty. (Yet five years for sale in New York State was at that time supposedly the minimum sentence.)

(2) A person charged with sale of narcotics was actually indicted for a felony in only one case out of two.

(3) If there was an indictment, sentence was suspended in one case out of four, and in two out of four cases the sentence was less than one year.

This study is supported by data indicating that over 95 per cent of those arrested for drug felonies are actually tried for a lesser felony or a misdemeanor. And the data apply equally to marihuana, LSD, heroin, and Methedrine offenses. The result of all this is that young people do not believe our society will back up its laws. If it is all one big game, and arraignment on a felony charge does not mean prosecution on a felony charge, then why respect the laws? Disrespect is fed by the fact that the majority of those arrested for marihuana offenses have the charges dismissed and never come to trial, often because the initial arrest was patently unjust. If the laws are neither applied as written nor vigorously implemented, it is hardly surprising that young people do not respect them and tell their peers not to worry about them. This is especially true in regard to marihuana laws.

There have been other legal problems. In many jurisdictions no distinction is made between the user of illicit drugs and the seller. In New Jersey, for example, possession of LSD or amphetamines has ordinarily been punishable only by a fine. The seller of LSD (also considered a disorderly person) was subject to the same penalty as the possessor. The same applied to heroin and marihuana; in New Jersey possession of these drugs until 1971 was a high misdemeanor punishable by two to fifteen years in jail, and the penalty structure for sale, of any amount, was identical. Other states have similar laws.

The point in question is whether we can revise these laws to make them realistic, sensible, and fair enough to be generally applied. Clearly there is no readily accepted answer. The majority of states have recently amended their drug laws or are about to do so. Some are moving toward harsher laws, but most are mitigating the penalty structure, especially in regard to marihuana possession. Many argue that very strict laws will only make the drug problem worse; others argue that repressive statutes is the only effective answer. It seems to me that we could reduce drug use if we had harsh laws directed against users and applied these laws relentlessly. The rock festivals of August, 1969, seem to support this notion. At Bethel, New York, it seemed as if all 450,000 participants were stoned on marihuana and none feared the consequences. That same month at a smaller festival in Texas the prevalence of drug use appeared to be appreciably less. This was true in large part because the participants feared the stern Texas laws and long sentences handed out in their courts, as well they might. In Texas, sentences of fifteen years have been meted out for possession of one marihuana cigarette, and the sale of several cigarettes has resulted in 40- to 50-year sentences. And in the summer of 1970 a twenty-seven-year-old man was imprisoned for 1,500 years in that state for selling about $15 worth of heroin to an undercover agent. We could reduce drug use nationwide by having cruel laws throughout the country, but by the same token we could markedly reduce the incidence of automobile drivers jumping red lights if the penalty for driving through a stoplight were 5 to 50 years in jail. Of course we would not invoke such laws for automobile drivers, and we should not for drug users. Cruel laws are the hallmark of tyranny and an anathema to democracy. After all, the object of laws under our form of government is to make the punishment fit the crime. Indeed, democracy can not survive if its laws are allowed to remain irrational and vicious. Besides, as I have already indicated there is generally a reluctance to apply our current laws because of their harshness. Were they made more severe that reluctance would surely increase.

The various arguments concerning how to change our drug laws can be separated into the following five categories:

1. Do not make the laws more lenient. Indeed, for certain categories (e.g., possession of LSD or Methedrine, sale of heroin, sale of marihuana to a minor) make the laws harsher. Opponents of this approach say the laws are now damaging enough to many young people who have offended society only minimally; and

surely, we should not compound the problem. Besides, how can we, in educating against drugs, point out that marihuana is a minor-league drug nobody really needs, and then treat possession of marihuana as if it were tantamount to rape, mayhem, or murder? We simply cannot. If we keep our drug laws as they are or make them harsher, our whole educative effort, the bulwark of the anti-drug battle, will fail.

2. Remove all criminal sanctions from marihuana, making possession punishable by a small fine. In other words, treat marihuana possession as if it were a traffic offense. The argument here is that since marihuana is for most people a mild and enjoyable drug, we must stop making criminals of our young people who have opted for this escape mechanism. The proponents of this view feel that the harm resulting from arrest and possible jail sentence for hundreds of thousands of young people each year far outweighs the dangers of marihuana itself. I believe there is much merit in this view, and adopting it would not preclude revision of our laws in general. But I am not entirely sanguine about such a change at this time. I feel it would increase marihuana use and thus increase the number of individuals hurt by this drug directly and those hurt indirectly through progression to more dangerous agents. In addition, such laws would lead to driving under the drug's influence, and this at a time when we cannot measure the presence of marihuana in an individual's blood or urine. Some say this should not matter because anyone causing an accident should be punished regardless of whether or not he used marihuana. However, without the capability to accurately detect marihuana use, we could not punish driving while intoxicated by the drug. Nor could we assess its influence on the prevalence of automobile accidents. Furthermore, if one removes criminal sanctions from marihuana possession, why not remove them from illicit possession of drugs such as the amphetamines, since two amphetamines are no more harmful than one marihuana cigarette? It seems to me that this proposal also moves us a step closer to adding marihuana to our totally legal intoxicants, and in doing so it ignores

the possibility that marihuana popularity may be only a transient fad. Finally, the proposal does not take into consideration the desirability or undesirability of adding even more intoxicants to an already intoxicated society.

3. Remove all penalties for possession and use of any drug. This is the old "What I put in my body is my business" proposal. It may attract many young people, but it is really a cruel proposal in the guise of individual freedom. It ignores two vital facts: First, under this proposal the user would have to carefully weigh the potential pleasures and dangers of the drug in order to come to a sensible decision about its use. Yet few users are likely to spend time and effort studying the medical and psychiatric literature to obtain accurate information on potential dangers. Today's user generally knows appallingly little about the drugs he inhales, ingests or injects. Second, because adequate self-education would be lacking, the potential user would be at the mercy of irresponsible drug proselytizers determined to turn others on. Many of these people have little knowledge of the drugs they use and no desire to attain it. They simply know that they like the feeling of drug intoxication and they want to persuade others to use the same drugs regardless of the consequences.

Additionally, a considerable proportion of our society simply cannot handle drugs. After all, one in ten persons in this country will spend some time in a mental hospital during his lifetime. Such individuals should not be exposed to mind-altering drugs, yet they and the very young gravitate toward the use of illicit drugs. It is ridiculous to suggest that the emotionally immature, those with unstable personalities, or the very young can use mind-altering drugs safely. They cannot. There are millions of young persons who would be in grave danger should they be exposed to potent drugs or even to the repetitive use of milder agents such as marihuana. This proposal is an invitation to disaster and should be firmly rejected.

4. Legalize marihuana. The argument here is threefold: the arrest of marihuana users unduly hurts many young people, appli-

cation of the marihuana laws is too expensive in terms of the benefits produced, and marihuana is really harmless anyway. Proponents of this proposal have had for the most part virtually no contact with people who are in trouble because of marihuana use. The legalization question is one of balancing the harm of current laws and the dangers of the drug itself. Yes, it is true that millions of Americans smoke marihuana and many thousands have their lives marred by arrests or jail sentences for the trivial offense of possessing small amounts of a relatively mild drug. But what of the other half of the equation? What of the thousands who become dependent on marihuana and damage themselves psychologically? What of the thousands whose minds do not function normally on even moderate amounts of the drug? What of the thousands who start with marihuana and drift into use of multiple mind-altering drugs that are far more dangerous? This is the half the "legalize marihuana" clique deliberately ignores. Let them see substantial numbers of young people strung out on the drug, with vacant stares and aimless existences because of their dependence on it. Let them see the tragedies that arise from recreational use of marihuana that has led to severe involvement with LSD, Methedrine, or heroin. Then perhaps this clique would not be so glib. I am not opposed to the concept of legalizing marihuana. I am opposed to those who in advocating legalization deliberately dismiss the data on potential harm. Legalization of marihuana can be considered only by examining the total picture of intoxicants in our society and where we are heading in regard to all mind-altering drugs. In my opinion it can considered seriously only after carefully balancing the damage resulting from arrest and the damage the drug itself may directly or indirectly do to the user. And I should think the entire question cannot be seriously contemplated until we have a method of detecting the drug in the body. This does not mean, as many insist, that legalization of marihuana would destroy our youth. It would not, nor would legalization be an overwhelming tragedy for our society. But it would increase our public health problems resulting from the use or misuse of intoxicating agents. Some say that those who now start with marihuana and move to other drugs do so because the entire gamut of drugs is being sold by the same pusher, and consequently, if marihuana were legalized, the user would no longer have contact with those selling other drugs and would not move on to LSD, Methedrine, or heroin. This is, of course, an unproven hypothesis. I believe that for many people marihuana has a built-in escalation mechanism, and legalizing it would take away neither the availability of more potent agents nor the desire to move on to them. If we legalized marihuana on the basis of this hypothesis and the hypothesis proved incorrect, we would merely have added an intoxicant, increased the number of users, and increased the number of people in trouble from the drug itself without reducing the problem of escalation to more dangerous drugs.

5. Markedly mitigate the penalties for possession, reclassify all the drugs, and deal severely with certain purveyors of the more dangerous agents. This is the approach I favor. I think we can devise equitable and potentially effective drug laws. I would propose that legislators and the public consider revising the entire drug law structure in accordance with the following outline:

(1) *Marihuana.* Marihuana and all other naturally occurring cannabis products including hashish must have their current legal marriage with heroin dissolved. The possession of drugs in this category should be labeled an offense. Upon conviction the offender could be fined from $500 to $1,000 or alternatively could be assigned to a local worthwhile program such as tutoring deprived or handicapped children or working in a poverty program. In order not to interfere with either work or school, the convicted individual could be assigned at night or on weekends or both for a period of perhaps twelve to fifteen weeks. Upon completion of the prescribed sentence the conviction would be expunged from the public record. The penalty for a second such offense would be similar. On third or subsequent convictions the individual

would be liable to a period in jail not to exceed 90 days. Sale of marihuana might carry a penalty range of one to ten years in jail. This would provide enforcement officials and judges with enormous flexibility, in that a young offender who sold a small amount of marihuana could be sentenced to a year in jail, whereas a major distributor or importer could get ten years. There should be provisions in the law for probation and suspension. Dr. Helen Nowlis offers an alternative proposal for possession of marihuana: The user would be subject to a point system similar to that used for traffic offenses in some states. Conviction of possession would result in no public record, but rather the offender would be given a specified number of points. If one accumulated a certain number of points, one would be considered an antisocial individual and could receive an appropriate jail sentence.

(2) *Potent hallucinogens such as LSD, mescaline, dimethyltryptamine, and psilocybin.* This category would also include synthetic cannabinol substances such as tetrahydrocannabinol. These are potentially very dangerous drugs, and possession would be a misdemeanor with a potential jail sentence of up to six months with provisions for probation and suspension. Sale would be a felony with a penalty range of two to ten years in jail. For both the possession of potent hallucinogens and marihuana (or any other illicit drug), if there were major psychological maladies, the judge should have the option to impose no penalty, but rather to order psychiatric treatment.

(3) *Opiates.* Possession of heroin, morphine, opium, or similar drugs would be a misdemeanor with a maximum sentence of six months in jail. Alternatively, where drug programs are available, the judge should have the option of having the convicted possessor of heroin civilly committed for attempted rehabilitation with a total institutional and aftercare supervision period of up to three years. The total time period seems reasonable, since a great deal of data indicate that considerable time is needed for the young, poorly motivated heroin

user to respond favorably to any rehabilitative and aftercare program. Sale of heroin by someone medically proven to be dependent on the drug would carry a flexible penalty of two to ten years in jail, with the judge having the option of assigning the individual to civil commitment, surveillance in an institution, and aftercare for a total of five years.

There should be a separate penalty structure for sale of a substantial amount of heroin by an individual who is not dependent on opiates or by importers, distributors, or major pushers. This penalty should be very severe indeed. I would personally recommend twenty years to life. The profits from heroin importation and sale are stupendous, and the toll in ruined lives and death is staggering. It is high time our society markedly increased the risk-to-profit ratio for this particular drug, and the only way to do this is to hand out extraordinarily severe sentences. Were this done, many of the major criminal elements would soon leave the heroin trade and the amount of heroin addiction in this country would be greatly reduced.

It is important to realize that codeine, although an opiate, is a mild narcotic with a very limited potential for causing addiction. Consequently, illicit possession of this drug should be punished by a fine not to exceed $500 and illicit sale by a maximum penalty of one year in jail.

(4) *The stimulant group.* Here again it is extremely important to carefully formulate the law so that it deals fairly with offenses that range from taking a few pills by mouth, not inordinately dangerous, to taking large amounts by vein, which can induce profound mental derangement and probably longstanding brain damage. I would make the illicit possession of modest numbers of pills or capsules of amphetamines or phenmetrazine (or other similar drugs) punishable by a fine of up to $500. On the other hand, possession of large numbers of pills or capsules or any amount of a liquid stimulant for use by injection would be considered a misdemeanor pun-

ishable by up to six months in jail. Sale of pills or capsules would be punished by jail sentences of one to three years, whereas sale or manufacture of the far more dangerous liquid preparations for intravenous use would be punished by two to ten years in jail. Cocaine, basically a stimulant, would be included in this category.

(5) *Sedatives and tranquilizers.* Illegal possession would on conviction subject the offender to a maximum fine of $500; conviction for the sale of these drugs would carry a maximum sentence of one year in jail. On the other hand, illegal diversion of large numbers of tranquilizers or sedatives from legal sources of supply or illicit manufacture of the drugs would carry a maximum sentence of five years in jail.

If an individual manufactured or sold capsules, tablets, or liquids for injection that contained combinations of agents including one or more of the above-listed drugs, his potential sentence upon conviction would be determined by the most dangerous drug in the combination. Furthermore, if anyone were to administer to another person a drug that has the capacity to produce hallucinations or otherwise profoundly alter consciousness and he does this without the other's knowledge, he should be subjected upon conviction to a jail sentence of up to ten years. There is no more reprehensible crime than that of giving a drug such as LSD to an individual without his knowledge. He suddenly experiences shattering ego deterioration; he often feels overwhelming panic or becomes convinced that he is going insane. And he has no knowledge that such terrifying things are happening because he surreptitiously was given a potent drug. He will frequently experience prolonged mental derangement, with recurrent panic reactions for months afterward. This kind of victimization must not be tolerated by society, and the only way to curb it is to hit the perpetrators with heavy sentences.

All laws that make it a crime to be where drugs are being used even if one does not possess the drugs should be done away with.

They are grossly unfair. And use of a drug (as contrasted to possession) should not be a crime, for such laws are too susceptible to misapplication. Besides, there are so many deceptions in the market that the user may have actually taken none of the drug and his reactions may be purely psychological. Consequently laws directed against use that are not predicated on blood or urine tests or analysis of the drug used are unjust. Sharing one's drugs, or selling a tiny amount to a friend, should ordinarily be treated as a possession offense if little profit is involved. In contrast, there should be severe penalties for injuring others while under the influence of mind-altering drugs. Our courts are enamored of the notion of temporary insanity. People have killed others under the influence of glue or LSD and been let off on the grounds that the drug made them temporarily insane. This is patently ridiculous. An individual who was sane when he took a drug should be responsible for his actions while under its influence unless he was unaware he was actually taking the drug or can demonstrate that there was no way he could have been expected to know he might injure another under the drug's influence. The latter would be rare, but I know of a case in which an individual killed a person under the influence of marihuana. I would think his lawyer could justifiably argue that the case was virtually unique in the United States, and that his client could not have been expected to know that such extraordinarily violent behavior might result.

People now travel so rapidly and frequently between countries that our laws on transporting dangerous drugs must be reconsidered. If a person is caught crossing United States with small amounts of a drug for his own use, he should be charged with possession. Only if he sells the drug or can be shown to be part of a criminal conspiracy to import drugs should severe penalties be invoked. This would obviate the imposition of ridiculous sentences such as that handed out to Timothy Leary in Texas on March 2, 1970.

I hold no brief for Leary, especially in view of his current activities. Nevertheless he was on trial for having a tiny amount of marihuana on his person, and in his case the possession offense was converted by our current legal structure to a smuggling offense. Clearly whatever he possessed was either for his own use or to share with friends. To saddle him with a ten-year sentence for possessing a small amount for his own use and carrying it across state and international borders was patently unjust. According to my proposals, he would have been found guilty of possession and sentenced to at most ninety days in jail. That would be a sensible penalty for a minor offense.

The above scheme seems to me to be entirely reasonable. It is fair to drug users, and it simultaneously protects society. It would allow police and district attorneys to enforce the laws, and because the potential punishment is carefully tailored to fit the crime, they could do so without feelings of either guilt or ambivalence. It would allow the judiciary to apply the penalty provisions in the most effective and sensible fashion. Certainly, the above outline is far more rational than our current potpourri of confused, archaic, and unjust state laws. Already some states have moved in the direction I have indicated, especially in regard to marihuana. At least seven states now have six months or less as the maximum penalty for possessing small amounts of marihuana and New York State is carefully considering reducing this to ninety days. And the Supreme Court of New Jersey has decided that first offenders convicted of marihuana possession should not be given a jail sentence.

Some would say the penalties for possession are too lenient—that users are often small-time sellers, and that because it is often difficult to document sale even by a known pusher, the only way to adequately punish user-sellers is to give them long sentences for possession. It seems to me that these are inadequate reasons for having a harsh legal structure. For the most part, those who possess illicit drugs are not guilty of a horrible offense. They are disrupting what society believes to be its orderly functioning, but if they have bad reactions from the drugs, they are ordinarily hurting themselves more than society. Furthermore, three to six months in jail for one used to personal freedom is in point of fact a very substantial penalty.

It is possible to come to grips with the problem of possession of large amounts of a drug. If the individual possesses more than an average one-week supply, the presumption should be it is not solely for his use but rather for sale; and the penalty could be intermediate between that for possession and that for documented selling. Liberally interpreting a week's supply, amounts of marihuana exceeding fifty cigarettes, amphetamines exceeding 30 grams, heroin exceeding 2.5 grams, and LSD exceeding 10 milligrams would fall into this category. Some would object to this because many marihuana users who do not sell might buy enough marihuana for 100 or even 1,000 cigarettes for their own use. Obviously that is true, but there is no way of avoiding a greater penalty for possession of large amounts of an illicit drug. The user silly enough to be caught with, say, 200 marihuana cigarettes would have to accept the necessity for trying to convince judge and jury that he should be treated leniently because he did not in actuality intend to sell his supply.

The reluctance of legislators to change anachronistic laws is based in part on fear of political retaliation by their constituents and potential political opponents. Unfortunately, this is abetted by lawmakers, often young and often novices, who deliberately introduce the most radical alterations in the drug laws in a flagrant bid for publicity. Thus, for example, new members of the New York State Legislature come to me before each session, indicate that the marihuana laws are atrocious, insist they should be strikingly mitigated, and conclude by saying they will introduce legislation to legalize the use of marihuana. Each time I point out to them that marihuana is not likely to be legalized in the near future and that there are cogent reasons they obviously have not carefully considered for not legalizing it. We spend considerable time together, and by the end of our talk they uniformly acknowledge that legalization proposals at the present would be ineffective and counter-productive. They then say they will introduce realistic legislation that has a good chance of passage. I tell them that if they would introduce legislation along the lines I have outlined in this chapter, many of us involved in attempts to reduce our burgeoning drug problem would vigorously and publicly support them.

They leave my office vowing to introduce realistic legislation but, possessed by an overwhelming desire for publicity, they subsequently propose legislation that calls for the immediate legalization of marihuana. This action may get them one or two days of publicity, but it antagonizes those legislators who wield control over which laws shall be brought to the floor and which buried in committee. Proposals urging the legalization of marihuana are almost uniformly relegated to obscurity by being assigned to committees from which they will never emerge. The unfortunate part of these petty acts of small personal aggrandizement is that many other proposals that would considerably mitigate the laws get lost along with the unrealistic proposals for immediate legalization of marihuana. Thus the neophyte legislator gets his publicity and enhances his reputation as a dedicated liberal, but he simultaneously manages to kill all constructive revision of the drug laws. It is high time that constructively inclined middle-of-the-road legislators take it upon themselves to reject, on the one hand, the publicity seekers and their thoughtless proposals and, on the other, those who intransigently attempt to preserve the status quo. A total reassessment and revision of our drug statutes is needed immediately. If it does not occur, the incongruities and inequities of our current legal structure will ineluctably increase the severity of our drug problem.

An additional difficulty is that our legal structure is often terribly unfair to those who are indicted, because there tends to be an inordinate time lapse between indictment and trial. Many young people cannot pay the bail charges and have to remain in jail; some of their experiences there may be far worse than the potential dangers of the drugs they are accused of using. A speedy trial is a must if we are to be fair to the drug offenders. In this regard, those accused of possession of small amounts of marihuana should ordinarily be released on their own recognizance and should not have to post bail. If this works for marihuana it can be expanded to possession of other illegal drugs. Rapid resolution of the charges is particularly necessary if the offender is a student, for the school often cannot act effectively until the trial is completed.

The revision of our drug laws is only the beginning. There is another important problem, that of our judiciary. It is notably inconsistent. Some judges are harsh, others are lenient, and most are appallingly unknowledgeable about the individual drugs. Thus part of the game for prosecutors is to try to get a tough judge, whereas the defense lawyers attempt to manipulate the trial to have the case tried by a jurist with a reputation for leniency. Indeed, in many ways the biggest stumbling block to a sane and effective approach to illicit drugs has been the judiciary. Judges often have failed to adequately distinguish among drugs, especially heroin, and they have at times been extraordinarily cruel to users and small-time purveyors of marihuana. All one needs for proof of this is a copy of the June–August, 1969, issue of the *Marijuana Review*. The magazine contains a heavy black-bordered box with the headline "Atrocities—Major Casualties in the Marijuana War." These are among the cases cited:

> Larry Belcher, 31. Detroit writer sentenced late 1968 to 20–30 years for the sale of $5 seeds and twigs to nark [narcotic officer].
>
> Samuel Williams, 32. Sentenced in Seattle for 20 years for sale of $1 joint to a 16-year-old.
>
> Richard Dorsey, 58. Sentenced in Dallas to 50 years for selling $5 matchbox to nark.
>
> Matthew Culmore, 19. Student at San Diego State sentenced in March 1969 to 16 years for possession of "several bags" of grass.

James Johnson, 18. Sentenced May 20, 1969 in Prince George, Virginia to 20 years and $500 for possession.

These sentences are worthy of the Inquisition rather than a just democracy.

Overly lenient sentences for sale of drugs such as heroin are as flagrant as atrociously severe marihuana penalties. Only a minority of the worst of the organized criminal elements receive more than ten years on conviction. A typical case was recently noted in a story in the *New York Times:* "A 32-year-old Frenchman convicted of being a member of a 30 million dollar heroin smuggling ring was sentenced to 8 years in prison. He could have got 40 years and $40,000 in fines."

I have had an opportunity to review the sentences of the most venal drug purveyors tried in Federal courts. In the four-year period from 1962 to 1965, less than one-third received sentences of over twelve years in prison. Surely we should be as harsh as the law allows on those members of organized criminal cartels who purvey heroin, a drug that leads large numbers of young people to degradation and death. In the last three years the situation in Federal courts appears to have improved somewhat, but there is still ample room for further improvement. In state courts the chaos appears unrelieved and is compounded by judicial inability to separate sale from possession.

The following table summarizes drug sentencing data from Newark, New Jersey, in 1967 and 1968. It may be seen that probation was given more frequently for possession, but where jail sentences were imposed, there was no major difference between those convicted of possession and those convicted of sale. Indeed, in the three most severe penalty categories almost half were convicted of possession, not sale. If a major revision of our drug laws is to take place, the Federal government most likely will have to take the lead. Fortunately, the Nixon administration has just completed a major revision of federal statutes. The new law makes possession of any illicit drug a misdemeanor with maximum sen-

NEWARK, NEW JERSEY—NARCOTIC AND MARIHUANA SENTENCES

	Per cent receiving each penalty (rounded to nearest full per cent)			
	1967		*1968*	
Sentence	Possession	Sale	Possession	Sale
6 months	0	0	1	0
1–2 years	1	0	0	0
2 years	32	22	30	27
2–3 years	42	30	40	33
3 years	3	0	1	0
3–5 years	13	32	17	22
5–7 years (or 4–6 years)	7	6	10	16
5–9 years	0	0	1	0
8–10 years	2	4	2	0
10–12 years	0	4	1	0
Suspended sentence or probation	50	21	46	14

tence of a year in jail. The penalty for heroin or cocaine sale is up to fifteen years in jail, and the penalty for sale of LSD, marihuana or amphetamines is up to five years in jail.

The penalty provisions of the bill are still unsatisfactory in five respects: First, the penalty for marihuana possession is still too severe. The penalty should not be identical to that for possession of LSD, heroin, or Methedrine, and it should not be over ninety days in jail. Second I believe possession of these other drugs should carry maximum sentences of six months. Third, there are inadequate provisions for expunging a conviction for possession from the public record. Fourth, there is inadequate classification of the drugs. Cocaine, a stimulant, is put in the narcotic category and treated just like heroin. Methedrine, another stimulant, is placed with marihuana and LSD in the penalty provisions, sale incurring a maximum five-year sentence. Sale of Methedrine for intravenous use should join the harsh penalty category, whereas sale of marihuana should be kept in a lesser category. Fifth, the penalties for sale of drugs such as heroin would be less severe than in the present laws. Theoretically, the sentence for major sellers could be doubled if a criminal conspiracy could be documented, but this would be hard to do. In essence, what the law does is allow inadequate punishment for the worst purveyors of the most dangerous drugs. Despite its defects, however, the bill deserves widespread support. It will serve as a model for individual states and will allow our laws to be completely reorganized at every judicial level. This is absolutely essential.

It is also important that laws mitigating possession penalties do not insist, as a concession to hard-liners, that offenders be compelled to undergo treatment for a presumed mental abnormality. Recently several states have lessened marihuana penalties, but insisted that those guilty of possession undergo treatment in a mental-health or psychiatric unit. Some need such help but most, especially marihuana users, do not, and, not infrequently, such "rehabilitation" can create emotional problems that did not exist previously.

9.

Final Thoughts

Lincoln Steffens once said, "The only thing worth having in earthly existence is a sense of humor." One of the most striking aspects of the current youth rebellion movement and the youth drug movement is their dour façade. No vestige of humor is allowed to creep into the endless polemics carried on by members of the drug subculture. The antidrug crusaders react equally sternly and unbendingly. If the acerbic debate were allowed to be touched by humor, a great deal more could be done about mitigating this national epidemic.

Nowhere is the angry, self-righteous, and intolerant attitude more evident than in treatment programs for heroin addicts. In New York City the entire panoply of anti-addiction efforts has been helplessly bogged down in the most maddening internecine warfare. The methadone program is attacked by therapeutic communities as an ineffectual prolongation of addiction; the people favoring the methadone program in turn claim that it alone is curing addicts and that the official city rehabilitation program is a farce; the city program insists the methadone program and other therapeutic communities have exaggerated their successes. The anti-addiction field is filled with zealots, each ridiculously convinced that he has the best, perhaps the only, program that will reach addicts. They squabble over everything. It reminds one of Robert Burns's poem:

> O ye who are so good yourself
> So pious and so holy
> Ye've naught to do but mark and tell
> Your neighbors' faults and follies.

In Newark, New Jersey, the New Jersey College of Medicine and Dentistry has moved to place all anti-addiction programs in the city under a single academic umbrella in hopes that the programs, though functioning independently, will work for a common goal without squabbling. In order to remain unbiased, the medical school will accept the responsibility for evaluating and coordinating the programs but will not itself treat addicts.

The concept of evaluation is terribly important. The problem of addiction is an emotional one, and every program quite naturally develops an emotional proprietary interest in its own methods. Because this is true, no program can assess itself adequately. Yet we desperately need effective evaluation if we are to make valid judgments relating to public health policy and if we are to spend large sums of public money wisely. No longer can panegyrics by the programs themselves substitute for good extramural analysis. Every anti-addiction program that requests funds or consideration for wide application of its methods should have an independent, accredited evaluation mechanism that would gather data on its own, establish criteria for recovery, and utilize statistical methodology. In New York City only the methadone maintenance project has an adequate evaluation mechanism, and even it could stand some modification, since the evaluating committee has been compelled to rely too heavily on figures provided by the project instead of collecting its own data independently. Despite the clear need for evaluation, few funds have been available for this purpose. Literally millions of dollars can be obtained from the Federal government for treating addicts or establishing drug registries but, at least in the 1966–1970 period, the granting agencies have not been able to provide the money to evaluate the efficacy of the treatment programs they support. This must be changed. It is wasteful and, in the long run, unproductive.

In the absence of extramural evaluation, the media have sometimes taken over this role themselves, even though they may possess neither expertise nor the facts. For example, one excellent newspaper insisted editorially in 1967, 1968, and 1969 that methadone was the answer to heroin addiction and that it was proven as a general treatment modality. It was impossible to persuade the editorial staff that the drug was still experimental. Abruptly, in 1970, one of the therapeutic communities got the ear of the editorial staff, and with marvelous ease the newspaper began to question methadone, indict the official city program, and advocate the therapeutic community. In one article, a member of the editorial staff attacked the city program as unevaluated, without apparently recognizing that the therapeutic community the editors advocated had no evaluation mechanism at all.

To be blunt, the newspaper knew perilously little about methadone when it supported that concept, or about the city program it condemned, or about the therapeutic community it espoused. It failed to note the limitations of methadone when urging rapid expansion of that treatment modality, ignored the admittedly limited success of the city program, and then accepted with open arms and closed eyes a program that made extreme claims based on unsubstantiated data.

I want to make it clear I am not attacking the particular therapeutic community. Perhaps it is great, but at the time of the newspaper's enthusiasm, the program's allegation of success was in actuality a well-planned publicity campaign to obtain more funds and power. The newspaper unwittingly became a pawn in a power struggle. Here, then, is a perfect example of a newspaper assuming the role of extramural evaluation and, in doing so, running the risk of performing a great disservice in the drug rehabilitation field.

In all fairness I should note that after its initial burst of enthusiasm, the editorial staff of the newspaper began to look at all figures with skepticism, and now the paper takes a very careful and realistic look at all claims of treatment success. The problem is not so much that treatment programs are dishonest; rather they often select the denominator they like best. If 1,000 people go through the earliest phases, 500 actually enter therapy, 200 remain in the program after three months, and 150 of the 200 do well, then it claims a 75 per cent success rate (150/200). But in point of fact the success rate should be calculated on a denominator of 1,000 or 500, which would make it at most 30 per cent.

When asked about such figures, program directors say that anyone who leaves the program during the first three months doesn't count. But in calculating success rates, all who enter treatment must be considered or a program cannot be compared with other programs such as civil commitment which must count everyone who enters treatment. If the data are viewed from the point of view of the total number entering treatment, parole, probation, civil commitment, and most therapeutic community programs have about the same success rate. Only the methadone program at Beth Israel Hospital in New York City has a success rate conspicuously higher than other programs, and it may well be selecting for treatment the addicts with greatest likelihood of success.

The difficulties Mayor John Lindsay experienced in 1965 serve as a perfect example of the difficulties in judging programs without a careful evaluation mechanism. During his first campaign for mayor, Lindsay, who was greatly concerned about addiction in New York City, vacillated from day to day about which program the city should adopt if he should be elected. His views on any given day depended on who talked to him the day before about a given program. This is entirely understandable because there were no valid evaluation data available to him and, as a result, he was caught between the emotional testimonials of a program's proponents and the equally emotional views of those implacably opposed to it. Here then was a man about to be mayor who was vitally interested in drug abuse but unable to fall back on any reliable data to use in formulating an effective program for the city.

Many rehabilitation programs are afraid of extramural evaluation. They need not be. There is no facile solution to heroin addiction, especially that of persons residing in depressed urban ghettos. If a program is valid, it is more than welcome. The point is that certain addicts respond better to one type of therapy than to another. A program that speaks only to the needs of 1 or 2 per cent of the addict population can be of great help to that small percentage of addicts but will be a complete waste for the rest. If evaluation allowed the addict to be matched to the program prior to his treatment, the recovery rate for each program would be substantially greater.

Of course, the heroin problem in our urban slums will not disappear until a concerted attempt is made to alleviate depressing environmental conditions. If substandard education, underemployment, inadequate sanitation, and dilapidated housing persist, so will heroin—or it will be replaced by equally undesirable drug abuse patterns or by still other antisocial behavior. For the most part, heroin abuse in city slums is caused by the interaction between an inadequate personality and a miserable environment. The heroin addict from these communities tends to be immature, angry, unable to establish goals, and intolerant of the frustrations inherent in everyday life. In short, he has personality defects and is hard to rehabilitate, especially if he is under thirty years of age. It is especially the ghetto addict that should be directed to the program most suited to his particular need. He needs a multifaceted approach that includes diminishing the availability of drugs, modifying the milieu he lives in, and restructuring his life pattern. It is important to recognize that the objective in drug rehabilitation is to help the drug user mature and acquire a life pattern that is both constructive and satisfying to him. All too often rehabilitation programs rigidly insist on casting the drug-dependent individual into a specific inflexible mold. This inevitably limits the success of a program and reduces its value to drug users.

Much of the drug abuse problem that exists today is in the nine- to eighteen-year-old age group, but almost always rehabilitative efforts are limited to those over sixteen years of age. Furthermore, the emphasis is on heroin addiction, but heroin abuse, although increasing rapidly, is still only a small part of the picture. The major drug problems in the very young come from use of stimulants, euphoriants (such as marihuana), hallucinogens, bizarre agents, and combinations of various drugs. This means priorities will have to be realigned. The only treatments for the use of non-opiates are psychiatric therapy, counseling and, for some, group therapy. Most experimenters do not need and will not accept formal psychiatric help. A minority of the stimulant, hallucinogen, and euphoriant users either have lost control over their drugs or use them because of major psychological abnormalities. These users need psychiatric aid, but there are not nearly enough psychiatrists, most of them know very little about illicit drugs, and even under the best of circumstances treatment often fails. Sweden has just begun to treat its abusers of stimulants by placing them in therapeutic communities in which group therapy is the mainstay of treatment, but American data suggest this technique will succeed in only a small percentage of cases. For some drug abusers, counseling may help, but most of the experimenters don't even need that. Although more treatment centers for the young and for non-opiate drug abusers must be established, it is even more important to concentrate on prevention, and this means a combination of education, counseling, and elimination of drug supply. The last is mandatory; if supply is reduced, use will inevitably decline. To reduce supply, we need fair laws that are applied vigorously and are directed sternly toward the seller and distributor. It is crucial to recognize that we must attack these various fronts simultaneously. No single approach will suffice: education cannot succeed unless the supply of drugs is reduced, and decrease of supply plus education will fail unless the laws are made just.

Once the laws are revised, it will be imperative that potential users and sellers be made aware that they will indeed be punished. One way of doing this would be for newspapers to have a daily listing of disposition of criminal cases after trial. The penalties imposed could also be carried on television and radio. If convictions and sentences were widely publicized, they would serve as warnings to potential lawbreakers. At present there is extensive publicity given to arrests but only haphazard reporting of sentences. Many young people are convinced that one may get arrested but that conviction is infrequent and substantial jail sentences are rare no matter what the offense.

Another problem in dealing with the drug scene is the tendency to approach it as an isolated phenomenon. This just doesn't work. Drug abuse doesn't occur in a vacuum. There is an undeniable connection between drug use and family strength, individual personality structure, society's standards, and the degree of ferment in the community.

In the United States in 1968 there were over 580,000 divorces and in 1969 the figure increased to 660,000; 1 in 3 marriages ends in divorce. To put it another way, the family unit continued to deteriorate from 1968 to 1969 just as it has every year since World War II. If drug use is to be reduced, the family structure has to be maintained and strengthened. A recent estimate suggests that actually 75 per cent of marriages are unhappy. I personally believe that we need formal courses, starting in junior high school and continuing in some form through high school and into college on the family, the history of its development, and its importance. Currently there are few such courses, and they are often used in considerable part for sex education. Additionally, a great deal more effort and money must be spent on family courts and family counseling services. The ones that exist are characteristically inept or merely act as traffic directors; they offer little effective guidance. There is very little public knowledge on where to turn if family disruption is imminent. I would suspect that if discord threatened to terminate a marriage, very few who read this book would have any idea of where to turn for expertise (family physicians and clergy excluded).

Now let us look at drug abuse in connection with the quality of society's present standards. Over the last two decades we have become increasingly pleasure-oriented. As the pleasure principle became predominant, society became more permissive. But in doing so, it did not set forth new standards; it merely indicated that the old ones were no longer applicable. Society has offered no new, liberalized guidelines. The best way to illustrate this is to look at nudity and sex in motion pictures and theater. At first, the ban on the naked breast seemed inordinately strict, and this was relaxed. But no new standards were issued and, overjoyed with the relaxed and undefined guidelines, motion picture and legitimate theater producers began to exploit nudity and sex, in the name of art but usually for box office receipts. As of today, we are being inundated with movies depicting sexual intercourse and plays such as *Oh! Calcutta!* that are acted in the nude. To many observers these entertainments are merely smut undiluted by taste or appeal to anything but prurience. Sexual acts that many feel are the individual's own business if performed in private have suddenly been thrust into the public forum by those who unconsciously or intentionally are subverting the age-old concept of a clear separation between private and public morality. The point here is not whether sexual exhibitionism in itself is good or bad. The point is that drug use inevitably will flourish in a milieu that has at its core an anything-goes ethic where standards have been abandoned rather than revised.

There are three reasons why drug use will increase as sexual pleasure and voyeurism become a major focus of our society: First, if anything that stimulates and pleases is totally accepted, illicit drugs, which surely give sensate pleasure, will also be accepted. Second, some people will take drugs in the hope of enhancing the sexual experience. Third, some will take drugs either to lose inhibitions in order to participate in sex more extensively or to withdraw from sexual confrontation foisted on them by society's new mores. After all, if one is not willing or able to play society's sex games, what better way to withdraw than by taking drugs and saying, "I'm getting my kicks from my drug experience; who needs sex?"

Thus it is impossible to divorce society's lack of standards from drug use. The more hedonistic society becomes, the more difficult it will be either to educate against or suppress drug use. One can educate all one wants against drugs, but if society, through its motion pictures and theaters, says that life is just one big sex orgy and if one's peers insist sex is better under the influence of certain drugs, what good will education do? I would emphasize that I am not advocating a reduction in pleasure but rather urging that pleasure be placed in perspective within a framework of goal-directed activity and within established guidelines.

But it is not just truncated standards that are of concern. The whole fabric of our society is in an upheaval. We appear to have lost our goals and are suffering from mass bewilderment. This sickness can best be cured with inspiring leadership. We need leaders who will define and articulate our major problems, establish goals, offer constructive solutions, and then forcefully lead our nation, especially the young, toward those objectives. At present, this country has too few such leaders, and at every level of our political structure we are dominated by self-aggrandizers and publicity seekers, by mediocrity, ineptitude, corruption, and laziness. We assassinate or ignore our best potential leaders, allow political office to be a playground for the rich, reward incompetence or political servitude by promotion to a judgeship, encourage our prosecutors to use their offices for political gain, and select our leaders on the basis of charisma, demagoguery, and shibboleth.

Perhaps our educational institutions should accept the responsibility for training a cadre of potential leaders for our ever-growing bureaucracy. It might be well, for example, for every high administrative official at municipal, state, or Federal level to take specific courses before running for office or to receive a certificate of expertise based on an examination from an educational institution; or alternatively, it might be well to hold our elections in late September and require those victors who have no acceptable training or expertise to take a special three-month course in administration prior to taking office on January 1.

However it is done, we must have more competent leaders at all levels or the malaise that permeates our society will persist. And if it does, drug abuse will increase. Nothing promotes malaise among young people more than political campaigns such as that in the fall of 1970. Directed against people, focused on personalities rather than issues, the tone of the campaign was generally shrill and acrimonious. In the long run nobody gains from this type of politics. It causes young persons to become disillusioned with the entire political system. Disillusion results in withdrawal from involvement in the system, withdrawal leads to apathy, apathy to boredom and in our society boredom thrusts the young into the drug scene. Obviously we cannot afford apathy among the young. In our complex modern society the issues are so immense that failure to do something about problems such as urban decay, pollution, malnutrition, the population explosion, and the nuclear arms race will surely mean our eventual destruction. It boils down to the fact that we can't afford pleasure and drugs if they predominate to such an extent that we fail to attack our most pressing national and international problems.

Perhaps the trouble our democracy now is in is the inevitable turmoil that besets any democracy that has survived a substantial period of time. Benjamin Disraeli predicted our plight in 1850. He said: "If you establish a democracy, you must in due time reap the fruits of a democracy. You will in due season have great impatience of the public burdens, combined in due season with great increase in the public expenditure. You will in due season have wars entered into from passion and not from reason; and you will in due season submit to peace ignominiously sought and ignominiously obtained which will diminish your authority and perhaps endanger your independence. You will in due season find your property is less valuable and your freedom less complete."

Whatever the reason, we are discontented and harboring a growing disdain for the laws and regulations that have governed us. The drug laws are defied by students and by many who purport to teach them in schools and colleges; teachers ignore valid court injunctions; labor unions strike in direct defiance of court orders; and so it goes, each of these acts of lawlessness sanctified by endless rationalization. But whatever the justification, the fact is that disregard for the law creates a climate of anarchy that promotes not only drug abuse but also corruption and violence. A biblical saying has it that "the law is good, if a man use it lawfully." Today our laws are not being used lawfully. More and more, each person is doing his own thing and the laws be damned. Surely our educational institutions have the obligation to inculcate the necessity for laws instead of permitting themselves in some cases to be turned into revolutionary and incendiary workshops.

If a return to law is to occur (and this would be the greatest deterrent to drug abuse), adults will have to act as irreproachable examples to young people. Our climate is such that many young people don't use the faults of older generations to establish better standards for their own generation. Instead, they seize on the peccadillos, foibles, excesses, and indiscretions of older generations to justify their own misbehavior and defiance of laws. At a pragmatic level this means that parents will have to be very circumspect about their own behavior if they expect to demand responsible and law-abiding activities on the part of their children. Cheating on income taxes, euchering business acquaintances, visible philandering, or virtually any form of fraud will be eagerly seized upon by the young as an excuse to use illicit drugs. At the same time, it is each adult's obligation not to let the younger generation use adult misbehavior to rationalize its own misbehavior. And it must be pointed out forcefully that the example the younger generation is giving in regard to drugs to those even younger is propelling the eight- to sixteen-year-old group to try anything and everything regardless of laws or the physical and mental consequences.

Of course our drug problem is compounded by our refusal to admit that we are a drugged society; we should carefully examine to what extent we are dependent on tobacco, caffeine, and alcohol. Were we to admit openly that we are a drugged society, then we could focus better on the crucial issue of how many intoxicants a society can tolerate and where the line should be drawn. We could then avoid parochial considerations such as the dangers or non-dangers of marihuana, marihuana versus alcohol, and marihuana versus tobacco and instead could concentrate on the more important broader issues. Once we have done that we can make a hard-nosed, unemotional decision whether to add marihuana to our legal intoxicants. As I have already indicated, my own conviction is that we have enough intoxicants and the last thing we should do is add more. But this may change dramatically if the campaign against tobacco is successful. Already at least half of our young people say they never intend to smoke, and over half of the members of Harvard's class of 1949 who answered a query on smoking said they had discontinued cigarettes by the time of their twentieth class reunion in 1969. The big question is what will replace tobacco. Whenever addicts stop heroin, a certain percentage become dependent on other drugs such as stimulants or alcohol. How many of the millions who smoke tobacco heavily will simply stop this oral and emotional gratification without turning to something else? Tobacco does harbor established dangers including bronchitis, emphysema, heart disease, and cancer, but the risk to the person who smokes less than a pack a day is quite limited. If tobacco is proscribed, how many will turn to alcohol? Or to marihuana? Or to some other drug? Or to overeating with the attendant risk of obesity, which is if anything more dangerous than smoking? There are 90 million users of alcohol in the United States, 6 to 9 million of whom are alcoholics. The question is how many additional heavy users we would have if tobacco use was interdicted. Some say marihuana might be a good substitute for tobacco or for alcohol. I think the evidence opposes marihuana, since its unpredictability, capacity to cause accidents, ability to reduce ambition, especially in the young, and its other dangers are enough to classify it as potentially as dangerous as either tobacco or alcohol.

It may well be that we ought to assiduously search for less dangerous intoxicants rather than merely educate or legislate against currently used legal or illegal ones. With our prolific pharmaceutical companies and extraordinary biochemical expertise, we should be able to find virtually innocuous substances. Betel, khat, and kava are three worthy of investigation, since slight modification of the active ingredients might provide a drug with mild stimulating, relaxing, or euphoriant qualities without significant toxicity. A few million dollars a year spent by the Federal government on research in this area could be tremendously rewarding in the long run. The sole objective would be to develop new intoxicants so that those wanting the pleasures of drug-induced intoxication could have them with the smallest possible risk to themselves and society.

Finally, it might be well to discuss just where our society is heading. There can be no question that a sensate, hedonistic era is upon us and drugs are used in an attempt to enhance the pleasures for which our society unceasingly searches. And our hedonism is abetted by an inordinate amount of leisure time that will surely increase. Recently it has been suggested we should have a three-day work week with four days of free time; several major companies are already starting to implement this. If the three-day work week comes to pass, it will be mandatory for governments to devote considerable thought and money to providing constructive activities so that the leisure created by our affluence and technology can be beneficial, not harmful.

The unrestrained proliferation of intoxicants could burden our society with increasing numbers of drug-induced dropouts. Even more seriously, persons harmed by powerful agents such as LSD could be inordinately susceptible to suggestion from or control by others. In the name of individuality and personal freedom the psychedelic guru well could be leading his acolytes to a state of drug-induced mind control. This is not nearly so preposterous as it sounds, and LSD-like drugs are likely to be only the first in a long line of agents able to increase suggestibility and reduce the will to resist. Tiny amounts of such drugs introduced into the food, water supply, or air of a community might well be far more effective than the chemical and biological warfare weapons so much discussed today.

But the possibility of an external power deliberately using mind-altering drugs to subjugate a nation is remote. More ominous is the possibility that young people, either from disillusionment, despair over uncontrollable events, or acceptance of sensate pleasure as the major objective in life, will opt for drug-induced joys at the expense of goal-directed activities and individuality.

A mass move toward mind control may well have already started. At Bethel, New York, in 1969, as I mentioned in the introduction to this book, some 450,000 rock music fans endured with amazing equanimity all sorts of miseries including hunger, thirst, mud, rain, and traffic jams, and were applauded by police, news media, and politicians for their good manners and nonviolence. Nonviolence is of course desirable, but in this case, according to a variety of observers, the calm was very likely due primarily to the effects of a welter of drugs including marihuana, LSD, hashish, Methedrine, and mescaline—a kind of mass crowd control by pharmacological agents. The implications boggle the mind. Even that segment of our society that does not use illicit drugs, and ordinarily despises their use applauded Bethel and may in the future accept, even encourage, drug-induced passivity because it fears violence and places a higher value on property than on the integrity of the human mind.

By the year 1980 the search for serenity, tranquillity, and feelings of pleasure may have gone beyond drugs to electrical control. Astounding as it may seem at first, electrical control of emotions is entirely feasible. Indeed, in a few cases, exactly this has been achieved. The following is taken from an article entitled "Striatal

Influence on Facial Pain" by neurosurgeons and psychiatrists from the renowned Massachusetts General Hospital in Boston:

> The patient was a 63-year old white male with far advanced invasive carcinoma involving the pharynx, sinuses and base of skull. There was no central nervous system involvement. He was referred from our tumor clinic for surgical alleviation of pain after exhaustion of radiation and chemotherapeutic procedures and after many months of management on narcotic medication. He was at the time of our procedures poorly and transiently relieved of pain by 100 mg. of meperidine hydrochloride given parenterally every three hours.
>
> Chronic electrodes were stereotactically implanted in posterior and anterior thalamus . . . and an additional electrode implanted near the base of the medial caudate. . . . After preliminary workup, the effects of long term stimulation of this presumed caudate electrode were investigated after a thorough parametric exploration. It was noted that the use of frequencies between 10 and 40 cycles per second with one msec pulse duration produced after 15 to 20 minutes an apparent mood elevation in this usually dour and surly individual, that there was less objective appearance of distress and that on direct questioning, he reported an absence of pain. This effect would persist throughout the stimulus period and indeed, after 45 to 60 minutes of such stimulation there seemed to be an outlasting effect for six to eight hours often giving rise to pain-free nights of sleep without need for medication which was an unusual occurrence in this individual. Because of this salutary effect of stimulation, we chose to allow this patient access to chronic stimulation rather than submitting him to a destructive brain lesion. We, therefore, constructed for him a small battery powered transistor stimulator which could be carried in his shirt pocket and connected to his electrodes at will. This stimulator when turned on produced a 30 sec train of pulses at 30 per second once every minute at that level which had been found effective in the laboratory. This stimulus intensity produced no immediate subjective sensory effect nor were there any objective indicators of the stimulus until some 15 to 20 minutes after onset. Several double blind studies were carried out, both de-

> liberately and accidentally, by having leads become disconnected, and there was adequate control for placebo effect. Both in the hospital and later at home, the patient was carried without narcotic medication except for 30 mg. of codeine two to three times a day supplemented by the use of his self-stimulator which he used ad lib, in general turning it on for one to two hours, three times a day toward the termination of his illness. He became quite dependent on this stimulation, felt it an important aspect of this alleviation of both his pain and to some extent his subjective suffering and used it as the primary control rather than drugs for about the last six weeks before death from his carcinoma. During the latter part of this period, his family noticed that after a prolonged stimulation, he would appear to them somewhat "drunk" showing slightly slurred speech and diminished awareness and a mild euphoria. He himself described the subjective effects of stimulation as being like "two martinis," although the pain-relieving effect seemed to far exceed the usual effects of this socially acceptable analgesia.

It has even been suggested that the operative scars from this treatment will be so small that women will use them as beauty marks.

It is not known how many people will embrace domination by mind-altering drugs or will choose to have electrodes implanted. But a surprisingly large number well may do so either as relief from an unpleasant environment or as a positive value in itself. In any case, if and when this occurs, the end of Western civilization as we know it cannot be far behind. Drug or electrical withdrawal from the immense problems that beset us will not solve or mitigate them. The implication is clear. We as a society must establish guidelines for use of pleasure-giving drugs, and these standards must neither be unfairly restrictive nor permit unlimited access to pharmacological or electrical intoxicants. Our decision in this regard must be made with great care, without hysteria, and must be guided by concern for the public health and by a determination that our society will cope with its problems and not withdraw from them. It is tragic indeed that so many young people recognize the issues and use their recognition, not to attack the problems, but rather to rail at society and withdraw from commitment to improving things.

Once we decide which drugs to legitimatize and which to interdict, our drug controls must be implemented by fair laws, reasonable regulations, and above all intensive and faultlessly honest education. But it is folly to depend too much on preventive education. There are far too many drug proselytizers spewing out facile generalities and false information in their perpetual attempts to turn others on. The drug subculture urges drug experimentation in the name of love and freedom, but it promotes drugs that may cause withdrawal from love and reduction of freedom. It is appallingly indifferent to those harmed by mind-altering agents; it knows people who have become potheads, acid-heads, speed freaks, and heroin addicts, and others who have drifted into a sad world of drug-induced narcissism, confusion, and lethargy. Yet the drug proponents act as if such tragedies are not a matter of great concern and try to exonerate themselves with statements such as, "Oh well, he should never have taken that drug." Such explanations are totally unacceptable. The drug subculture cannot free itself from responsibility for the extraordinary number of individual and family tragedies caused by drugs. And yet many young people listen uncritically to its spokesmen and close their minds to the educational efforts of those they feel represent the Establishment. This being so, the most salutary influences should and must come from the user's peer group. To this end, responsible young persons must be asked to join in planning antidrug education programs, and, even more important, they should play a major role in developing constructive alternatives to drug use. The large group of young persons who do view drug abuse as unhealthy, the growing number who recognize the potentially disastrous influence their own drug use might have on the very young, and the substantial proportion who are educable if given the facts must no longer remain silent, but must make it clear to the drug subculture that they themselves do not believe illicit use of mind-altering drugs is acceptable behavior. Until such time, we adults can keep the lid on through our educational efforts, laws, regulations, reduction in supply, and other techniques. But that is all we can do. Drug abuse will continue to plague our society until our young people themselves decide that commitment to the drug scene is a waste of time and effort. Then and only then will the use of intoxicants be placed in proper perspective. And, hopefully, the youth of our society will then decide to commit their energies and minds to solving the enormous problems that threaten the very viability of our civilization.

I would like to end on a hopeful note. Although our drug problems get progressively worse, prospects for getting our young people away from drugs are paradoxically improving. It's the hated Vietnam war that has done it. Millions of young people have become involved in protest against our continued involvement in a vicious war. Whether the young people's protest is right from a historical perspective is unclear, but from the point of view of drug abuse, it doesn't matter. What does matter is that they did get aroused. Sooner or later, however, the war will end. Then what will happen? Since the war protest is against an action rather than a commitment to achieve permanent peace for our world, the conclusion of the war could leave the protesters with a gigantic void. As the combat has dragged on, many of the antiwar activists and others have begun to find other reasons for protest. Perhaps the most visible and dramatic is the protest against our polluted environment, but this, unlike the Vietnam protest, is both against the current contamination and for a cleaner, more healthy environment for all. Because there are such strong positive aspects to this protest, there is a potential for long-term constructive commitment here. If young people turn to this kind of involvement, they themselves will reject the drug scene. But it will not happen by itself.

The Vietnam war mobilized the young, and now many of them are asking for support and leadership in positive battles such as that against environmental contamination. It is up to our society to provide that support, for the condition of our world in

1980–2000 may well depend on whether we encourage and direct our young people in 1970–1972. If we should fail them now, they may well flit from one ephemeral cause to another without continuing commitment, and the vital problems affecting our society will continue to grow unabated, creating a vicious cycle. The larger the problems, the larger the number of young persons who, feeling frustrated, will withdraw; and the larger the number of young persons who withdraw, the smaller the chance that the problems will be ameliorated. Eventually they will appear insurmountable, the young will be largely uncommitted, and extensive drug use will be the norm.

The other possibility is that we will provide the leadership and direction that will convince young people that we are still a meliorist society and that none of our problems is insoluble. Once they are fully committed to solving our major problems, the abuse of drugs will surely diminish, and the peer group pressure will be to use legal intoxicants in such a manner as to maximize pleasure and minimize harm.

The alternatives are clear; the unanswered question is how our society will react.

Appendix
The Drugs

1. *Lysergic acid diethylamide (LSD)—"acid."* The prototype of the powerful hallucinogen category, LSD was synthesized in 1938 but it was not until 1943 that Albert Hofmann, the noted Swiss chemist, discovered its hallucinogenic potential. The basic component of LSD is lysergic acid, an alkaloid derived from the fungus *Claviceps purpurea.* Lysergic acid is extremely difficult to synthesize and is not a hallucinogen, but any moderately adroit amateur chemist can convert it to the potent lysergic acid diethylamide. LSD can be administered either by mouth or by injection. Most of it is metabolized in the liver; only tiny amounts reach the brain.

Despite a welter of experiments performed over the last twenty-five years, LSD's precise mechanism of action remains an enigma. It appears to act at the juncture of the brain cells, inhibiting some parts of the brain and facilitating nerve-impulse transmission in other parts. Along with behavioral changes, certain biochemical and physiological events occur, but it is not clear whether these merely accompany the hallucinations or cause them. The substance most often implicated is serotonin (chemically: 5-hydroxytryptamine). It is known that LSD antagonizes serotonin, a naturally occurring substance in the body, and further, it is known that serotonin builds up in certain parts of the brain cells after LSD has been administered. However, other substances that similarly antagonize serotonin or cause it to increase in brain cells do not produce hallucinations. Consequently, the exact mechanisms underlying the overwhelming mental effects of LSD are not known.

The usual dose is 200 to 700 micrograms, the mental change starts thirty to sixty minutes after ingestion, and the duration of the experience is six to twelve hours. Untoward effects include intentional or unintentional suicide (rare), accidents, attempts at homicide (rare), profound panic, feelings of persecution, acute and occasionally chronic mental breakdown in some normal persons, precipitation of prolonged mental breakdown in predisposed individuals, and potential genetic damage (not yet entirely proven). Unpleasant trips may recur months or even years later.

Morning-glory seeds contain lysergic acid amides that are hallucinogenically active but far less powerful than LSD.

2. *Dimethyltryptamine* (*DMT*). This is a naturally occurring or easily synthesized hallucinogen that chemically is closely related to serotonin and psilocybin. It is far less potent on a weight basis than LSD, but it can produce extraordinary effects if given in dosages of 20 to 60 milligrams. Either smoked or injected, it produces a so-called businessman's trip, meaning that the onset is rapid (fifteen to thirty minutes) and duration usually short (two to four hours). The experience is so profound many call it the granddaddy of all hallucinogens. The trip also may be very rocky, with intense feelings of fear and panic. The drug is found extensively in Latin America, where it is utilized by many primitive tribes in the form of snuff for purposes of prophecy, ritual, or warfare; medicine men frequently use the drug in healing rites. The toxicity is not fully known, but DMT can produce acute mental derangement similar to that found after LSD use. There is no adequate information on genetic harm.

3. *Psilocybin.* Used for centuries by certain Mexican tribes in crude form (ingestion of the sacred mushroom, *Psilocybe mexicana*), psilocybin and its close relative psilocin are chemically related to serotonin and dimethyltryptamine. Although ordinarily taken by mouth, psilocybin can also be injected, and the experience mimics that of LSD. Many of the early Harvard experiments on potent psychedelics were actually performed with psilocybin.

Psilocybin is not nearly as potent as LSD. The usual dose is 8 to 40 milligrams. As with DMT, the toxicity of psilocybin is not fully known, but it can produce severe mental derangement. Preliminary data suggest a real possibility of genetic harm.

4. *Mescaline* (*peyote*). Mescaline is the most active principle in peyote, the hallucinogenic cactus used for centuries by Mexican and American Indians. The active substance was isolated in 1898 and chemically synthesized in 1926. Chemically it is related to adrenalin. It is usually taken by mouth in dosages of 200 to 500 milligrams. The experience is similar to the LSD experience, but illusions tend to be more florid and better structured, often containing astoundingly precise details. Aldous Huxley wrote extensively about this drug. It was used in Germany in the early 1900s in psychiatric therapy, but this vogue didn't last long.

Possible adverse effects on American Indians have not been adequately explored. Similarly, the untoward effects of the drug if taken promiscuously by young people are not fully known. But it is known that mescaline can produce severe mental aberration. Its potential for genetic harm has not been adequately explored.

5. *STP.* The initials stand for serenity, tranquillity, and peace. First synthesized by the Dow Chemical Company, the formula was stolen and introduced to the public by a notorious underground chemist. Chemically it is 2,5-dimethoxy-4-methylamphetamine. Taken by mouth in pill or capsule form in dosage of up to 20 milligrams, STP produces intense hallucinations lasting for four to twenty-four

hours. There are reports of people who ingested STP, hallucinated, fell asleep, and upon awakening had the hallucinatory experience begin again, this time even more intensely. Pure STP was studied by Drs. Solomon Snyder, Louis Faillace, and Leo Hollister and was found to have limited toxicity (*Science,* November 3, 1967). The substance sold as STP on the street has produced severe mental derangement characterized by mania, as well as blurred vision, dry mouth, difficulty in swallowing, difficulty in breathing, and in several cases lethal respiratory paralysis. Furthermore, the "antidote" for LSD, if given to a person who has ingested STP, makes the situation worse; the manic psychosis is aggravated, and on rare occasions fatal vascular collapse has been reported.

The use of STP diminished rapidly because the hippie community into which it was introduced objected to the many adverse effects. Nevertheless, small numbers of psychedelic acolytes continue to play around with the drug.

6. *Marihuana.* Marihuana cigarettes are composed of leaves, tops, and often stems of the ubiquitous hemp plant, *Cannabis sativa.* It is mainly the female plant that contains the active resin in the flowering tops. Contrary to widely held opinions, the male plant also has some active material. Marihuana and other cannabis products of similar potency can be smoked or taken in a variety of drinks or foods. Cannabis has been known since antiquity, and it is estimated that more than 200 million persons in the world use some form of it, usually the milder ones such as bhang (India), kif (Morocco), dagga (South Africa), or marihuana (U.S.A., Mexico).

Little is known of the distribution of marihuana in the body, the manner in which the drug is metabolized or excreted, or how it acts on the nervous system. Ordinarily the experience lasts from one to eight hours. Toxicity is limited; adverse manifestations include depression, panic, paranoia, and loss of goals.

Penalties for possession of marihuana in many states are similar to those for heroin and cocaine: possession, two years in jail; sale, a minimum of five years in jail. Some states, such as New York, are more flexible; in New York possession of small amounts is a misdemeanor, punishable by a maximum of one year in jail.

7. *Hashish.* Like ganga or charas, hashish is relatively pure cannabis resin and about five to eight times as powerful as marihuana. It is usually smoked and can produce frank hallucinations. The untoward manifestations also occur more frequently. These include anxiety, panic, depression, and sometimes psychosis requiring hospitalization.

8. *Tetrahydrocannabinol (THC).* This is the active principle in marihuana. THC can be readily synthesized in any moderately sophisticated chemical laboratory. A tiny amount of it produces a marihuana-like reaction. If the dose mimicking marihuana is increased three- to fourfold, in most individuals an LSD reaction occurs, characterized by hallucinations, illusions, and delusions.

THC is now being used to study the tissue distribution and mechanisms of action of the cannabis drugs. It is still remarkably unstable, and thus it is not used widely in the drug subculture. But the problem of instability should be solved in the near future. This surely will be followed by a great deal of abuse. In 1968 to 1970, THC tablets each of which allegedly was equivalent to five marihuana cigarettes were sold but people who paid $1 to $5 per dose actually received no active THC because the active substance had deteriorated on exposure to air.

9. *Amphetamines—"bennies," "ups," "speed."* These are the central stimulants, available in pill form for ingestion or liquid form for injection. Normally they are administered by physicians, in dosage of 5 to 15 milligrams daily by mouth—for obesity, depression, and lethargy. Their use for appetite suppression in overweight persons is not proven. Amphetamines can also be taken by

injection for a disease called narcolepsy, which is characterized by an inability to stay awake, and paradoxically they have been used successfully in the treatment of some hyperactive children.

The potential for abuse is enormous. Dosage is crucial: illicit users often take from 20 to 200 pills daily or inject by vein 150 to 15,000 milligrams.

A more subtle form of promiscuous use occurs among adults who initially use stimulants on a physician's prescription, then begin taking the pills on their own without medical indication. Sometimes after starting with two to four pills daily, they build up to gargantuan dosage, often alternating with sedatives (barbiturates) or tranquilizers. Tolerance develops slowly but predictably, so that a heavy intravenous user may have to increase the dose tenfold during a fourteen-day jag in order to keep getting the same kick. Adverse effects of large amounts taken repetitively, especially by injection, include paranoia and possibly brain damage. As with heroin, injection by unhygienic techniques frequently produces an infection of the liver. Methamphetamine taken by vein can be extraordinarily dangerous; it decreases inhibition, increases energy, stimulates sexual activity, and induces paranoia, and this can result in rape, mayhem, or murder.

Abuse has increased substantially in the United States during the last three years. Under Federal law illicit use is a misdemeanor, and sale is a felony punishable by up to five years in jail. In most states, sale and possession are misdemeanors.

10. *Ritalin.* This is a synthetic central stimulant (chemically: methylphenidate) similar in action to the amphetamines. Popular in Sweden, its use is growing in the United States, especially on the West Coast. It can be taken by mouth or injected. Toxicity is the same as with the amphetamines.

11. *Preludin.* This is the most popular of the central stimulants used in Sweden, where the stimulant problem is by far the worst of any country. The generic name of Preludin is phenmetrazine.

It was originally imported into Sweden for use in weight reduction; its use is now legally proscribed.

The usual dosage is 25 milligrams (one tablet) three times daily. Abusers take 20 to 400 pills by mouth; or, more frequently, they add water, allow the crude suspension to settle, and then inject the upper, clear part of the mixture. The usual pattern is four to six injections a day totaling 1,800 to 3,000 milligrams. This may be taken in jags of up to fourteen days at a time, using increasing amounts, sleeping and eating little, then injecting a barbiturate, sleeping for forty-eight hours, and upon awakening starting all over again.

Like amphetamines, Preludin induces delusions of persecution and other forms of mental derangement. Permanent brain damage has been suspected but has not yet been fully documented. Paranoia is so frequent in Sweden that users call it "noia" and fully expect it.The drug may produce a true addiction with abdominal pain and tremors on abrupt withdrawal (in heavy users). The number of habitués doubles about every two years in Sweden. There is also an increasing problem in the United States, but the major stimulants abused still are the amphetamines.

12. *Opiates.* These are the only true narcotics. Included in the group are opium, morphine, heroin, Demerol, methadone (Dolophine), and codeine. All except codeine have a marked addiction potential.

Neophytes often take heroin nasally or by injection under the skin. Confirmed users almost always turn to intravenous injection. Tolerance usually develops, but this has been much overrated. A user can build up six injections daily, taking a total of 18 to 75 milligrams of heroin, but more often he stops at two to four injections daily, using 6 to 50 milligrams. Habitués may never exceed this dose or may inject the drug only on weekends and still obtain a high from it. If tolerance uniformly developed to a marked degree, consistent elevation of the dosage would be observed more frequently. Currently heroin is so adulterated that even those using four to six injections daily may not be addicted; that is, on abrupt cessation of the drug, significant symptoms (vomiting, nausea, chills, diarrhea, aches, fever) will not be observed. Experimentation with heroin in the United States is increasing markedly among junior high school, high school, and college students and among those in the drug subculture who primarily use hallucinogens and euphoriants.

Complications include overdose, bloodstream infections, liver infection, skin infection, tetanus, and clots in veins that are repeatedly used to inject the narcotic. The last is particularly evident if one injects paregoric, a medication for diarrhea that contains opium and camphor. Those who use paregoric almost invariably suffer from extensive clots in veins, and they often turn to injecting the drug directly into the larger veins of the neck. In these people, as one might expect, the infection rate is very high.

Narcotic addiction can be detected by a Nalline (nalorphine) test. In this test the user is placed in a darkened room and given a small amount of Nalline; if the individual has used heroin recently the constricted pupils of the eyes will dilate. However, this test is now obsolete. A far better method of detection is a urinalysis, using the chemical technique of chromatography.

Laws governing opiates are for the most part similar in all of the various states. In general, conviction for illicit possession results in a jail sentence of two to five years, and conviction for sale or possession of large amounts results in a sentence that ranges from five years to life, the severity depending on the individual state. Parole or probation is usually denied except for first-offense possession conviction.

13. *Nutmeg*. Obtained from the evergreen tree *Myristica fragrans,* nutmeg is ingested in dosage of one to three whole nutmegs or one to three teaspoons or tablespoons of the grated material. Indonesia and the Caribbean are major sources of nutmeg supply. Chemically the active principle is myristicin, which bears structural similarities to mescaline and adrenalin. Nutmeg is primarily

an excitant and stimulant. Use goes back to the first century A.D. In folk medicine, somewhat incongruously, nutmeg has been used as a hypnotic, sedative, and analgesic. It has also been advocated to bring on menses and to increase virility.

Nutmeg has not become very popular, in large part because its ingestion often is followed by adverse effects including an unpleasant detached feeling, restlessness, shortness of breath, palpitations, and abdominal discomfort. Nutmeg poisoning has been recognized since the sixteenth century; in one reported case, ingestion of two nutmegs produced coma and death.

Although stimulation is the usual result of nutmeg ingestion, hallucinations or illusions can occur.

14. *Cocaine.* Primarily a stimulant, cocaine is used by millions of impoverished people in South America, who chew it in crude form to achieve relief from incredibly hard lives characterized by overwork and malnutrition. Although many decry the use of cocaine in this fashion, nobody has really attempted to eliminate the appalling conditions under which these poverty-stricken people are compelled to exist.

In developed countries, especially the United States and the United Kingdom, cocaine is taken in the form of snuff or by injection for purely hedonistic purposes. The "rush" from cocaine occurs shortly after injection and is described as a pleasant, often erotic feeling that is frequently centered in the lower abdomen or genitalia. Cocaine habituation is considered to be a rich man's habit because the effects are short-lived. Consequently, cocaine users tend to take large amounts over a short period of time.

Adverse effects include delusions, illusions, and paranoia. The last, as with other stimulants, is quite characteristic. The habitué often has marked judgmental lapses and may experience profound auditory hallucinations such as imagining angry voices or laughter. Lilliputian hallucinations have also been described, in which the user sees tiny persons or animals. Chronic, heavy use occasionally may be associated with convulsions.

The delusions of persecution induced by cocaine may cause a user to attack another person. The habitué is often extraordinarily tremulous, jittery, and emotionally labile. Sweating, cramps, abdominal pain, and severe depression may occur on withdrawal. Injection of a large dose of cocaine may produce instantaneous death.

Cocaine can be detected in the urine. Sometimes it is injected with heroin; this combination is called a speedball. The laws covering it are similar to those governing heroin.

15. *Catnip.* A member of the mint family, catnip, or *Nepeta cataria,* has been used for centuries for a variety of purposes including mild stimulation, tranquilization, and relief of amenorrhea. A few cases of catnip smoking have been reported in the United States. The reaction is generally marihuana-like, but may be more prolonged. Until further cases are reported, the potential for harm will not be clear.

16. *Khat.* The active principle in khat (or kat) is related to ephedrine, a modest stimulant. Used by millions in Arabia and Africa, the drug technically known as *Catha edulis* is chewed or drunk in tea. Use results in stimulation and talkativeness. Khat can also produce insomnia, constipation, loss of appetite, and stomach irritation, but it does not appear to have major toxicity when taken by mouth. Although many more studies are needed, thus far khat appears to be a relatively mild and harmless stimulant when taken in moderation by mouth.

17. *Kava.* Used in Polynesia, Samoa, West Guinea, and adjacent Pacific areas, kava comes from the roots of the plant *Piper methysticum.* Its active principle is methisticin (5, 6-dihydro-alpha-pyrone). The root is pulverized or chewed and made into a drink that is consumed in ceremonial fashion. Kava is usually a mild intoxicant with sedative and soporific effects, but it can produce substantial intoxication characterized by mouth numbness,

staggering gait, and weakness of the legs. Although data are incomplete, use of kava does not appear to be followed by major adverse manifestations. Chronic use does produce a yellowing of the skin.

18. *Betel.* Used in New Guinea and Southeast Asia, betel is chewed. There are usually three ingredients: the nuts (or seeds) of a feather palm, dried leaves of a vine, and lime. These are chewed together and provide a mild stimulating effect. No significant toxicity has been described, but betel does color saliva red and teeth black.

19. *Soma.* Soma was a legendary hallucinogen used in India around 1000 B.C. This substance disappeared, never reappeared, and thus has never been identified. Recently the noted ethnopharmacological explorer Gordon Wasson has suggested that soma and fly agaric are identical. The latter is derived from the fungus *Amanita muscaria* and has the capacity to induce prolonged hallucinations. For some time it was thought that the active substance was bufotenine, which is chemically closely related to the naturally occurring neurohumor serotonin and to the hallucinogens dimethyltryptamine (DMT) and psilocybin. Currently other substances in fly agaric, notably muscimol and ibotenic acid, are thought perhaps to be the hallucinogenic materials. Fly agaric is still used on the Kamchatka Peninsula in Siberia; three tribes there use the mushroom for pleasure, to facilitate contact with spirits, and to assuage their harsh environment. Typically, wives chew the bitter-tasting mushrooms, then pass the quid to their husbands who, after swallowing the material, undergo an intense hallucinatory experience characterized by excitement, euphoria, hallucinations, visualizations of spirits, nausea, and then stupor.

Toxic manifestations have not been adequately studied. Fly agaric is at present not used in the United States.

Bibliography

RECOMMENDED BOOKS

Blum, R. and Associates, *Students and Drugs II: College and High School Observations.* Jossey-Bass, Inc., San Francisco, 1969. A fine sociological analysis of drug use—the best of its kind.

Chein, I., *The Road to H.* D. L. Gerard, R. S. Lee, and E. Rosenfeld, Inc., Basic Books, New York, 1964. The best book available on the personality and family patterns of young heroin users in deprived communities.

Cohen, S., *The Beyond Within: The LSD Story.* Atheneum, New York, 1964. Highly readable and enjoyable account of the discovery and ascendancy of LSD; written before use of LSD became widespread and its dangers known.

Cohen, S., *The Drug Dilemma.* McGraw-Hill, New York, 1969. Comprehensive, well-written, brief (120 pages); has the virtue of presenting the data in unbiased fashion.

Cole, R., J. H. Brenner, and D. Meagher, *Drugs and Youth.* Liveright Publishing Co., New York, 1970. Well-balanced and well-written.

Fort, J., *The Pleasure Seekers.* Bobbs-Merrill, Indianapolis, 1969. Puts the use of escapist and pleasure-giving drugs in reasonable perspective.

Fuller, J. G., *The Day of St. Anthony's Fire.* Macmillan, New York, 1968. The story of an LSD-like ergot epidemic in France; although tangential to the drug scene, there is a loose connection, and the story is so magnificently unfolded it belongs on this reading list.

Goode, E., *The Marihuana Smokers.* Basic Books, New York, 1970. Based on a careful study of 200 marihuana smokers.

Kaplan, J., *Marihuana: The New Prohibition.* World Publishing Company, Cleveland, 1970. An extensive analysis of the marihuana controversy from a lawyer's point of view.

Lewin, L., *Phantastica, Narcotic and Stimulating Drugs.* Routledge & Kegan Paul, London, 1964. By the leading authority on the psychedelic field. First printed in 1924 and now hard to get, it has lost none of its delight or luster; a must for anyone truly interested in the subject.

Lingeman, Richard, *Drugs from A to Z: A Dictionary.* McGraw-Hill, New York, 1968. Just what the title says: a concise summary of each drug of abuse and of colloquial terms used in the United States and England.

Louria, D. B., *The Drug Scene.* McGraw-Hill, New York, 1968. I think it's great, but I could be a bit biased.

Marin, P. and A. Y. Cohen, *Understanding Drug Use.* Harper and Row, New York, 1971. Sort of a long letter to parents.

Smith, D. E., *The New Social Drug.* Prentice-Hall, Englewood Cliffs, N.J., 1970. A good marihuana compendium.

Taylor, N., *Narcotics: Nature's Dangerous Gifts.* Dell, New York, 1963. An absolutely delightful analysis of everything from tobacco to fly agaric; superbly written.

U.S. Public Health Service Publication 1645, *Ethnopharmacologic Search for Psychoactive Drugs.* Government Printing Office, Washington, D.C., 1967. Filled with an enormous amount of data on mind-altering drugs including the harmaline group, DMT, fly agaric, and soma. A lot is technical and chemical, but this is a thorough treatise well worth the effort for the nondilettante.

Wittenborn, J. R., H. Brill, J. P. Smith, and S. A. Wittenborn, *Drugs and Youth.* Charles C Thomas, Springfield, Ill., 1969. Quite a few good papers from a 1968 symposium.

ADDITIONAL WORTHWHILE BOOKS

DeBold, R. C. and R. C. Leaf (eds.), *LSD, Man and Society.* Wesleyan University Press, Middletown, Conn., 1967. Nine papers, most of them good, summarizing the data on the controversy surrounding LSD.

Goode, Erich, *Marihuana.* Atherton, New York, 1969. A reasonably good compendium on marihuana; quite well balanced.

Kalant, O. J., *The Amphetamines.* University of Toronto Press, Toronto, 1966. An interesting summary of amphetamine toxicity.

Kolb, L., *Drug Addiction.* Charles C Thomas, Springfield, Ill., 1962. Relatively old but full of solid basic information.

Maurer, D. W. and V. H. Vogel, *Narcotics and Narcotic Addiction.* Charles C Thomas, Springfield, Ill., 1962. Relatively old but full of solid basic information.

Mills, J., *The Panic in Needle Park.* Farrar, Straus, & Giroux, New York, 1966. Heroin addiction in New York City; well-written in reportorial style.

Moscow, Alvin, *Merchants of Heroin.* Dial, New York, 1968. A well-written story of the international heroin business.

Nowlis, Helen H., *Drugs on the College Campus.* Anchor Doubleday, New York, 1968. A nice summary of drugs and students from the point of view of a thoughtful educator.

Solomon, D. (ed.), *The Marihuana Papers.* Bobbs-Merrill, Indianapolis, 1966. Biased, but not a bad compilation; has the 1944 Mayor's report from New York City, which is very worthwhile.

Ungerleider, J. T., *The Problems and Prospects of LSD.* Charles C Thomas, Springfield, Ill., 1968. A reasonably good review of LSD.

Wilson, C. W., *Adolescent Drug Dependence.* Pergamon, New York, 1968. Based on a major conference in London in 1967; contains a great deal of helpful data.

PAMPHLETS AND ARTICLES

Bass, M., "Sudden Sniffing Death." *Journal of the American Medical Association,* Vol. 212 (June 22, 1970), 2075.

Cheek, F. E., S. Newell, and M. Joffe, "Deceptions in the Illicit Drug Market." *Science,* Vol. 167 (February 27, 1970), 1276.

Clark, L. D. and E. N. Nakashima, "Experimental Studies of Marihuana." *American Journal of Psychiatry,* Vol. 125 (1968), 379.

Cohen, A. Y., "Psychedelic Drugs and the Student: Educational Strategies." *Journal of College Student Personnel* (March, 1969).

Connell, P. H., "The Use and Abuse of Amphetamines." *The Practitioner,* Vol. 200 (1968), 234.

Drug Abuse: Escape to Nowhere. Smith, Kline and French, 1967.

Einstein, S., *The Use and Misuse of Drugs.* (Belmont, Calif.: Wadsworth, 1970).

Espelin, D. E. and A. K. Done, "Amphetamine Poisoning." *The New England Journal of Medicine,* Vol. 278 (June 20, 1968), 1361.

Garson, R. M. and M. K. Robson, "Studies in a Patient with Acute Leukemia after Lysergide Treatment." *British Medical Journal,* Vol. 2 (June 28, 1969), 800.

Geber, W. F. and L. C. Schramm, "Effect of Marihuana Extract on

Fetal Hamsters and Rabbits." *Toxicology and Applied Pharmacology,* Vol. 14 (1969), 276.

Glatt, M. M., D. J. Pittman, D. G. Gillespie and D. R. Hills, *The Drug Scene in Great Britain.* (London: Edward Arnold, Ltd., 1967).

Goode, Erich, "Multiple Drug Use Among Marijuana Smokers." *Social Problems,* Vol. 17 (1969), 48.

Grossman, W., "Adverse Reactions Associated with Cannabis Products in India." *Annals of Internal Medicine,* Vol. 70 (1969), 529.

Hallucinogenic Agents: A Concise Review. (Bloomfield, N.J.: Schering Corp., 1968).

Hecht, F., R. K. Beals, M. H. Lees, R. Jolly, and P. Roberts, "Lysergic Acid Diethylamide and Cannabis as Possible Teratogens in Man." *Lancet,* Vol. 2 (1968), 1087.

Hirschhorn, K., "LSD and Chromosomal Damage." *Hospital Practice,* Vol. 4, No. 2 (1969), 98.

Hollister, L. E., J. Shelton, and G. Krieger, "Controlled Comparison of Lysergic Acid Diethylamide (LSD) and Dextroamphetamine in Alcoholics." *American Journal of Psychiatry,* Vol. 125 (April, 1969), 1352.

Isbell, H., Gorodetzsky, C. W. and Jasinski, D., "Effects of $(^{-})A^{9}$ Trans tetrahydrocannabinol in Man." *Psychopharmacologia,* Vol. 11 (1967), 184.

Keeler, M. H., C. B. Reifler, and M. B. Liptzin, "Spontaneous Recurrence of Marihuana Effect." *American Journal of Psychiatry,* Vol. 125 (1968), 384.

Krippner, S., "Drug Deceptions." *Science,* Vol. 168 (1970), 654.

Louria, D. B., T. Hensle, and J. Rose, "The Major Medical Complications of Heroin Addiction." *Annals of Internal Medicine,* Vol. 67 (July, 1967), 1.

Louria, D. B., "LSD: A Medical Overview." *Saturday Review,* April 22, 1967.

Louria, D. B., *Nightmare Drugs.* (New York: Pocketbook Specials, Inc., 1966).

Ludwig, A., J. Levine, L. Stark, and R. Lazar, "A Clinical Study of LSD Treatment in Alcoholism." *American Journal of Psychiatry,* Vol. 126 (July, 1969), 59.

McGlothlin, W. H., "Hallucinogenic Drugs: A Perspective with Special Reference to Peyote and Cannabis." *Psychedelic Review,* No. 6 (1965), 16.

Press, E. and A. K. Done, "Solvent Sniffing: Physiologic Effects and Community Control Measures for Intoxication from the Intentional

Inhalation of Organic Solvents." *Pediatrics,* Vol. 39 (March, 1967), 451 and Vol. 39 (April, 1967), 611.

Saltman, J., *Marihuana and Your Child.* (New York: Grosset and Dunlap, Inc., 1970).

Smith, D. E. (ed.), "Speed Kills: A Review of Amphetamine Abuse." *Journal of Psychedelic Drugs,* Haight-Ashbury Medical Clinic, Vol. 2, Issue 2, 1969.

Solursh, L. P. and W. R. Clement, "Hallucinogenic Drug Abuse." *Canadian Medical Association Journal,* Vol. 98 (1968), 407.

Talbott, J. A. and J. W. Teague, "Marihuana Psychosis." *Journal of the American Medical Association,* Vol. 210 (1969), 299.

Tijo, J., W. N. Pahnke, and A. A. Kurland, "LSD and Chromosomes." *Journal of the American Medical Association,* Vol. 210 (1969), 849.

Weil, A. T., "Adverse Reactions to Marihuana." *The New England Journal of Medicine,* Vol. 282 (1970), 997.

Weil, A. T., "The Use of Nutmeg as a Psychotropic Agent." *United Nations Bulletin on Narcotics,* Vol. 18, No. 4 (1966), 15.

Weil, A. T., N E. Zinberg, and J. M. Nelsen, "Clinical and Psychological Effects of Marihuana in Man." *Science,* Vol. 162, No. 3859 (December 13, 1968), 1234.

Zinberg, N. E., and A. T. Weil, "Marihuana and Personality: A Comparison of Marihuana Users and Non-Users." *Nature,* Vol. 226 (1970), 119.